THE ESSENTIAL MORENO
*Writings on Psychodrama, Group Method,
and Spontaneity by J. L. Moreno, M.D.*

J.L. Moreno, M.D., 1889-1974

THE ESSENTIAL MORENO

Writings on Psychodrama, Group Method, and Spontaneity by J. L. MORENO, M.D.

Jonathan Fox, *Editor*

SPRINGER PUBLISHING COMPANY • NEW YORK

87 88 89 90 91 / 5 4 3 2 1

Library of Congress Cataloging-in-Publication Data

Moreno, J. L. (Jacob Levy), 1889–1974.
   The essential Moreno.

   Bibliography: p.
   Includes index.
   1. Psychodrama.   2. Group psychotherapy.
3. Spontaneity (Personality trait).   I. Fox, Jonathan.
II.   Title.
RC489.P7M575   1987.   616.89'1523   87-20667
ISBN 0-8261-5820-X
ISBN 0-8261-5821-8 (pbk)

Printed in the United States of America

Grateful acknowledgment is made to the following for permission to reprint Moreno's work:

For Chapter 6, "The Role Concept, A Bridge Between Psychiatry and Sociology," *American Journal of Psychiatry 118*, 518–523, 1961. Copyright © 1961, the American Psychiatric Association. Reprinted by permission.

For the sections "Playing God," "Young Man in Search of a Calling," "A Life of Service," "Among the Prostitutes," and "Superintendent of a Refugee Camp," from Chapter 17 from Moreno's unpublished *Autobiography*, to Zerka T. Moreno. Used with permission.

For the section entitled "A Religious Experience" in Chapter 17: from *Healer of the Mind*, edited by Paul E. Johnson. Copyright © 1972 by Abingdon Press. Used by permission.

And for all other selections from Moreno's works, comprising those from the books, *Group Psychotherapy: A Symposium* (1945), *Psychodrama*, Vols. 1 (1946) & 3 (1969), *Sociometry, Experimental Method and the Science of Society* (1951), and *Who Shall Survive?* (1953), Beacon House, Ambler, PA, as well as the journals, *Sociometry 1, 3, 14, Group Psychotherapy, Psychodrama and Sociometry 3, 26, 28*, and *International Journal of Sociometry and Sociatry 1*.

Contents

Foreword

The effort to understand the growth of the human individual as a whole rather than as a body or as an intellect or a social organism has been very difficult to clarify. Sigmund Freud, in his massive research, became convinced that the important issue was individuation—that the person became more himself the more he separated from the dependencies of childhood and was self-activating. Years later Fritz Kunkel described in some detail what he called the evolution of "we-ness"—the primary "we" with the mother, the secondary "we" with the father or another significant other, and the tertiary "we-ness" with the social set. Thus a child moved, if you will, from the biopsychosocial (with the mother) to the psychosocial (with the father) to the social (with the community).

In many years of working exclusively with families, it has gradually become a part of my belief system that the process of growth is a dialectic one. One cannot grow to be a full person by endless individuation because that produces isolation. One cannot grow to be a full person by constant dependent investment with the family because that becomes a kind of psychological enslavement. In fact, the dialectical evolution of personhood consists of an endless process of symbiosis and isolation, belongingness and defiance, or separateness. Each state contains anxiety; each pushes for an escape to the other side of the dialectic; and there is no resolution. There is only a gradual increasing comfort in the reverberations from one state to the other and back again.

Jonathan Fox has made a heroic effort to put together the writings, philosophy, theories, and accomplishments of an important contributor to our understanding of this process of human growth—J.L. Moreno. Dr. Moreno was one of the seminal figures in the world of psychiatry. He was probably more clearly responsible for the move from individual therapy to the understanding of interpersonal components of psychological living than any other single psychiatrist in the field. Jake had a combination of the hyopomanic qualities that made Karl Menninger such a remarkable contributor to the world of psychological understanding; the creativity of Picasso; and characteristics that made those who produced the theater of the absurd so invasive of our inner world. He had a unique ability to open himself to others. His preoccupation with spontaneity and creativity was only matched by his dedication to behavior, to action rather than words. He discovered that we are all actors on the stage of life, and at the same time he exposed a great deal of our endless stage phobia.

He almost single-handedly discovered the power and significance of the Here and Now moment and the spontaneous creative encounter, and may well have been one of the originators of the movement to discover that words are not things but only symbols. His use of the theater patterns of role reversal, the alter ego, role playing, and role simulation was the beginning of his development of a theory of embodiment and enactment. He wrote very extensively about the struggles of grouping, triangulation, subgroups, alienation, and domination. He wrote about the use of the social universe, about work, about play, about learning, about citizenship, and about the whole concept of the social atom and social space. He was also unique in being one of the first to develop the concept of the patient as co-therapist rather than the victim of the "helper." By this process he evolved the theory of spontaneity into a theory of action. He was tremendously significant in rupturing the dogma of culture and the modes of enslavement that were programmed by the family. As early as 1940 he was involved in an effort to understand the therapeutic triangles in marriage and the interrelationship of roles in premarital, early marriage, and later marriage phases.

Because of his openness and his freedom to transcend the process of the living moment on the stage, he developed the capacity to transcend stress and taught those people he worked with how to laugh at themselves (which Harold Searles calls the cure for schizophrenia). He did indeed work many, many years with psychotics— and with great success—in hospitals around the country, in his workshops, and in his own hospital and outpatient clinic on the banks of the Hudson. His move from focusing on the delusion system and the hallucinatory problems of the psychotic to the imaginary stage roles was remarkably valuable. Moreover, his pattern of participation included the free expression of his own belief system, which made his work such a personal experience for everyone connected with him.

This book records not only Moreno's theoretical evolution of psychodrama, sociodrama, and sociometry, but also his understanding of authority and democracy. He extrapolated the processes of group dynamics just as

Freud did with individual dynamics. One of the great qualities of this compendium is the presence of a great many long samples of Moreno at work, quoting in detail the give-and-take between him and the auxiliary egos, the patients and the audience-observers. Jake's status in the United States was somewhat limited because he spent a great deal of his time in Europe, where he is still revered and is the model of much of the group therapy work in the European Economic Community. He was an exciting man, with a wonderful combination of Genet, Fritz Redl, Freud, and Picasso, and this is an exciting book. It is not the usual book on psychiatry, psychotherapy, or psychopathology. It is a book about living, and the massive contribution of a true master.

CARL A. WHITAKER, M.D.

Jonathan Fox, M. A., teaches at the State University of New York, College at New Paltz, where he directs a program in Theatre for Education and Human Services. He is a former managing editor of the *Journal of Group Psychotherapy, Psychodrama, & Sociometry*. A Fellow of the American Society for Group Psychotherapy and Psychodrama, he is a certified Trainer, Educator and Practitioner (T.E.P.) and has taught at many psychodrama institutes in the United States and abroad. He is also the founder of Playback Theater, an approach based on the spontaneous enactment of personal story.

Acknowledgments

This book benefited from the kind assistance of many individuals. First I would like to express my gratitude to the Executive Council of the American Society of Group Psychotherapy and Psychodrama for asking me to undertake the task, especially the chair of the Publications Committee, Jonathan D. Moreno, who assisted in a number of ways. Dinah Hawkin, Fred Harris, and John Pitre helped with early research. For bibliographical assistance I am indebted to Anne Ancelin Schützenberger, Adam Blatner, Dalmiro M. Bustos, Pierre J. Fontaine, George Gazda, Ann Hale, Annette Henne, Kei Kudo Maeda, René Marineau, John Nolte, Bjørn K. Rasmussen, Ottavio Rosati, and James M. Sacks. The following responded with suggestions for what *was* the essential Moreno: Giovanni Boria, Dale Richard Buchanan, Christina Hagelthorn, Linnea Carlson-Sibelli, Elaine Eller Goldman, Marcia J. Karp and her students, Yvonne Kennedy, Donnell Miller, Karen Finucane McNamara, Peter Mendelson, Ray Naar, Warren Parry, Peter Pitzele, and Ken Sprague. Richard Wolfe, Curator, Rare Books and Manuscripts, Countway Medical Library, Harvard University, where Moreno's papers are deposited, was unfailingly helpful. The work of his assistants in cataloguing the Moreno material made my work much easier: Christopher Kraus, Joni Clouse, and Pat Sherman. I am grateful to A. Paul Hare for permission to draw from the bibliography of Moreno's works that forms the basis of the Countway list, as well as for his bibliographical suggestions. For reviewing either all or parts of the manuscript, I wish to thank most earnestly Rodney E. Donaldson, editor of Gregory Bateson's papers and correspondence; Elaine Goldman, Ph.D., director of the Psychodrama Program of Camelback Hospital in Phoenix, AZ; Alan Kraus, C.S.W., Division Chief, Department of Mental Hygiene, Dutchess

County, NY; and René Marineau, Ph.D., Professor of Clinical Psychology, Université du Québec à Trois Riviéres. I am appreciative of Bette D. McKenna for proofreading. Jo Salas gave important support in many ways. Finally, I wish to thank Zerka T. Moreno for her unfailing generosity and support. Any errors or omissions are, of course, my own responsibility.

JONATHAN FOX

Introduction

J.L. Moreno was a large man with a large vision. His scope went beyond the development of a comprehensive philosophical system; he originated methods of psychotherapeutic treatment, sociological investigation, and training. Today Moreno is known primarily as the originator of psychodrama, a form of therapy based on role playing. But he originally achieved prominence for his innovative work with groups. Interested in neither the mob nor the individual, he took a middle way, focusing on the small group, which he analyzed and treated according to a sophisticated theory of group process called sociometry. He thus spanned the line between sociology and psychology and was a pioneer in the development of the group approach to problems of social organization and mental health.

The essence of sociometry lies in the idea that groups have an internal life of their own and that this life can best be understood by examining the choices members make at any given moment with regard to each other. Such knowledge—who is rejected, who is the "star," where are the cliques—can then be used to institute a program for positive change. Every group, Moreno insisted, has underneath its visible structure an internal, invisible structure that is "real, alive, and dynamic." Furthermore, Moreno believed that all groups have the capacity for a transcendent interconnectedness. This state of loving and sharing can rarely be accomplished, however, without a skillful management of sociometric processes.

Underlying all Moreno's work in sociometry (the measure of relationship), in sociodrama (the drama of the group) and in psychodrama (the drama of the individual) are certain common themes, the first of which is an emphasis on acting and action. "Man is a role player," Moreno stated. Moreno's concept of mental health was based on the idea of the multi-role personality, the individual with a large repertoire of roles and the flexibility to act the right way at the right time. Action was also the essence of his approach to therapy. "The essential feature of the psychodramatic dream technique is that the dream is not told but acted out," he wrote. Even in a sociometric test, in which group members express preferences on paper, the emphasis is on concrete change in the status quo: "The true sociometric test as we planned it is a revolutionary category of investigation. It upsets the group from within. It produces social revolution on a microscopic scale." Without such a commitment to *act* on its results, sociometry becomes "a harmless, poverty-stricken instrument."

This "science of action," as Moreno called it, is a direct refutation of psychoanalysis (Freud was Moreno's senior by a generation). Moreno found Freud's approach distasteful for a number of reasons—one being his lack of interest in group treatment. But what was most unpalatable about Freud for Moreno was the verbal emphasis of psychoanalysis. A number of times in his writings Moreno referred disparagingly to the "couch" as a locus for therapy. In contrast he was willing to treat his patients anywhere, even, he claimed, "on the street." Moreover, he demanded that therapy be conducted "face-to-face," even advocating that the therapist become a "friend" of the patient.

Basically, Moreno believed in encounter rather than transference as a principle of cure. This means a controversial intensity of engagement among therapist, therapeutic aides, and patient. Encounter means "meeting, contact of bodies, confrontation, countering and battling, seeing and perceiving, touching and entering into each other . . . in a primary, intuitive manner . . a meeting on the most intense level." The emphasis is on relation rather than words, on a physically rather than verbally induced catharsis. There is also an appreciation of the immediacy of the therapeutic moment that anticipated Gestalt psychology.

Moreno's active, highly personalized, group-oriented focus was a radical turn for psychiatry in the 1920s and 1930s. A personal incident is revealing: As a young man in Vienna, just having completed his medical degree, he saw a prostitute arrested on the street. The incident disturbed Moreno, and he became involved. He had no interest in imposing his own view of normal or acceptable behavior—i.e., in "curing" the "sickness" of this particular woman. Moreover, he was not interested merely in her individual case. What Moreno did was to initiate a series of weekly meetings in the prostitutes' own setting, which functioned rather like what we might today call a consciousness-raising group. He was concerned with helping them identify their own problems and stimulating their own motivation to find solutions. (Of course, Moreno was not alone in defending prostitutes; another notable example was Wilhelm Reich).

Moreno believed that our social world, what he came to call the social atom, was highly significant to our sense of well-being. In a constantly shifting pattern, we reach out towards or reject individuals in our social atom, and they do the same towards us. If we are isolated, our sociometric status is low and we are prone to injury. Much of Moreno's work was directed toward improving the position of the isolate.

It was a corollary of Moreno's emphasis on interaction that psychological problems often have an interactive basis. This finding was another stimulus to moving beyond treatment of the individual alone. From inception of Moreno's tenure as director of a psychodrama treatment center, Beacon Hill, which he founded in a Hudson River town north of New York City in 1936, he demanded, whenever possible, treating not only the individual sent for therapy, but members of the patient's social atom as well—the spouse, the parents, even the lover (see Chapter 9 for an article on this early appearance of the systems approach to treatment).

He was also not loathe to treat many clients at once, even different types of clients. In fact, from personal reports and what one can glean from the literature, he had an Ericksonian genius for treating an entire gathering—patient, assistants, and audience (see Part III, "Protocols"). Despite Moreno's emphasis on the group, however, the methods he developed pay high respect to personhood. What he returns to again and again in his writings is the capacity of everyone to be creative and spontaneous. In fact, for Moreno, spontaneity was a byword. We all have the capacity to act not only readily, but also *appropriately* which implies doing something new, better, more creative than ever before.

Even the isolate has this capacity. In fact, Moreno's interest in the isolate had a deeply ethical basis. He was not a conventionally religious man in later life, but during his adolescence he went through a Hassidic period. He and a band of friends wore beards, refused payment for services, and opened a shelter for refugees (see Part IV, "Autobiographical Selections"). It was at this time that he adopted "Moreno" as a surname instead of his patronymic, "Levi." Moreno, which was a family name, also means "chief rabbi" and is contained in Jewish prayer. The Judeo-Christian tradition finds value, even sanctity, in the humble and powerless. It was thus no accident that Moreno's methods were developed while working with young children, prostitutes, displaced persons, prisoners, and delinquent adolescents—readily contained populations handy for research, perhaps, but also groups deserving of our ethical concern.

In psychodrama a patient, called the protagonist, is invited to share his or her *Eigenwelt*, or private, inner world, no mattter how idiosyncratic; in the process, individuality is validated. Moreno was criticized for abetting patients' delusions, but he actually believed that his permission-giving was the opposite of escapism. For the severely disturbed, it is a first step towards making contact, towards a meaningful encounter between therapist and patient, without which no therapeutic progress is possible (see Chapter 8 for an article on the treatment of psychoses). It was most likely his understanding of spontaneity that gave Moreno the courage and skill to work with psychotics; he was able to enter their world as would R.D. Laing decades later.

For the neurotic and even for the healthy individual seeking personal growth, psychodrama is an invitation to self-liberation. Its power is immense, causing exhilaration in the ready and terror in the faint of heart. Moreno was aware of psychodrama's potency. He wrote that we are liable to "fear our own spontaneity as our ancestors feared fire," a point similar to Fromm's concerning the human tendency to want to flee the prospect of freedom. Moreno was not one to be intimidated by convention. He wanter to offer "all forms of subjective existence, including the prophetic and the deviate, a place to fulfill and perhaps transform themselves, unencumbered by the restrictions of the prevailing culture. " In fact, he felt that the "megalomania normalis" of the child is a quality to hold on to in adulthood, and his psychodrama stage at Beacon included a balcony so that the protagonist would be able to play God. He urged his clients not merely to tell, but to act out their dream—first in the therapeutic theater, then in the theater of life.

BIOGRAPHICAL DETAILS

Moreno was born in 1889 in Rumania but grew up in Vienna, capital of the Hapsburg Empire—a double refugee because of his Jewishness. He was the eldest of six, bright, very much a child of his age if also an isolate. Turn-of-the-century Vienna, strained by the increasingly ineffective government of a rigid monarchy (Franz Joseph celebrated 50 years of rule in 1908), was like a Luna Park with antiquated equipment—pulsating with excitement and deadly dangerous. Its culture was full of contradictions. The only possible hero was "The Man Without Qualities," the title of Robert Musil's celebrated novel, whose principal character was poised on a fulcrum between picaresque serendipity and existential despair. Hitler grew to adulthood in this city, as did Theodor Herzl. The *Wiener Werkstaette* produced gay, brilliant decorative art, while Schiele and Kokoschka turned to a seething expressionism. Kokoschka, by the way, started out as a playwright but gave up word-making for painting. He was one of many involved in a debate about the utility of language (understandable in a decadent, dying regime) that achieved its most elevated expression in Wittgenstein's *Tractatus logico-philosophicus,* the final sentence of which work, "Whereof one cannot speak, thereof one must be silent," would find a parallel in Moreno's contention that the act comes before the word. It is interesting that the role of the imagination was also hotly debated in this period. Karl Kraus, editor of the influential satirical magazine

Die Fackel, criticized Freud's emphasis on the antisocial demands of the unconscious as just another manifestation of the sickness of the age. In contrast, Kraus agreed with Schoenberg that fantasy is the *"fons et origo* of creativity." Moreno was clearly on the side of Kraus, Schoenberg, and the "dreamers," including Viktor Frankl, who discovered in World War II that his capacity to imagine a positive future, even under unimaginably hopeless circumstances, made possible a here-and-now choice for spiritual freedom and physical survival.

While Moreno studied medicine and psychiatry at the University of Vienna during the epoch of World War I, he directed his *Stegreiftheater* (theater of spontaneity), first using children, then adults, as actors. Moreno considered this theater work very important (after emigrating, he rented a studio in Carnegie Hall to conduct presentations of what he called "Theater of the Impromptu"). Despite the publication of a book on the subject as early as 1923, however, his writing on theater is not as cogent as his other work. Thus his contribution to theater consisted of personal influence upon a likeminded few who were not interested in artistically produced plays but in native inventivness and spontaneous dramas "as they spring up in everyday life, in the minds of simple people."

As a young thinker and professional, Moreno wrote and published essays with provocative titles like "Godhead as Actor" and "The Silence." He also edited a journal called *Daimon*, which included among its contributors Franz Werfel and Martin Buber. He published most of his writing anonymously, a paradoxical gesture very much in the contemporary spirit, since despite Vienna's cosmopolitanism, everyone seemed to know everyone else. By the time Moreno—by now a practicing doctor and psychiatrist with most of his basic ideas already formed—came to the United States in the wake of one of his brothers, he was ready to make his name. His rise to prominence was astonishingly fast. As the 1930s began, he was being recognized for his sociometric work at Sing Sing Prison, published under the title "Classification of Prisoners According to the Group Method" (1931). His statements were quoted in *The New York Times*: A 1929 article, for example, carried the headline "Impromptu Plan Used in Education." By 1940 he had opened his sanitarium in Beacon (it was to be the premier psychodrama treatment facility for 31 years), written his magnum opus, *Who Shall Survive? A New Approach to the Problem of Human Interrelations*, and started a journal, *Sociometry*.

For Moreno the 1930s and 1940s were a fecund period. Students either in New York City or Beacon included Fritz Perls, Marion Chace, Eric Berne, Theodore Sarbin, and Ronald Lippitt. Karl Menninger visited and subsequently had a psychodrama theater installed at Winter General Hospital in Topeka. The editorial board of *Sociometry* included Read Bain, John Dewey, Gardner Murphy, Wesley C. Mitchell, and George Murdock. Margaret Mead wrote for it, as did George Gallup, Adolf Meyer, Paul Lazarsfeld, Rudolph Dreikurs, Kurt Lewin, and Charles P. Loomis (an agricultural economist who implemented sociometric procedures in planning resettlement communities for the Tennessee Valley Authority). Reading *Sociometry* issues published during these years, one cannot but get a sense of Moreno's driving, inspiring influence on a wide circle of curious and committed people. It was during this period, as well, that he wrote many of his most significant articles.

In 1942 Moreno founded the American Society for Group Psychotherapy and Psychodrama, which became the new field's professional association. A psychodrama theater had already been built at St. Elizabeths Hospital in Washington, D.C. During the decade he dedicated a theater at Harvard University, founded a second major journal, initially called *Sociatry*, then renamed *Psychotherapy, Psychodrama, and Sociometry*, and published the first of three volumes intitled *Psychodrama*.

He also married Zerka Toeman, who had come to Beacon Hill to seek help for her sister. Zerka Moreno became her husband's principal administrative assistant and auxiliary ego (therapeutic aide). She was to have a significant influence on the development of the psychodramatic method (volumes two and three of *Psychodrama* were co-authored by her). That the contemporary practice of psychodrama has developed considerably beyond Moreno's written description of it owes a great deal to Zerka Moreno's leadership; specifically, Moreno, with his abiding sociometric perspective, favored a horizontal, social system approach (see Chapters 15 and 16 for examples), while Zerka Moreno favors a vertical approach that concentrates directly on a primal past experience. Zerka Moreno played a decisive role in training the modern generation of students in the cathartic form of psychodrama that is today considered "classical."

Having established sociometry and psychodrama in the United States, Moreno turned his focus to the international arena: 1954, the First International Congress of Group Psychotherapy, Toronto; 1964, First International Congress of Psychodrama, Paris; 1968, First International Congress of Sociometry, Baden, Austria. In 1959 he made the first of two lecture tours to the Soviet Union, and in 1969 he received an honorary degree from his alma mater, the University of Vienna. A plaque was ceremoniously placed on his former home in Bad Voslau, a town outside Vienna where he had lived and served as Public Health Officer just prior to his departure for the United States.

Moreno died as he had lived, with considerable intentionality. As a young man he had written, "I had no fear"; he faced his end at home, without medicine, and eventually without food. He left this world an honored man, his work translated into over a dozen languages.

Despite the sense of greatness—even genius—felt by many who came into his orbit, however, Moreno was a problem personality. Perhaps especially since he had been so creative, his megalomania normalis knew no bounds. In fact, there was a fundamental contradiction between his credo of unconserved spontaneity and what Ernest Becker would call his "Oedipus Project," his inability to distinguish between himself and his creations. In his confusion Moreno oscillated between magnanimity and paranoia, between generous gestures and accusations of professional theft.

Moreno's need to have it all may have contributed to an inability to limit his focus on a particular project to either clinical practice or experimental research. His frequent claim that his work was both "operational" *and* "observational" put off potential sympathizers accustomed to a more rigorous approach. It was also not easy to accept a dualistic philosophical position that embraced both logical positivism and religious existentialism.

His egotism notwithstanding, it is incontrovertible that Moreno was a seminal practitioner at the forefront of the encounter movement and the group-oriented approach to psychotherapy. The range and complexity of what he developed made it inevitable that his discoveries be adopted piecemeal and often in containable, simpler formats. There was certainly misuse, such as the administration of sociometric tests that did not include an action segment (sometimes called "cold" sociometry and almost always a manipulation), encounter groups that valued expressiveness over transcendence, and role playing that ignored the key technique of role reversal.

It is another philosophical contradiction that Moreno was driven to put his ideas down on paper despite his allegiance to action over intellect. For this we can be grateful, and yet the blessing is a mixed one. While the corpus of Moreno's written work is considerable, for the most part he self-published. His works were not professionally edited or distributed—to the growing frustration of those interested in his ideas. The goal of this volume is thus to provide the reader with a basic sense of Moreno's work in a compact format. Nevertheless, Moreno's scope was wide, and there is a considerable amount of interesting material that could not be included.

In the selections included in this volume Moreno argues forcefully and at times eloquently for his methods. But despite his commitment to science, evidenced by the technical nature of his language, Moreno never lost the philosophical and religious beliefs of his youth. Indeed, the practices and methods described herein are based on a philosophy of service, courage, and compassion that ultimately, perhaps, cannot be described and conserved but must be lived to be fully understood.

ARRANGEMENT, SELECTION, AND EDITING OF ITEMS

Part I of this volume is a general introduction to Moreno's ideas, designed for the newcomer to the field. Part II covers more technical subjects and roughly follows a progression from psychodrama to sociometry. Part III consists entirely of protocols that show Moreno at work directing psychodrama and sociodrama. Part IV contains autobiographical fragments. The book concludes with a section of Notes, a Chronology, and two Bibliographies: a list of Moreno's published books and a list of relevant books in the field.

While editing this volume, I have kept in mind the danger and delicacy of making improvements. Nevertheless, an unusual number of interventions have been necessary. My editorial policy is outlined below. I do take some comfort from the fact that unlike the situation brought about by the medieval scribes, who often discarded their source after copying and brought about the extinction of the original, Moreno's books are available for comparison and further research in libraries or from the current distributor, Beacon House, Ambler, Pennsylvania.

The date of writing of each selection is cited under the title at the beginning of each chapter. The source is indicated in a footnote. Since Moreno reprinted his own writing frequently, often under another title or amalgamated with new work, I have listed sources for other versions of the selected articles when they exist, to the extent that I am aware of them.

I have corrected incorrect or inconsistent punctuation and spelling; made sentences grammatical when necessary; and omitted passages that are unduly confusing, disorganized, self-serving, or topical, when such omissions do not lessen the value of the article as a whole. Thus all selections contain slight omissions, marked by ellipses in the conventional manner when substantive.

A problem has been the sexual stereotyping typical of Moreno's milieu and legion in the text. Despite the awkwardness of Moreno's constant use of "he" and "man" to mean both men and women, changing this usage seemed too much a violation of his own thought and sentence structure; so I have let it stand.

The above general policy also applies to the Notes: They have been edited for clarity and consistency. The list of Moreno's publications has been limited to his books and the journals founded by him. Most of Moreno's articles can be found in these journals. A full bibliography is on file at the Countway Medical Library at Harvard University, where Moreno's papers are located. Moreno published a series of pamphlets before his emigration to the United States, which for the most part remain untranslated. Only one has been listed in the Bibliography [*Einladung zu einer Begegnung* (Invitation to an encounter)], even though some European scholars feel they contain important material. The others include *Das Kinderreich* (The children's realm), 1908, later reedited as *Das Reich der Kinder*, 1914; *Homo Juvenis* (Man as youth), 1908; *Die Gottheit als Komodiant* (The godhead actor), 1911; *Der Bericht* (The report), 1915; and *Das Schweigen* (The silence), 1915—all published in Vienna by the Anzengruber Verlag. Published in *Daimon* and *Der Neue Daimon* were

Die Gottheit Autor (The godhead as author), 1918; and *Die Gottheit als Redner* (The godhead as preacher), 1919. The Verlag Gustav Kiepenheuer in Berlin and Potsdam published *Der Augenblick* (The moment), 1922; *Rede über die Begegnung* (Speech on the encounter),1924; *Der Konigsroman* (The kings novel), 1923; *Die Rede vor dem Richter* (Speech before the judge), 1925. The Secondary Bibliography is confined to journals that have carried frequent articles on psychodrama and published books. The journals are listed first. Additional articles in journals as well as unpublished theses on psychodrama and related fields can be traced through the standard reference channels. I have included a brief listing of foreign-language books on the grounds that the vigor of the psychodrama movement worldwide has produced significant writing that demands attention from the English-speaking student. Good sources for foreign-language bibliographies are translations of Moreno as well as the works of the major non-American authors, whose identity is readily distinguishable from the listing.

PART I: An Overview

"My position was threefold: first, the hypothesis of
spontaneity-creativity as a propelling force in human progress . . . second, the hypothesis of having
faith in our fellowman's intentions . . . of love and
mutual sharing as a powerful, indispensable working principle of group life; and third, the hypothesis of a superdynamic community based upon
these principles."

(From *Who Shall Survive?, xv*)

CHAPTER 1

Moreno's Philosophical System

1966

> *Editor's note: Moreno often stated his philosophical position from as early as the 1920s, but this late expression represents the best synthesis of some fundamental beliefs: the importance of living one's truth in action; the validity of subjective reality; the premise of a living here-and-now encounter between individuals (including client and therapist); and a deep egalitarianism.*

. . .The objective of psychodrama was, from its inception, to construct a therapeutic setting which uses life as a model, to integrate into it all the modalities of living, beginning with the universals—time, space, reality, and cosmos—down to all the details and nuances of life.

PSYCHOTHERAPY AND PSYCHOPATHOLOGY OF TIME

Let us start with time, one of the great universals. What has happened with the function of time in the course of psychotherapy in our century? I do not speak of time as a philosophical, mystical, or phenomenological concept, but

From Psychiatry of the Twentieth Century: Function of the Universalia: Time, Space, Reality, and Cosmos, *Psychodrama,* Vol. 3 (1969), 11–23. Also *Sociometry* 3 (1940); *Group Psychotherapy, Psychodrama & Sociometry* 19 (1966).

as a therapeutic concept. From the point of view of therapeutic procedures, to what extent does the time dimension enter into and function in psychotherapeutic settings? Man lives in time—past, present, and future. He may suffer from a pathology related to each. The problem is how to integrate all three dimensions into significant therapeutic operations. It is not sufficient that they figure as "abstract" references; they must be made alive within treatment modalities. The psychological aspect of time must reappear in toto.

Let us look first at psychoanalysis. When I speak of psychoanalysis, I refer to the orthodox Freudian position. Time, in the psychotherapeutic doctrine, is emphasized in terms of the past. Freud, an exponent of genetic psychology and psychobiology, found going back and trying to find the causes of things of particular interest. Often the farther back he went, the more he thought he would find something which is worthwhile as a causation. And soon, psychoanalysts began to go farther and farther back, into the womb, and if possible, even beyond that, until they got tired of the futile "recherche du temps perdu," and began to come back.

However important that past is as a dimension of time, it is a one-sided position, a "reduced time," which neglects and distorts the total influence which time has upon the psyche. Here we come to my first conflict with the Freudian view. I have pointed out that time has other phases which are important. One of them is the present, the dynamics of the present, of the Here and Now, hic et nunc. The experiences which take place continuously in the context of the Here and Now have been overlooked, distorted, or entirely forgotten. Therefore, early in my writings . . . I began to emphasize the moment, the dynamics of the moment, the warming up to the moment, the dynamics of the present, the Here and Now, and all its immediate personal, social, and cultural implications. But again, I considered these not only from the point of view of philosophy and phenomenology, but from the viewpoint of the therapeutic process as it takes place in connection with patients and in patient groups—the encounter. The encounter is a telic phenomenon. The fundamental process of tele* is reciprocity—reciprocity of attraction, reciprocity of rejection, reciprocity of excitation, reciprocity of inhibition, reciprocity of indifference, reciprocity of distortion . . . .

> A meeting of two: eye to eye, face to face.
> And when you are near I will tear your eyes out
> and place them instead of mine,
> and you will tear my eyes out
> and will place them instead of yours,
> then I will look at you with your eyes . . .
> and you will look at me with mine.[1]

---

* For a definition of tele, see Chapter 3. (Ed.).

There is another dimension of therapeutic time which has been neglected until recently—the future. Yet it is an important aspect of living, for we certainly live more in the future than in the past. Since early this morning, I have been concerned with being on time to meet you.* But it is one thing to consider the expectancies of future happenings in our own minds and another thing to "simulate" them, to construct techniques which enable us to live in the future, to act as if the future is at hand, right here, "a la recherche du temps de l'avenir." For instance, via our therapeutic future techniques, I can act out a situation which I expect to happen tomorrow, with a new friend, or an appointment with a prospective employer, to simulate the morrow as concretely as possible, so as to predict it, or perhaps to be better prepared for it.

I have often had clients who suffered from an employment neurosis or an unemployment neurosis, who are anxious about getting a job, or having an interview with a boss to ask for higher wages. Often we rehearse such a client a week in advance of what may happen; it is a sort of "rehearsal for life." This rehearsal for life technique is also effective with clients concerned about an affair of the heart—whether it be a prospective marriage, divorce, new baby, or whatever. The problem is how to integrate these expectancies and concerns of the client into the therapeutic operation as actualities, so as to be of value for both client and therapist.

The importance of the future as a perception and as a dynamic meaning has been emphasized by others—for instance, Adler, Horney, and Sullivan. But the special configuration around and inside the future situation remained unstructured and impersonal.

Thus all three dimensions of time—past, present, and future—are brought together in psychodrama, as they are in life, from the point of view of functional therapy.

PSYCHOTHERAPY AND PSYCHOPATHOLOGY OF SPACE

Now let us go into the concept of space. Space, too, has been almost entirely neglected in all the psychotherapies, not semantically and psychologically, but, again, as part of the therapeutic process. If you go into a psychoanalytic office, you find an abstract bed, a couch, but the rest of the office space is not related to the therapeutic process. The client is language-centered and the therapist is centered to listen. Yet, despite the fact that all therapies have noticeably neglected the element of space, the physicists, the astronomers, and the astronauts have not. In the cosmic affluence of our time, space and

---

*This article was originally delivered as a speech at the Second International Congress of Psychodrama in Barcelona. (Ed.)

physical communication through it have become enormously important categories in the mind of man, in his vision of life and of the universe as he plans to travel to the moon, the planets, and eventually the stars.

If you go into an office in which any of the current varieties of psychotherapy are practiced, you may find only a chair. The space in which the protagonist experiences his traumas has no place in that setting. The idea of a psychotherapy of space has been pioneered by psychodrama, which is action-centered and comprehensively tries to integrate all the dimensions of living into itself. It is a sort of "recherche de l'espace concrét, vécu." If a client steps into the therapeutic space, we insist on a description, delineation, and actualization of the space in which the ensuing scene is to be portrayed— its horizontal and vertical dimensions, the objects in it, and their distance and relationship to one another.

Here is an illustration of an actual case: The client is a teenage boy. He tells me, "Doctor, I'm afraid to go home tonight." I ask him: "Why, what happened?" "Well, this afternoon my mother and father had an argument and my father hit my mother and made her fall down the stairway. I saw her there, at the bottom of the stairs and became so furious at my father that I hit him. But then I got scared, took my bag of clothes, and ran away. Here I am, and I don't dare go home."

Now what do we do? How do we start psychodramatizing the incident? I ask the boy, "Jack, where is the stairway? And where is your mother?" Jack moves about on the stage, points out the location of the stairway, places it in relationship to the front door, the bedrooms, living room, et cetera, moving around in the space in which he experiences this episode, structuring it before our eyes.

At this point we use a future technique. "Jack, you go home now, but instead of really going to Brooklyn, where you live, you are going home right here in this room. Let's say you will be home in about an hour from now. Set up all the spatial configurations as closely as possible. Who is home when you arrive and where are they located in space?" Jack explains and physically constructs the spatial arrangement: "Well, first of all I come in at the front door, here, into the living room. I expect my father to be over there, in his chair in the corner of the room, angry. My mother is in the bedroom upstairs, crying." Now Jack proceeds to set up the rest of the space . . . [including] all things which he feels to be significant. He warms up more and more and gets increasingly involved in the situation. Soon he begins to see pictures on the walls; he noticed that mother wears a certain dress, father smokes a cigar. In other words, immediately the configurations of the space itself become a parameter for a therapeutic setting.

There is no point in dwelling on the details too much. However, I cannot emphasize sufficiently that in our research the configurations of space as a part of the therapeutic process are of utmost importance. It warms up the protagonist to be and to act himself in an environment which is modeled after that in which he lives.

PSYCHOTHERAPY AND THE PSYCHOPATHOLOGY OF REALITY

We come now to the third universal, reality. That, also, has undergone quite a change in the last thirty or forty years. As our psychiatry takes place more and more in the community, rather than in hospitals, reality begins to attain new meanings. The trend is very much along the lines of confrontation and concretization.

One may say that the reality in a psychoanalytic office, from the point of view of the therapeusis, is a sort of "reduced reality," an "infra-reality." The contact between doctor and patient is not a genuine dialogue, but a sort of interview, a research situation or projection test. Whatever is happening to the patient—for example, a suicidal idea or a plan to run away, is not a phase of direct actualization and confrontation but remains on the level of imagining, thinking, feeling, fearing, and so forth. To an extent, this is also true of the reality in the office of the client-centered, existential, or interview therapist.

The next step is the reality of life itself, of the everyday lives of you and me and of all ordinary people, how we live in our own homes, in our businesses, and in our relationships to one another . . . .

However, the manner in which we live in reality, in our relationships with the significant people in our lives, may be defective or inadequate, and we may wish to change—to attempt new ways of living. But change can be both threatening and extremely difficult, to such an extent that we stay in our familiar ruts rather than risk a calamity which we cannot handle. Thus a therapeutic situation is needed in which reality can be simulated, so that people can learn to develop new techniques of living without risking serious consequence or disaster . . . .

We come to yet another level of structuring, representing the intangible, invisible dimensions of intra- and extrapsychic life, which I have called surplus reality. When I coined this term, I was influenced by the term "surplus value" which Marx used in Time *Das Kapital* to indicate that the capitalists absorb the surplus earnings of the working man. This became for him one of the reasons why an economic revolution was needed—to restore the right of the working man. However, surplus does not quite have the same meaning in psychotherapy. Surplus reality is only an analogous term; in our case it means that there are certain invisible dimensions in the reality of living, not fully experienced or expressed, and that is why we have to use surplus operations and surplus instruments to bring them out in our therapeutic settings.

One of the most popular surplus reality techniques in psychodrama is that of role reversal. If, for instance, a husband and wife fight in the reality of daily life, each remains in his own role, in his own life situation. The perceptions, expectations, fears, disappointments, or whatever of each remain unchanged. And even if both parties come to some point of agreement or disagreement, they still maintain the same relative status which they have in life. The husband remains the husband, the wife remains the wife. But in role reversal we request the wife take the part of the husband, and the husband take the part of the wife. We expect them to do this not only nominally, but to make an effort to go through the actual process of reversing roles, each one to try and feel his way into the thinking, feeling, and behavior patterns of the other.

Of course, this is particularly useful in situations which are provoked by stress. Let us quote a specific case: It is eight o'clock in the morning and the husband, who is employed as the head of a sales office, comes down the stairs, rushes into the kitchen, and says to his wife: "Mary, what's the matter with you. Are you crazy? Why didn't you wake me up? It's already eight o'clock and you know I have to be in my office by 8:15!" She begins to cry, "But I'm just fixing your eggs. I knocked on your door three times and you didn't wake up! Why do you have to yell at me? I'm doing the best I can. What's the matter with *you*?" Then she bursts into tears and he has a temper tantrum. This is the critical moment for role reversal. At this point the therapist steps in and says: "Now, Bob, you take the part of Mary, and Mary, you take the part of Bob." And now you see Bob, in the role of his wife, standing over the stove trying to fix the eggs and crying bitterly because Mary, in the role of the husband, is such a sadist. She is now the one who has the temper tantrum, who comes rushing down the stairs into the kitchen shouting, "You damn fool! What's the matter with you. Are you crazy?"

Now it is not always easy to establish identity with one's own self at a certain time in one's life, to recapture feelings and behavior in a crucial episode—for instance as a child or adolescent, but it is at least plausible. But how can one establish identity with another person, as one is requested to do in role reversal? Yet we have found that this is possible, especially between individuals who have lived a long time together in intimate ensembles, such as husbands and wives, mothers and children, fathers and sons, sisters and brothers, or very close friends.

Just recently I spoke before a group of theologians who asked me, "What is the difference between the old Christian hypothesis, 'Love your neighbor' and your hypothesis?" I answered, "Well, we have not really improved very much on 'Love your neighbor' except that we have added, 'by means of role reversal.'"

We do not practice such surplus reality techniques as role reversal in life itself; that is why we have started them in therapy. However, I predict that some day they will be just as popular as some of the jet airplanes which fly from one part of the country to another and from one part of the world to another. In the distant future people will begin to play the game of role reversal among themselves and with the inhabitants of other planets. But in the present we need these methods to improve our techniques of human interaction.

One of the basic instruments in constructing a patient's psychodramatic world is that of the auxiliary ego, which is the representation of absentee individuals, delusions, hallucinations, symbols, ideals, animals, and objects. They make the protagonist's world real, concrete, and tangible. However, in the course of making this world real and dynamic, numerous problems emerge, such as the use of bodily contact. Now bodily contact has been, to some extent, a taboo in all psychotherapies. Yet when a nurse sees a patient suffering, she cannot help but touch him and say, "Now Jack, don't worry, it will be all right." Her touch may mean more to the boy than the words she speaks, not in an overtly sexual way, but as a sort of maternal, protective approach to him. But a psychoanalyst who would become in any way physically personal with his patient would be ostracized.

However, in the psychodramatic approach to human relations we are interested in following the model of life itself, and within limits in making therapeutic use of the bodily contact technique. This technique is obviously contra-indicated if it is used to gratify the need of the therapist, but most indicated if it gives the patient the warmth and immediacy of pulsating life in an area in which he is in need—not only in words, but in action.

For instance, if you have a young woman patient who suffers a profound alienation from her husband or from her family, you will give her an auxiliary ego, and whether it be male or female, you will expect him or her to be warm and personal, to put his or her arm around the patient's shoulder, and if indicated, even to go beyond that. Where to draw the ethical, aesthetic, and therapeutic limitation is a very great problem. But you cannot be an auxiliary ego, a mother, a father, a son, or whatever, unless you live it. If you do not live it, it becomes abstract, unfeeling, and untherapeutic. Of course the therapist can get into real trouble this way, and as a warning I would like to tell you about an actual case in a big hospital in the U.S.A. It involved a young woman patient who was engaged to be married; she was profoundly depressed and in need of affection. She was given an auxiliary ego to portray the man to whom she was engaged. According to the rules, the auxiliary fiancé became very warm, put his arms around her, and kissed her. He did not go too far, I assure you, but still, far enough to arouse the ire of her father, who happened to be a Senator. When he heard about the session he immediately called up the Superintendent of the hospital and asked him, "What's the big idea, allowing a perfect stranger to make love to my daughter on a stage!" The Superintendent answered, "Senator, this is therapy. It isn't anything but therapy. We are trying to treat your daughter. Don't you send her or your wife to gynecologists, obstetricians, and other specialists when they need professional attention, and don't these doctors use all kinds of methods which may be a little embarrassing? What do you have against psychotherapy when it become a little bit real?" And so the whole thing was smoothed over, the daughter improved, and a good method was found to calm down even a Senator.

Role playing is another important surplus reality technique. Here a person may be trained to function more effectively in his reality roles—e.g., employer, employee, student, instructor, parent, child, mate, lover, or friend. In the therapeutic setting of psychodrama, the protagonist is free to try and fail in a role, for he knows he will be given the opportunity to try another alternative, and another, until he finally learns new approaches to the situations which he fears, approaches which he can then apply *in situ*, in life itself?

Simulation of reality techniques, which we use so often in psychodrama, are now being employed to train astronauts. Astroengineers simulate, in a laboratory setting, the actual conditions of space. You have seen television pictures of the astronauts being trained to float in space, to live in space ships, to meet other space ships in space, et cetera . . . .

PSYCHOTHERAPY AND PSYCHOPATHOLOGY OF THE COSMOS

Now we come to the forth universal—the cosmos. Early in the twentieth century, during my youth, two philosophies of human relations were particularly popular. One was the philosophy that everything in the universe is all placed in the single individual, in the individual psyche. This was particularly emphasized by Sigmund Freud, who thought that the group was an epiphenomenon. For Freud, everything was "epi"; only the individual counted. The other philosophy was that of Karl Marx. For Marx, everything ended with the social man, or more specifically, the socio-economic. It was as if that were all there was to the world. Very early in my career I came to the position that there is another area, a larger world beyond the psychodynamics and sociodynamics of human society—cosmodynamics. Man is a cosmic man, not only a social man or an individual man . . . .

Since time immemorial, man has tried to understand his position in the universe at large, and if possible, to control the phenomena that determine this position-evolution, birth, death, sex, and the function of the Creator of the world. To do this, man has, in the past, invented religions, myths, fables. He has submitted himself to stark regimentation in order to comply with the laws of the universe as he conceived them. Buddha's Rules, the Ten Commandments of Moses, the numerous rituals of the various illiterate cultures are all testimony of the profound need for man to comply with an invisible value system.

Since we have entered the age of the atomic bomb and the computer, the conceptions of man have changed radically. The pronouncement that God is dead may be meaningless; he may never have existed. But it is important that we may be able to create him in our image. The evolution of the future is wide open for speculation. Birth and death may not be terminal but may attain new meaning through scientific discoveries. Even the difference between the sexes may not be fixed, but may be transitory. One's sex may be changed. The possibility of millions of other beings on other planets raises questions which we have never confronted as clearly as now.

Just like the functions of time, space, and reality, the function of the cosmos must be so integrated into the therapeutic setting that it has experiential and existential value for the protagonist. Within the framework of psychodrama, by means of its numerous methods, cosmic phenomena can be integrated into the therapeutic process. A therapeutic method which does not concern itself with these enormous cosmic implications, with man's very destiny, is incomplete and inadequate. Just as our forefathers encountered these changes by means of fables and myths, we have tried to encounter them in our time with new devices. It is at this point that surplus reality techniques in cosmodynamics come to the fore. In the psychodramatic world the differentiation between the sexes is overlooked and surpassed. There is no sex in psychodrama. The differences in age are overlooked. There is no age in psychodrama. The actualities of birth and death are overlooked. There is no death in psychodrama. The unborn and the dead are brought to life on the psychodrama stage . . . .

The externalizations are, however, closely related to the subjectivity and imagining of the protagonist. A woman who wishes she were born a man may play a man on the psychodrama stage, and so correct the injustices of the universe as she perceives them. In reverse, a man may play a woman. An old man may play a child and so correct the loss of childhood or experience the childhood which he feels he never had. Anatomies and physiologies and biologies do not matter. What matters is the expansion of man in relation to the needs and fantasies he has about himself. He becomes the master of anatomy and physiology instead of the servant. A man can, in the psychodramatic cosmos, also embody animals—dogs, tigers, bears, fish, birds, insects—any form of actual or imaginary beings, not as a form of regression, but as creative involvement. He is free from the fetters of facts and actuality, although not without the highest respect for them. And he has a good foundation for believing, as science has repeatedly taught us, that things are changing and can be further changed, even conditions which seemed for millennia absolutely fixed. This is not a plea for "illusionism" or an escape from reality, but, just the opposite, a plea for the creativity of man and the creativity of the universe. It is, therefore, through man's faith in the infinite creativity of the cosmos that what he embodies in the psychodramatic world may one day actually become true. And so just as Goethe's Faust, at the end of his life, looked into the future and said, "What will be, then, someday in the distant future, I am already experiencing now," psychodrama makes it possible for man to anticipate life . . . . He has the future reality hic et nunc.

One of the greatest dilemmas of man in our time is that he has lost faith in a supreme being, and often in any superior value system as a guide for conduct. Is the universe ruled by change and spontaneity only? The psychodramatic answer to the claim that God is dead is that he can be easily restored to life. Following the example of Christ we have given him and can give him a new life, but not in the form which our ancestors cherished. We have replaced the dead God by millions of people who can embody God in their own person.

This may need further explanation. The outstanding event in modern religion was the replacement, if not the abandonment, of the cosmic, elusive, Super-God by a simple man who called himself the Son of God—Jesus Christ. The outstanding thing about him was not scholarship or intellectual wizardry, but the fact of *embodiment*. There lived in his time many men intellectually superior to Christ, but they were flabby intellectuals. Instead of making an effort to embody the truth as they felt it, they talked about it.

In the psychodramatic world the fact of embodiment is central, axiomatic, and universal. Everyone can portray his version of God through his own actions and so communicate his own version to others . . . . It is no longer the master, the great priest, or the therapist who embodies God. The image of God can take form and embodiment through every man—the epileptic, the schizophrenic, the prostitute, the poor and rejected. They all can at any time step upon the stage, when the moment of inspiration comes, and give their version of the meaning which the universe has for them. God is always within and among us, as he is for children. Instead of coming down from the skies, he comes in by way of the stage door.

CHAPTER 2

Psychodrama and Sociodrama

1946

> *Editor's note: Moreno thought enough of this basic description of psycho-drama, his principal method of treatment, and sociodrama, its adaptation for group issues, to distribute it to each new visitor to the Moreno Institute.*

THE FIVE INSTRUMENTS OF PSYCHODRAMA

Psychodrama can be defined as the science which explores the "truth" by dramatic methods. It deals with interpersonal relations and private worlds.

The psychodramatic method uses mainly five instruments—the stage, the subject or actor, the director, the staff of therapeutic aides or auxiliary egos, and the audience.* The first instrument is the stage. Why a stage? It provides the actor with a living space which is multi-dimensional and flexible to the maximum. The living space of reality is often narrow and restraining; he may easily lose his equilibrium. On the stage he may find it again due to its

---

From *Who Shall Survive?* (1953), 81–89. Another version appears in *Psychodrama*, Vol. 1 (1946).

* Today in psychodrama the universally used term for subject is "protagonist." In his writings, Moreno does not begin to use this term until about 1950. (Ed.)

methodology of freedom—freedom from unbearable stress and freedom for experience and expression. The stage space is an extension of life beyond the reality test of life itself. Reality and fantasy are not in conflict, but both are functions within a wider sphere—the psychodramatic world of objects, persons, and events. In the logic [of psychodrama] the ghost of Hamlet's father is just as real and permitted to exist as Hamlet himself. Delusions and hallucinations are given flesh and an equality of status with normal sensory perceptions. The architectural design of the stage is made in accord with operational requirements. Its circular forms and levels . . . stimulate relief from tensions and permit mobility and flexibility of action. The locus of a psychodrama, if necessary, may be designated anywhere, wherever the subjects are, the field of battle, the classroom, or the private home, but the ultimate resolution of deep mental conflicts requires an objective setting, the psychodramatic theatre.

The second instrument is the subject, or actor. He is asked to be himself on the stage, to portray his own private world. He is not an actor compelled to sacrifice his own private self to the role imposed upon him by a playwright. Once he is warmed up to the task, it is comparatively easy for the subject to give an account of his daily life in action, since no one is as much of an authority on himself as he is. He has to act freely, as things rise up in his mind; that is the why he has to be given freedom of expression, spontaneity. Next in importance to spontaneity comes the process of enactment. The verbal level is transcended and included in the level of action. There are several forms of enactment—pretending to be in a role, re-enactment or acting out a past scene, living out a problem presently pressing, or testing oneself for the future. Further comes the principle of involvement. We have been brought up with the idea that, in test as well as in treatment situations, a minimum of involvement with other persons and subjects is a most desirable thing for the subject. In the psychodramatic situation all degrees of involvement take place, from a minimum to a maximum. In addition comes the principle of realization. The subject is enabled not only to meet parts of himself, but the other persons who take part in his mental conflicts. These persons may be real or illusions. The reality test which is a mere word in other methods is thus actually made true on the stage. The warming up process of the subject to psychodramatic portrayal is stimulated by numerous techniques, only a few of which are mentioned here: self-presentation, soliloquy, projection, interpolation of resistance, reversal of roles, double ego, mirror, auxiliary world, realization, and psycho-chemical techniques. The aim of these sundry techniques is not to turn the subjects into actors, but rather to stir them up to be on the stage what they *are*, more deeply and explicitly than they appear to be in life. The patient has as dramatis personae either the real people of his private world—his wife, his father, his child, et cetera—or actors portraying them, the auxiliary egos.

The third instrument is the director. He has three functions: producer, counselor, and analyst. As producer he has to be on the alert to turn every clue which the subject offers into dramatic action, to make the line of production one with the life line of the subject, and never to let the production lose rapport with the audience. As director, attacking and shocking the subject is at times just as permissible as laughing and joking with him; at times he may become indirect and passive, and for all practical purposes the session seems to be run by the subject. As analyst he may complement his own interpretation by responses coming from informants in the audience— husband, parents, children, friends, or neighbors.

The fourth instrument is a staff of auxiliary egos. The auxiliary egos or participant actors have a double significance. They are extensions of the director, exploring and guiding, but they are also extensions of the subject, portraying the actual or imagined personae of his life drama. The functions of the auxiliary ego are threefold: to be an actor, portraying the roles required by the subject's world; to be a counselor, guiding the subject; and to be a social investigator.

The fifth instrument is the audience, which has a double role. They may serve to help the subject or, being themselves helped by the subject on the stage, the audience may become the "problem." In helping the subject they are a sounding board of public opinion. Their responses and comments are as extemporaneous as those of the subject; they may vary from laughter to violent protest. The more isolated the subject is, for instance, because his drama on the stage is shaped by delusions and hallucinations, the more important becomes, to him, the presence of an audience willing to accept and understand him. When the audience is helped by the subject, thus becoming the subject itself, the situation is reversed. The audience then sees itself—that is, one of its collective syndromes, portrayed on the stage.

THE PSYCHODRAMA PRODUCTION

In any discussion of psychodrama the important dynamics which operate should be considered. In the first phase of psychodramatic process the director may meet with some resistance from the subject. In most cases the resistance against being psychodramatized is small or nil. Once a subject understands the degree to which the production is of his own making he will cooperate. Nevertheless, the fight between director and subject is in the psychodramatic context extremely real; to an extent they have to assess each other like two battlers, facing each other in a situation of great stress and challenge. Both of them have to draw spontaneity and cunning from their resources. Positive factors which shape the relationship and interaction in the reality of life itself exist: spontaneity, productivity, the warming up process, tele, and role processes. The psychodramatist, after having made much ado to get the subject started, recedes from the scene. Frequently he does not take any part in it . . . . From the subject's point of view his object of transference, the director, is pushed out of the situation. The retreat of the director gives the subject a feeling that he is the winner. Actually it is nothing but the preliminary warm up before the big bout. To the satisfaction of the subject other persons enter the situation, persons who are nearer to him, like his delusions and hallucinations. He knows them so much better than this stranger, the director. The more they are in the picture, the more he forgets the director, who wants to be forgotten, at least for the time being. The dynamics of this forgetting can be easily explained. Not only does the director leave the scene of operation; the auxiliary egos step in and it is between them that his share of tele, transference, and empathy is divided . . . .

As the subject takes part in the production and warms up to the figures and figureheads of his own private world, he attains tremendous satisfactions which take him far beyond anything he has ever experienced. He has invested so much of his own limited energy in the images of his perceptions of the people in his world as well as in certain images which live a forgotten existence within him, delusions and hallucinations of all sorts, that he has lost a great deal of spontaneity, productivity, and power for himself. They have taken his riches away, and he has become poor, weak, and sick. The psychodrama gives back to him all the investments he had made in the extraneous adventures of his mind. He takes his father, mother, sweetheart, delusions unto himself and the energies which he has invested in them. They return by his actually living through the role of father or employer, friend or enemy. By reversing the roles with them he is already learning many things about them which life does not provide him. When he can be the persons he hallucinates, not only do they lose their power and magic spell over him, but he gains their power for himself. His own self has an opportunity to find and reorganize itself, to put the elements together which may have been kept apart by insidious forces, to integrate them and to attain a sense of power and relief, a catharsis of integration. It can well be said that the psychodrama provides the subject with a new and more extensive experience of reality, a "surplus" reality, a gain which at least in part justifies the sacrifice he has made by working through a psychodramatic production.

The next phase in psychodrama comes into play when the audience drama take the place of the production. The director vanished from the scene at the end of the first phase; now the production itself vanishes and with it go the auxiliary egos, the good helpers and genies who have aided the subject so much in gaining a new sense of power and clarity. The subject is now divided in his reactions. On the one hand he is sorry that it is all gone; on the other he feels cheated and mad for having made a sacrifice whose justification he does not see completely. The subject becomes dynamically aware of the presence of the audience. In the beginning of the session he was angrily or happily aware of them. In the warming up of the production he became oblivious of their existence, but now he sees them again, one by one, strangers and friends. His feelings of shame and guilt reach their climax. However, as he was warming up to the production, the audience in front of him was warming up, too. But when he came to an end they were just beginning. The tele-empathy-transference complex undergoes a third realignment of forces; it moves from the stage to the audience, initiating among the audio-egos intensive relations. As the strangers from the group begin to rise and relate their feelings as to what they have learned from the production, the subject gains a new sense of catharsis, a group catharsis. *He has given love and now they are giving love back to him.* Whatever his psyche is now, it was molded originally by the group; by means of the psychodrama it returns to the group, and now the members of the audience are sharing their experiences with him as he has shared his with them.

The description would not be complete if we would not discuss briefly the role which the directors and the auxiliary egos play in the warm up of the session. The theoretical principle of psychodrama is that the director acts directly upon the level of the subject's spontaneity—obviously it makes little difference to the operations whether or not one calls the subject's spontaneity his "unconscious"—so that the subject actually enters the areas of objects and persons, however confused and fragmented, to which his spontaneous energy is related. The director is not satisfied, like the analyst, to observe the subject and translate symbolic behavior into understandable, scientific language. He enters as a participant-actor, armed with as many hypothetical insights as possible, into the spontaneous activities of the subject, to talk to him in the spontaneous languages of signs and gestures, words and actions, which the subject has developed . . . . An elaborate system of production techniques has been developed by means of which the director and his auxiliary egos push themselves into the subject's world, populating it with figures extremely familiar to him—with the advantage, however, that they are not delusional but half-imaginary, half-real. Like genies, they shock and upset him at times, and at other times they surprise and comfort him. The subject finds himself, as if trapped, in a near-real world. He sees himself acting, he hears himself speaking, but his actions and thoughts, his feelings and perceptions do not come from him, they come, strangely enough, from another person, the psychodramatist, and from other persons, the auxiliary egos, the doubles and mirrors of his mind.

SOCIODRAMA

Sociodrama has been defined as a deep action method dealing with inter-group relations and collective ideologies.

The procedure in the development of a sociodrama differs in many ways from the procedure which I have described as psychodramatic. In a psycho-dramatic session, the attention of the director and his staff are centered upon the individual and his private problems. As these are unfolded before a group, the spectators are affected by the psychodramatic acts in proportion to the affinities existing between their own context of roles and the role context of the central subject. Even the so-called group approach in psycho-drama is in the deeper sense individual-centered. The audience is organized in accord with a mental syndrome which all participating individuals have in common, and the aim of the director is to reach every individual in his own sphere, separated from the others. He is using the group approach only to reach actively more than one individual in the same session. The group approach in psychodrama is concerned with a group of private individuals, which makes the group itself, in a sense, private. Careful planning and orga-nizing the audience is here indispensable because there is no outward sign indicating which individual suffers from the same mental syndrome and can share the same treatment situation.

The true subject of a sociodrama is the group. It is not limited by a special number of individuals. It can consist of as many persons as there are human beings living anywhere, or at least of as many as belong to the same culture. Sociodrama is based upon the tacit assumption that the group formed by the audience is already organized by the social and cultural roles which in some degree all the carriers of the culture share. It is therefore incidental who the individuals are, or of whom the group is composed, or how large their number is. It is the group as a whole which has to be put upon the stage to work out its problem, because the group in sociodrama corresponds to the individual in psychodrama. Sociodrama, therefore, in order to become effec-tive, has to assay the difficult task of developing deep action methods, in which the working tools are representative types within a given culture and not private individuals. Catharsis in the sociodrama differs from catharsis in psychodrama. The psychodramatic approach deals with personal problems principally and aims at personal catharsis; the sociodramatic approach deals with social problems and aims at social catharsis.

The concept underlying this approach is the recognition that *man is a role player,* that every individual is characterized by a certain range of roles which dominates his behavior, and that every culture is characterized by certain sets of roles which it imposes with a varying degree of success upon its membership.

The problem is how to bring a cultural order to view by dramatic methods. Observation and analysis are inadequate tools for exploring the more sophisticated aspects of intercultural relations. Deep action methods are indispensable. Moreover, the latter have proven to be of indubitable value and irreplaceable because they can, in the form of sociodrama, explore as well as treat in one stroke, the conflicts which have arisen between two separate cultural orders, and at the same time, by the same action, undertake to change the attitude of the members of one culture versus the members of the other. Furthermore, sociodrama can reach large groups of people, and by using radio or television it can affect millions of local groups and neighborhoods, in which intercultural conflicts and tensions are dormant or in the initial phases of open warfare . . . .

CHAPTER 3

Sociometry

1937

> *Editor's note: From the first, Moreno was interested in social relations. He believed that the structure of human groups was complex, highly dynamic, and only discernible by means of a pragmatic, hands-on method of investigation. His goal: the maximum participation of every individual concerned.*

Religious, economic, technological, and political systems have been constructed to date with a tacit assumption that they can be adequate and applicable to human society without an accurate and detailed knowledge of its structure. The repeated failure of so many plausible and humane remedies and doctrines has led to the conviction that the close study of social structure is the only means through which we may treat the ills of society.

Sociometry, a relatively new science developed gradually since the World War of 1914-1918, aims to determine objectively the basic structure of human societies . . . .

The difficulties in the way of attaining such knowledge are enormous and discouraging. These difficulties may be considered essentially in three categories: the large number of people, the need of obtaining valid participation,

---

From Sociometry in Relation to Other Social Sciences, *Sociometry* 1 (1937), 206-219. Another version appears in *Experimental Method & the Science of Society* (1951).

and need for arranging for continued and repeated studies. The difficulties may be considered in a bit more detail together with the steps thus far taken toward overcoming them in the development of sociometric techniques.

First, human society consists of approximately two billion individuals. The number of interrelations among these individuals—each interrelation influencing the total world situation in some manner, however slight—must amount to a figure of astronomical magnitude. Recognizing this fact, the field work of sociometry was started with small sections of human society, spontaneous groupings of people, groups of individuals at different age levels, groups of one sex, groups of both sexes, institutional and industrial communities. To date, various groups and communities, the total populations of which are more than 10,000 persons, have been sociometrically tested.[1] A considerable amount of sociometric knowledge has been accumulated. We may not forget, though, however much we may learn in the course of time, however accurate our sociometric knowledge of certain sections of human society may become, that no automatic conclusions can be carried over from one section to another and no automatic conclusions can be drawn about the same group from one time to another. Each part of human society must always be considered in its concreteness.

Second, as we have to consider every individual in his concreteness and not as a symbol, and every relationship he may [have] . . . we cannot gain a full knowledge unless every individual participates *spontaneously* in uncovering these relationships to the best of his ability. The problem is how to elicit from every man his maximum spontaneous participation. This participation would produce as a counterpart of the physical geography of the world a psychological geography of human society. Sociometry has endeavored to gain such participation by applying as a fundamental part of the procedure an important aspect of the actual social situation confronting the people of the community at the moment. This was made possible by broadening and changing the status of the participant observer and researcher so as to make him an auxiliary ego of that individual and all other individuals of the community—that is, one who identifies himself as far as possible with each individual's aims and tries to aid him in their realization. This step was taken after a careful consideration of the spontaneous factor in social situations. General definitions of the physical and mental needs do not suffice. There is such a uniqueness about each actual momentary position of an individual in the community that a knowledge of the structure surrounding and pressing upon him at that moment is necessary before drawing conclusions.

Third, as we have to know the actual structure of a human society not only at one given moment but in all its future developments, we must look forward to the maximum spontaneous participation of every individual in all future time. The problem is how to motivate men so that they all will give repeatedly and regularly, not only at one time or another, their maximum spontaneous participation. This difficulty can be overcome through fitting the procedure to the administration of the community. If the spontaneous strivings in regard to association with other persons or in regard to objects and values are aided officially and permanently by respective community agencies, the procedure can become repeatable at any time, and the insight into the structure of the community in its development in time and space can become constantly available.

In undertaking the study of the structure of human society, the first step has been to define and develop sociometric procedures which would surmount the difficulties described above. Sociometric procedures try to lay bare the fundamental structures within a society by disclosing the affinities, attractions, and repulsions operating between persons and between persons and objects.

TYPES OF SOCIOMETRIC PROCEDURES

Every type of procedure enumerated below can be applied to any group, whatever the development level of the individuals in it. If the procedure applied is, in degree of articulation, below the level of that which a certain social structure demands, the results will reflect but an infra-structure of that community. An adequate sociometric procedure should be neither more nor less differentiated than the assumed social structure which it is trying to measure.

One type of procedure is to disclose the social structure between individuals by merely recording their movement and positions in space with regard to one another. This procedure of charting gross movements was applied to a group of babies. At their level of development no more differentiated a technique could have been applied fruitfully. This procedure discloses the structure developing between a number of babies, between the babies and their attendants, and between the babies and the objects around them in a given physical space. At the earliest developmental level, the physical and social structures of space overlap and are congruous. At a certain point of development the structure of the interrelationships begins to differentiate itself more and more from the physical structure of the group, and from this moment onward social space in its embryonic form begins to differentiate itself from physical space . . . . A more highly developed structure appears when the children begin to walk. They can now move towards a person whom they like or away from a person whom they dislike, towards an object which they want, or away from an object which they wish to avoid. The fact of nonverbal, spontaneous participation begins to influence the structure more definitely.

Another development of the procedure is used in groups of young children who (before or after walking) are able to make intelligent use of simple verbal symbols. The factor of simple "participation" of the subject becomes more complex. He can choose or reject an object without moving bodily. A still further development of the procedure sets in when children are influenced in their making of associations by the physical or social characteristics of other people, such as sex, race, and social status. This factor of differential association signifies a new trend in the development of structure. Up to this point, only individuals have stood out and have had a position in it. From here on associations of individuals stand out and have a position in it as a group. This differentiating factor is called a criterion of the group. As societies of individuals develop, the number of criteria around which associations are or may be formed increases rapidly. The more numerous and the more complex the criteria, the more complex also becomes the social structure of the community.

These few samples may make clear that sociometric procedure is not a rigid set of rules, but that it has to be modified and adapted to any group situation as it arises. Sociometric procedure has to be shaped in accord with the momentary potentialities of the subjects, so as to arouse them to a maximum of spontaneous participation and to a maximum of expression. If the sociometric procedure is not attuned to the momentary structure of a given community, we may gain only a limited or distorted knowledge of it. The participant observer of the social laboratory, counterpart of the scientific observer in the physical or biological laboratory, undergoes a profound change. The observing of movements and voluntary associations of individuals has value as a supplement if the basic structure is known. But how can an observer learn something about the basic structure of a community of 1,000 people if the observer tries to become an intimate associate of each individual simultaneously, in each role which he enacts in the community? He cannot observe them like heavenly bodies and make charts of their movements and reactions. The essence of their situations will be missed if he acts in the role of a scientific spy. The procedure has to be open and apparent. The inhabitants of the community have to become participants in the project to some degree. The degree of participation is at its possible minimum when the individuals composing the group are willing only to answer questions about one another. Any study which tries to disclose with less than maximum possible participation of the individuals of the group the feelings which they have in regard to one another is near-sociometric. Near-sociometric procedures of the research or the diagnostic type are of much value in the present stage of sociometry. They can be applied on a large scale, and within certain limits without any unpleasantness to the participants. The information gained in near-sociometric studies is based, however, on an inadequate motivation of the participants; they do not fully reveal their feelings. In near-sociometric situations the participants are rarely spontaneous. They do not warm up quickly. Often an individual, if he is asked, "Who are your friends in this town?" may leave one or two persons out, the most important persons in his social atom, persons with whom he entertains a secret friendship of some sort which he does not want known. The observational method of group research, the study of group formation from the *outside*, is not abandoned by the sociometrist. This becomes, however, a part of a more inclusive technique, the sociometric procedure. In fact, sociometric procedure is operational and observational at the same time. A well-trained sociometrist will continuously collect other observational and experimental data which may be essential as a supplement to his knowledge of the *inside* social structure of a group at a particular time. Observational and statistical studies may grow out of sociometric procedures which supplement and deepen structural analysis.

The transition from near-sociometric to basic sociometric procedures depends upon the method of creating the motivations to more adequate participation. If the participant observer succeeds in becoming less and less an observer and more and more an aid and helper to every individual of the group in regard to their needs and interests, the observer undergoes a transformation . . . to auxiliary ego. The observed persons, instead of revealing something more or less unwillingly about themselves and one another, become open promoters of the project; the project becomes a cooperative effort. They become participants in and observers of the problems of others as well as their own; they become key contributors to the sociometric research. They know that the more explicit and accurate they are in expressing what they want, whether it is as associates in a play, as table mates in a dining room, as neighbors in their community, or as co-workers in a factory, the better are their chances to attain the position in the group which is as near as possible to their anticipations and desires.

The first decisive step in the development of sociometry was the disclosure of the actual organization of a group. The second decisive step was the inclusion of subjective measures in determining this organization. The third decisive step was a method which gives to subjective terms the highest possible degree of objectivity, through the function of the auxiliary ego. The fourth decisive step was the consideration of the criterion (a need, a value, an aim) around which a particular structure develops. The true organization of a group can be disclosed if the test is constructed in accord with the criterion around which it is built. For instance, if we want to determine the structure of a work group, the criterion is their relationship as workers in the factory, and not the reply to a question regarding with whom they would like to go out for luncheon. We differentiate therefore between an essential and an auxiliary criterion. Complex groups are often built around several essential criteria. If a test is near-sociometric—that is, inadequately constructed, then it discloses, instead of the actual organization of the group, a distorted form of it, a less differentiated form of it, an infra-level of its structure.

Within sociometric work several approaches can be distinguished: (1) the research procedure, aiming to study the organization of groups; (2) the diagnostic procedure, aiming to classify the positions of individuals in groups and the positions of groups in the community; (3) therapeutic and political procedures, aiming to aid individuals or groups to better adjustment; and finally, (4) the complete sociometric procedure, in which all these steps are synthetically united and transformed into a single operation, one procedure depending upon the other. This last procedure is also the most scientific of all. It is not more scientific because it is more practical; rather, it is more practical because it is more scientifically accurate.

The responses received in the course of a sociometric procedure from each individual, however spontaneous and essential they may appear, are material only and not yet sociometric facts in themselves. We have first to visualize and represent how these responses hang together. The astronomer has his universe of stars and of the other heavenly bodies visibly spread throughout space. Their geography is given. The sociometrist is in the paradoxical situation that he has to construct and map his universe before he can explore it. A process of charting has been devised, the sociogram, which is, as it should be, more than merely a method of presentation. It is first of all a method of exploration. It makes possible the exploration of sociometric facts. The proper placement of every individual and of all interrelations of individuals can be shown on a sociogram. It is at present the only available scheme which makes structural analysis of a community possible.

As the pattern of the social universe is not visible to us, it is made visible through charting. Therefore the sociometric chart is the more useful the more accurately and realistically it portrays the relations discovered. As every detail is important, the most accurate presentation is the most appropriate. The problem is not only to present knowledge in the simplest and shortest manner, but to present the relations so that they can by studied.* As the technique of charting is a method of exploration, the sociograms are so devised that one can pick small parts from the primary map of a community, redraw them, and study them as if under a microscope. Another type of derivative or secondary sociogram results if we pick from the map of a community large structures because of their functional significance, such as psychological networks. The mapping of networks indicates that we may devise on the basis of primary sociograms forms of charting which enable us to explore large geographical areas.

---

*See examples of sociograms in Chapter 15. (Ed.)

THE SOCIAL ATOM

Sociometry started practically as soon as we were in the position to study social structure as a whole and in its parts at the same time. This was impossible as long as the problem of the individual was still a main concern, as with an individual's relations and adjustment to the group. Once the full social structure could be seen as a totality it could be studied in its minute detail. We thus became able to describe sociometric facts (descriptive sociometry) and to consider the function of specific structures—i.e., the effect of some parts upon others (dynamic sociometry).

Viewing the social structure of a certain community as a whole, in so far as it is related to a certain locality, with a certain physical geography—a township filled with homes, school, workshops, and the interrelations between their inhabitants in these situations—we arrive at the concept of the psychological geography of a community. Viewing the detailed structure of a community, we see the concrete position of every individual in it, also a nucleus of relations around every individual which is "thicker" around some, "thinner" around others. This nucleus of relations is the smallest social structure in a community, a social atom. From the point of view of a descriptive sociometry, the social atom is a fact, not a concept, just as in anatomy the blood vessel system, for instance, is first of all a descriptive fact. It attained conceptual significance as soon as the study of the development of social atoms suggested that they have an important function in the formation of human society. Whereas certain parts of these social atoms seem to remain buried between the individuals participating, certain parts link themselves with parts of other social atoms and these with parts of other social atoms again, forming complex chains of interrelations which are called, in terms of descriptive sociometry, psychological networks. The older and wider the network spreads, the less significant seems to be the individual contribution towards it. From the point of view of dynamic sociometry these networks have the function of shaping social tradition and public opinion.

It is different and more difficult, however, to describe the process which attracts individuals to one another or which repels them, that flow of feeling of which the social atom and the networks are apparently composed. This process may be conceived of as *tele*. We are used to the notion that feelings emerge within the individual organism and that they become attached more strongly or more weakly to persons or things in the immediate environment. We have been in the habit of thinking not only that these totalities of feelings spring up from the individual organism exclusively, from one of its parts or from the organism as a whole, but also that these physical and mental states, after having emerged, reside forever within this organism. The feeling relation with regard to a person or an object has been called attachment or fixation, but these attachments or fixations were considered purely as individual projections. This was in accord with the materialistic concept of the individual organism, with its unity, and, we can perhaps say, with its microcosmic independence.

The idea that feelings, emotions, or ideas can "leave" or "enter" the organism appeared inconsistent with this concept. The claims of parapsychology were easily discarded as unfounded by scientific evidence. The claims of collectivistic unity of a people appeared romantic and mystical. The resistance against any attempt to break the sacred unity of the individual has one of its roots in the idea that feelings, emotions, ideas must reside in some structure within which it can emerge or vanish and within which it can function or disappear. If these feelings, emotions, ideas "leave" the organism, where then can they reside?

When we found that social atoms and networks have a persistent structure and that they develop in a certain order, we had extra individual structures—and probably there are many more to be discovered—in which this flow can reside. But another difficulty stepped in. As long as we (as auxiliary ego) drew from an individual the responses and material needed, we were inclined—because of our nearness to the individual—to conceive the tele as flowing out of him towards other individuals and objects. This is certainly correct on the individual-psychological level, in the preparatory phase of sociometric exploration. But as soon as we transferred these responses to the sociometric level and studied them not singly but in their interrelations, important methodological reasons suggested that we conceive this flowing feeling, the tele, as an interpersonal, or more accurately and broadly speaking, as a sociometric structure. We must assume at present, until further knowledge forces us to modify and refine this concept, that some real process in one person's life situation is sensitive and corresponds to some real process in another person's life situation and that there are numerous degrees, positive and negative, of these interpersonal sensitivities. The tele between any two individuals may be potential. It may never become active unless these individuals are brought into proximity or unless their feelings and ideas meet at a distance through some channel—for instance, the networks. These distance or tele effects have been found to be complex sociometric structures produced by a long chain of individuals, each with a different degree of sensitivity for the same tele, ranging from total indifference to a maximum response.

A social atom is thus composed of numerous tele structures; social atoms are again parts of a still larger pattern, the psychological networks, which bind or separate large groups of individuals due to their tele relationships. Psychological networks are parts of a still larger unit, the psychological geography of a community. A community is again part of the largest configuration, the psychological totality of human society itself.

SOCIOMETRY AND THE SOCIAL SCIENCES

A full appreciation of the significance of sociometry for the social sciences cannot be gained unless we analyze some of the most characteristic developments in recent years. One development is along Marxist lines as elaborated especially by Georg Lukács and Karl Mannheim.[2] The social philosophy of these students is full of near-sociometric divinations. They stress the existence of social classes and the dependence of ideology upon social structure. They refer to the position of individuals in their group and to the social dynamics resulting from the changing of the positions of groups in a community. But the discussion is carried on at a dialectical and symbolical level, giving the reader the impression that the writers had an intimate and authoritative knowledge of the social and psychological structures they are describing. They present social and psychological processes which are supposed to go on in large populations, but their own intuitive knowledge . . . shines through. These large generalizations encourage pseudo-totalistic views of the social universe. The basic social and psychological structure of the group remains a mythological product of their own mind, a mythology which is just as much a barrier to the progress from an old to a new social order as the fetish of merchandise was before Marx's analysis of it. The dialectical and political totalists have reached a dead-end. A true advance in political theory can not crystallize until more concrete sociometric knowledge of the basic structure of groups is secured.

The economic situation of a group and the dynamic influence it has upon the social and psychological structures of that group cannot be fully understood unless we also know the social and psychological characteristics of this group and unless we study the dynamic influence they have upon its economic situation. Indeed, from the sociometric point of view, the economic criterion is only one criterion around which social structure develops. Sociometric method is a synthetic procedure which through the very fact of being in operation releases all the factual relationships, whether they have an economic, sociological, psychological, or biological derivation. It is carried out as one operation. But it has several results: it secures knowledge of the actual social structure in regard to every criterion dynamically related to it; allows for the possibility of classifying the psychological, social, and economic status of the population producing this structure; and [permits] early recognition of changes in the status of the population. Knowledge of social structure provides the concrete basis for rational social action. This should not be surprising, even to staunch believers in the old dialectic methods. As long as it appeared certain that all that counts is the knowledge of economic structure, all other structural formations within society could be considered in a general manner intimating at random how the economic motive determines them. An economic analysis of every actual group was all that seemed necessary. Since the more inclusive sociometric technique of social analysis has developed which attacks the basic social structure itself, the possibility of a new line of development appears on the horizon. From the sociometric angle the totalism of the new-Marxists appears as flat and unrealistic as the totalism of Hegel appeared to Marx. Compared with the elan of the totalistic schools of thought, sociometric effort may seem narrow. Instead of analyzing social classes composed of millions of people, we are making painstaking analyses of small groups of persons. It is a retreat from the social universe to its atomic structure. However, in the course of time, through the cooperative efforts of many workers, a total view of human society will result again, but it will be better founded. This may be a deep fallback after so much dialectical conceit, but it is a strategic retreat, a retreat to greater objectivity.

A different sort of symbolism comes from other lines of development which deal largely with psychological theory. An illustration of this trend is the recent phase of the Gestalt school. Thus J. F. Brown schematizes social structures and social barriers which no one has empirically studied. A conceptual scheme may become just as harmful to the growth of a young and groping experimental science as a political scheme. There are many links in the chain of interrelations which cannot be divined. They have to be explored concretely in the actual group. It is not the result of a study which concerns us here—for instance, whether it approximates the probable factual relations or not—but the contrast between empirical and symbolical methods of procedure. We have learned in the course of sociometric work how unreliable our best divinations are in regard to social structure. Therefore we prefer to let our concepts emerge and grow with the growth of the experiment and not to take them from any a priori or any non-sociometric source.

SOCIOMETRIC CONSCIOUSNESS

The best test of the damage done by any sort of symbolic concept of social structure is to come face to face with the crucial experiment itself—a worker entering a group, however small or large, with the purpose of applying to it sociometric procedures. The introduction of sociometric procedure, even to a very small community, is an extremely delicate psychological problem. The problem is the more intricate the more complex and the more differentiated the community is. On first thought one would be inclined to minimize the difficulties involved. Sociometric procedures should be greeted favorably as they aid in bringing to recognition and into realization the basic structure of a group. But such is not always the case. They are met with resistance by some and hostility by others. Therefore a group should be carefully prepared for the test before submitting to it.

Sociometric techniques have to be fashioned according to the readiness of a certain population for sociometric grouping . . . which may vary at different times. This psychological status of individuals may be called their degree of sociometric consciousness. The resistance against sociometric procedures is often due to psychological and educational limitations. It is important for the field worker to consider the difficulties one by one and try to meet them.

The first difficulty which one ordinarily meets is ignorance of what sociometric procedure is. A full and lucid presentation, first perhaps to small and intimate groups, and then in a town meeting if necessary, is extremely helpful. It will bring misunderstandings in regard to it to open discussion. One reaction usually found is the appreciation of some that many social and psychological processes exist in their group which have escaped democratic integration. Another reaction is one of fear and resistance, not so much against the procedure as against its consequences for them. These and other reactions determine the degree of sociometric consciousness of a group. They determine also the amount and character of preparation the group members need before the procedure is put into operation.

In the course of its operation we can learn from the spontaneous responses of the individuals concerned something about the causes underlying their fears and resistance. In one of the communities tested some individuals made their choice and gave their reasons without hesitancy; others hesitated long before choosing; one or two refused to participate at all. After the findings of the test were applied to the group, a frequently chosen individual was much displeased. He had not received that man as a neighbor with whom he had exchanged a mutual first choice. It took him weeks to overcome his anger. One day he said smilingly that he liked the neighbor he had now and he would not change him for his original first choice even if he could. There was another individual who did not care to make any choice. When the chart of the community was laid out, it was found that in turn none of the other individuals wanted him. He was isolated. It was as if he guessed that his position in the group was that of an isolate; therefore he did not want to know too much about it. He did not have the position in the group he would like to have, and so he thought it better perhaps to keep it veiled.

Other individuals also showed fear of the revelations the sociometric procedure might bring. The fear is stronger with some people and weaker with others. One person may be most anxious to arrange his relationships in accord with actual desires; another may be afraid of the consequences. For instance, one remarked that it made him feel uncomfortable to say whom he liked for a co-worker: "You cannot choose all and I do not want to offend anybody." Another person said, "If I don't have as a neighbor the person I like—i.e., if he lives farther away, we may stay friends longer. It is better not to see a friend too often." These and other remarks reveal a fundamental phenomenon, a form of interpersonal resistance against expressing the preferential feelings which one has for others. This resistance seems at first sight paradoxical as it crops up in face of an actual opportunity to have a fundamental need satisfied. An explanation of this resistance of the individual versus the group is possible. It is, on the one hand, the individual's fear of knowing what position he has in the group. To be made fully conscious of one's position may be painful and unpleasant. Another source of this resistance is the fear that it may become manifest to others whom one likes and whom one dislikes, and what position in the group one actually wants and needs. The resistance is produced by the extra-personal situation of an individual. He feels that the position he has in the group is not the result of his individual make-up but chiefly the result of how the individuals with whom he is associated feel towards him. He may even feel dimly that there are beyond his social atom invisible tele-structures which influence his position. The fear about expressing the preferential feelings which one person has for others is actually a fear of the feelings which the others have for him. The objective process underlying this fear has been discovered by us in the course of quantitative analysis of group organization. The individual dreads the powerful currents of emotions which "society" may turn against him. It is fear of the psychological networks. It is dread of these powerful structures whose influence is unlimited and uncontrollable. It is fear that they may destroy him if he does not keep still.

The sociometrist has the task of breaking down gradually the misunderstandings and fears existing or developing in the group he is facing. The members of the group will be eager to weigh the advantages which sociometric procedure is able to bring them—a better balanced organization of their community and a better balanced situation of each individual within it. The sociometrist has to exert his skill to gain their full collaboration, for at least two reasons: the more spontaneous their collaboration, the more valuable will be the fruits of his research and the more helpful will the results become to them.

CHAPTER 4

Group Psychotherapy

1945

Editor's note: Here Moreno concerns himself primarily with a group of 26. He was interested in even larger groups, such as institutional populations and political communities, and he worked frequently with couples and families. All are examples of his commitment to the group approach—what he called the 3rd Psychiatric Revolution.

The late arrival of group psychiatry and group psychotherapy has a plausible explanation when we consider the development of modern psychiatry out of somatic medicine. The premise of scientific medicine has been since its origin that the locus of physical ailment is an individual organism. There treatment is applied to the locus of the ailment as designated by diagnosis. The physical disease with which an individual, *A*, is afflicted does not require the collateral treatment of *A*'s wife, his children, and friends. If *A* suffers from an appendicitis and an appendectomy is indicated, only the appendix of *A* is removed; no one thinks of the removal of the appendix of *A*'s wife and children, too. When in budding psychiatry scientific methods began to be used, axioms gained from physical diagnosis and treatment were automat-

From Scientific Foundations of Group Psychotherapy, *Group Psychotherapy: a Symposium* (1945), 77-84.

ically applied to mental disorders as well. Extra-individual influence, such as animal magnetism and hypnotism, was pushed aside as mythical superstition and folklore. In psychoanalysis—at the beginning of this century the most advanced development of psychological psychiatry—the idea of a specific individual organism as the locus of psychic ailment attained its most triumphant confirmation. The "group" was implicitly considered by Freud as an epi-phenomenon of the individual psyche. The implication was that if 100 individuals of both sexes were psychoanalyzed, each by a different analyst with satisfactory results, and were put together into a group, a smooth social organization would result; the sexual, social, economic, political, and cultural relations evolving would offer no insurmountable obstacle to them. The premise prevailed that there is no locus of ailment beyond the individual; that there is, for instance, no group situation which requires special diagnosis and treatment. The alternative, however, is that 100 cured psychoanalysands might produce a societal bedlam together.

Although during the first quarter of our century there was occasional disapproval of this exclusive, individualistic point of view, it was more silent than vocal, coming from anthropologists and sociologists particularly. But they had nothing to offer in contrast with the specific and tangible demonstrations of psychoanalysis except large generalities like culture, class, and societal hierarchy. The decisive turn came with the development of sociometric and psychodramatic methodology.

The change in locus of therapy which the latter initiated means literally a revolution in what was always considered appropriate medical practice. Husband and wife, mother and child are treated as a combine, often facing one another—because separate they may not have any tangible mental ailment. Facing one another deprives them of that elusive thing which is commonly called "privacy"; actually what remains "private" between husband and wife or mother and daughter is the abode where some of the trouble between them may blossom—secrets, deceit, suspicion, and delusion. Therefore the loss of personal privacy means loss of face and that is why people intimately bound up in a situation . . . prefer individual treatment. It is obvious that once privacy is lifted (as a postulate of individual psyche) for one person involved in the situation, it is a matter of degree for how many persons the curtain should go up. In a psychodramatic session, therefore, Mr. A, the husband, may permit that besides his wife, his partner in the sickness, the other man (her lover) be present; later his daughter and son; and some day, perhaps, they would not object to (in fact, they would invite) the presence of other husbands and wives who have a similar problem, sitting in the audience and looking on as their predicaments are enacted in order to learn how to treat or prevent their own. It is clear that the Hippocratic oath will have to be reformulated to protect a group of subjects involved in the same therapeutic situation. The stigma coming from unpleasant ailment and treatment is far harder to control if a group of persons is treated than if only one is.

But the change of locus of therapy has other unpleasant consequences. It revolutionizes the agent of therapy. The agent of therapy has usually been a single person, a doctor, a healer. Faith in him—rapport (Mesmer) or transference (Freud)—is usually considered indispensable to the patient-physician relation. But sociometric methods have radically changed this situation. In a particular group a subject may be used as an instrument to diagnose and as a therapeutic agent to treat the other subjects. The doctor as the final source of mental therapeusis has failed. Sociometric methods have demonstrated that therapeutic values (tele) are scattered throughout the membership of the group. One patient can treat the other. The role of the healer has changed from the owner and actor of therapy to its assigner and trustee. But as long as the agent of psychotherapy was a particular, special individual, a doctor or a priest, the consequence was that he was also the medium of therapy as well as the catalyzer of healing power . . . . It was always his actions, the elegance of his logic, the brilliancy of his lecture, the depth of his emotions, the power of his hypnosis, the lucidity of his analytic interpretation to which the subject responded . . . . In psychodramatic methods the medium is to a degree separated from the agent. The medium may be as simple and amorphous as a still or moving light, a single sound repeated, a puppet or a doll, a still or a motion picture, a dance or music production, finally reaching out to the most elaborated forms of psychodrama by means of a staff consisting of a director and auxiliary egos, calling to their command all the arts and all the means of production. The staff of egos on the stage are usually not patients themselves, but only the medium through which the treatment is directed. The psychiatrist as well as the audience of patients are often left outside of the medium. When the locus of therapy changed from the individual to the group, the group became the new subject (first step). When the group was broken up into its individual little therapists and they became the agents of therapy, the chief therapist became a part of the group (second step). Finally, the medium of therapy was separated from the healer as well as the group therapeutic agents (third step). . .

SOCIODYNAMIC EFFECT

All group methods have in common the need for a frame of reference for assessing the validity of their findings and applications. One of my first efforts was therefore to construct instruments by means of which the structural constitution of groups could be determined. An instrument of this type was the sociometric test, and it was so constructed that it could easily become a model and a guide for the development of similar instruments. My idea was also that if an instrument were good, its findings would be corroborated by any other instrument which had the same aim—that is, to study the structure resulting from the interaction of individuals in groups. After social groups of all types had been studied, such as formal and informal groups, and home and work groups, the question of the validity of group structure was tested by first using deviations from chance as a reference base, and second by control studies of grouping and regrouping of individuals.

A population of 26 was taken as a convenient unit to use in comparison with a chance distribution of a group of 26 fictitious individuals, and three choices were made by each member.[1] For our analysis any size of population, large or small, would have been satisfactory, but the use of 26 persons happened to permit an unselected sampling of groups already tested. Without including the same group more than once, seven groups of 26 individuals were selected from among those which happened to have this size population. The test choices had been taken on the criterion of table-partners, and none of the choices could go outside the group, thus making comparison possible. Studies of the findings of group configurations (resulting from the interacting individuals), in order to be compared with one another, were in need of some common reference base from which to measure the deviations. It appeared that the most logical ground for establishing such reference could be secured by ascertaining the characteristics of typical configurations produced by chance balloting for a similar sized population with a like number of choices. It became possible to chart the respective sociograms (graphs of interactional relations) of each experiment, so that each fictitious person was seen in respect to all other fictitious persons in the same group. It was also possible to show the range in type of structures within each chance configuration of a group. The first questions to be answered read: What is the probable number of individuals who by mere chance selection would be picked out by their fellows, or not at all, or once, twice, three times, and so on? How many pairs are likely to occur (a pair being two individuals who choose one another)? How many unreciprocated choices can be expected on a mere chance basis? The experimental chance findings followed closely the theoretical chance probabilities. The average number of pairs in the chance experiment was 4.3, and in the theoretical analysis, 4.68 (under the same condition of three choices within a population of 26 persons). The number of unreciprocated choices in the chance experiments was 69.4; the theoretical results showing 68.64 under the same conditions.

Among many important findings, two were most instructive. (a) A comparison of the chance sociograms to the actual sociograms showed that the probability of mutual structures was 213% greater in the actual configurations than in chance, and the number of unreciprocated structures was 35.8% rarer actually than by chance. The more complex structures, such as triangles, squares, and other closed patterns, of which there were seven in the actual sociograms, were lacking in the chance sociograms. (b) A greater concentration of many choices upon few individuals and a weak concentration of a few choices upon the majority of individuals skewed the distribution of the sampling of actual individuals still further than took place in the chance experiments, and in a direction it need not necessarily take by chance. This feature of the distribution is called the sociodynamic effect. The actual frequency distribution compared with the chance distribution showed the quantity of isolates to be 250% greater. The quantity of overchosen individuals was 39% greater, while the volume of their choices was 73% greater. Such statistical findings suggest that if the size of the population increases and the number of choice relations remains constant, the gap between the chance frequency distribution and the actual distribution will increase progressively . . . .

[In another case] two groups of individuals were compared. In the one group, *A*, the placement to the cottage was made hit or miss. In the second group, *B*, the placements were made on the basis of the feelings which the incoming individuals had for the cottage parent and for the other inhabitants of the cottage, and vice versa. Sociometric tests were then applied at intervals of eight weeks so that we could compare the structure of control group *A* with tested group *B*. Among other things it was found that the tested individuals underwent a quicker social evolution and integration into the group than the individuals who were placed in a cottage hit or miss. At the end of a 32 week period the control group showed four times as many isolated individuals as the tested group. The tested group *B* showed twice as many individuals forming pairs than the control group.*

---

*The section on "Housing Assignments" in Chapter 12 gives a fuller account of these findings. (Ed.).

PART II: Advanced Concepts and Techniques

"The first step to be taken must be with the consent
and the cooperation of the individuals concerned. It
must be made by them as if it were their own project—their own design for living. There is no other
way imaginable which can enlist the spontaneity, the
critical intelligence, and the enthusiasm of grown-up,
thinking people."

(From *Sociometry, Experimental Method, and the
Science of Society*, 187).

CHAPTER 5

Spontaneity and Catharsis

1940

Editor's note: What characterizes human nature is an unlimited capacity for spontaneous and creative action, Moreno believed, and as such his outlook is an optimistic one. However, the emotional "disequilibria" that come from living in the world will block spontaneity unless we experience an active catharsis, releasing the "true, naked emotions and feelings." Often another person is involved, in which case, to reach the core of the problem "both people are necessary . . . and must be brought together in a situation which is crucial for them." Here we have an early expression of the systems orientation to psychotherapy.

. . . Cultural conserves served two purposes: they were of assistance in threatening situations and they made secure the continuity of a cultural heritage. But the more developed cultural conserves became and the more attention there was given to their completion and perfection, the more rarely did the people feel the need for momentary inspiration. Thus the spontaneous component of the cultural conserves themselves were weakened at the core, and the development of the cultural conserve—although it owed its very birth to the operations of spontaneous processes—began to threaten and

---

From Mental Catharsis and the Psychodrama, *Group Psychotherapy, Psychodrama & Sociometry* 28 (1975), 5-32; Other versions appear in *Sociometry* 3 (1940), *Psychodrama*, Vol. 1 (1946).

extinguish the spark which lay at its origin. This situation called forth, as if to its rescue, the diametric opposite—the category of the moment. This event could only have occurred in our time, when cultural conserves have reached such a point of masterful development and distribution en masse that they have become a challenge and a threat to the sensitivity of man's creative patterns.

Just as an analysis and a reevaluation of the cultural conserve was forced upon me by the apparent decay of man's creative function when faced with the problem of our time, I was, in turn, forced to focus my attention from a new point of view upon the factors of spontaneity and creativity. The problem was to replace an outworn, antiquated system of values, the cultural conserve, with a new system of values in better accord with the emergencies of our time—the spontaneity-creativity complex.

My first step was to reexamine the factors of spontaneity and creativity and to determine their place in our universe. Although it was evident that a spontaneous creative process is the matrix and the initial stage of any cultural conserve—whether a technological invention, a work of art, or a form of religion—the mere confirmation of such a fact was barren of any kind of progress. It simply brought to the fore the relationship between the moment, immediate action, spontaneity, and creativity—in contrast to the customary link between spontaneity and automatic response. This first step led to a dead end.

The second step was far more rewarding. I started with the idea that the spontaneous creative matrix could be made the central focus of man's world, not only as the underlying source but on the very surface of his actual living; that the flow of the matrix into the cultural conserve—however indispensable this may appear to be—is only one of the many routes open to the historical development of creativity; and that a different route is perhaps more desirable, a route which would carry the spontaneous creative matrix to the periphery of man's actuality—his daily life.

At this juncture numerous questions arose which could not be answered by intellectual means. For instance—is it the fate of the spontaneous creative matrix always to end in a cultural conserve because of the fallibility of human nature? To this and other questions there was only one answer possible—systematic experiments which would permit a theory of spontaneity to grow as a theory of action.

Numerous theoretical preparations were made and many precautions were taken. All dogmatic assumptions were disregarded except those immediately needed to provide satisfactory conditions for the experiment. Some of the dogmas which were set aside may be worth discussion here since they indicate the atmosphere from which we had to free ourselves. One dogma, for instance, was the consideration of spontaneity as a sort of psychological energy—a quantity distributing itself within a field—which, if it cannot find actualization in one direction, flows in some other direction in order to maintain "equilibrium." Take, for instance, the concept of the libido in psychoanalytic theory. In accordance with this theory, Freud thought that if the sexual impulse does not find satisfaction in its direct aim, it must displace its unapplied energy elsewhere. It must, he thought, attach itself to a pathological focus or find a way out in sublimation. He could not even for a moment conceive of this unapplied affect vanishing because he was biased by the physical ideas of the conservation of energy.[1]

If we, too, were to follow this precept of the energy-pattern when we consider spontaneity, we should have to believe that a person has a certain amount of spontaneity stored up, to which he adds as he goes on living—but in smaller and smaller quantities the more he is dominated by cultural conserves. As he performs actions, he draws from this reservoir; if he is not careful he may use it all up—or even overdraw! The following alternative seemed to us to be just as plausible as the foregoing: this person is trained not to rely upon any reservoir of spontaneity; he has no alternative but to produce the amount of emotion, thought, and action a novel situation demands from him. At times he may have to produce more of this, say, spontaneity, and at others, less—in accord with what the situation or task requires. If he is well trained, he will not produce less than the exact amount of spontaneity needed (for if this were to happen he would need a reservoir from which to draw) and he will likewise not produce more than the situation calls for (because the surplus might tempt him to store it, thus completing a vicious circle which ends in a cultural conserve).

Another dogma whose acceptance we succeeded in avoiding—for we believed it to be only a half-truth—was that the climax of intensity of experience is at the moment of birth, and that the intensity is de-sensitized as living goes on and recedes to its lowest ebb towards the end of life. To a person who is comparatively passive, this may seem a plausible point of view. But for a person who acts upon the spur of the moment, who has no reservoir from which to draw energy—not consciously, at least—and who at the same time is faced with a novel situation—such a situation is for him very similar to that of birth. He has been trained to put himself (by means of the warming up process) into motion in order to summon as much spontaneity as the emergency with which he is faced requires. This whole process is repeated again and again, no matter with what rapidity one novel situation follows another. At every moment his training enables him to respond to a situation with the appropriate spontaneity.

SPONTANEITY TRAINING

This theoretical preparation led to several experimental methods in spontaneity. In one, the subject throws himself into a state—into an emotion, a role, or a relationship with another subject, any of these operating as a stimulus . . . . This does not mean that the units comprising the state are expected to be absolutely new and without precedent for the subject; it means that the experiment is so intended as to bring the subject, as a totality, to bear upon his act, to increase the number of possible combinations and variations, and—last but not least—to bring about such a flexibility of the subject that he can summon any amount of spontaneity necessary for any situation with which he can be faced. It is clear, therefore, that the factor (spontaneity) which enables the subject to warm up to such states is not, in itself, a feeling, emotion, thought, or act which attaches itself to a chain of improvisations as the warming up process proceeds. Spontaneity is a readiness of the subject to respond as required. It is a condition—a conditioning—of the subject, a preparation of the subject for free action. Thus freedom of a subject cannot be attained by an act of will. It grows by degrees as the result of training in spontaneity. It seems certain, therefore, that through spontaneity training a subject becomes relatively freer from conserves—past or future—than he was previous to the training, which demonstrates that spontaneity is a biological value as well as a social value.*

Another experimental method arose from the fact that the subject in action was often found to be controlled by remnants of roles which he had assumed at one time or another in the past, and these conserves interfered with or distorted the spontaneous flow of his action; or the subject, after having been liberated from old cliches in the course of spontaneity work, may have shown an inclination to conserve the best of the thought and speeches which he had extemporized, thus repeating himself. In order to overcome such handicaps to untrammeled spontaneity and in order to keep him as unconserved as possible by the influence of the conserves, he had to be deconserved from time to time. These and many other steps were taken before we could be sure that our subjects had reached the point at which they might begin to operate in a truly spontaneous fashion.

The term "spontaneous" is often used to describe subjects whose control of their actions is diminished. This is, however, a usage of the term "spontaneous" which is not in accord with the etymology of the word, which shows it to be derived from the Latin *sponte*, "of free will." Since we have shown the relationship of spontaneous states to creative functions, it is clear that the warming up to a spontaneous state leads up to and is aimed at more or less highly organized patterns of conduct. Disorderly conduct and emotionalism

---

*Moreno's most quoted definition of spontaneity can be found in *Who Shall Survive?*, 42: "[Spontaneity] propels the individual towards an adequate response to a new situation or a new response to an old situation." (Ed.)

resulting from impulsive action are far from being desiderata of spontaneity work. Instead, they belong more in the realm of the pathology of spontaneity.

Spontaneity is often erroneously thought of as being more closely allied to emotion and actions than to thought and rest. This bias probably developed because of the assumption that a person cannot really feel something without at the same time being spontaneous, and conversely, that a person who is thinking can have a genuine experience without spontaneity. But this is not the case. There seems to be a similar misconception that a person in action needs continuous spontaneity in order to keep going, but that no spontaneity is required by a person at rest. As we now know, these are fallacies. Spontaneity can be present in a person when he is thinking just as well as when he is feeling, when he is at rest just as well as when he is in action.

Another confusion—the difference between a cultural conserve and the spontaneous creative matrix of this conserve at the moment when it is springing into existence—should be cleared up. An example may help to clarify this difference. Let us imagine the music of the Ninth Symphony at the moment it was being created by Beethoven, and let us also image the same music as a work of art—a finished product—separated from the composer himself. On the surface it may appear as if the creative units which went into the Ninth Symphony—its musical themes, it climaxes, its harmonies, et cetera—must also have been in its original matrix, and that no difference exists between the one in its state in Beethoven's mind and the other in its conserved state—except only that of locus. It might seem as if it were merely a transposition of the same material—the same sum total of creative units—from one locus in time (the mind of Beethoven) to another (the musical score). Closer inspection, however, will show that this is not true. As Beethoven was walking though his garden trying intensively to warm up to his musical ideas, his whole personality was in an uproar. He made use of every possible physical and mental starter he could muster in order to get going in the right direction. These visions, images, thoughts, and action-patterns—both musical and non-musical inspirations—were the indispensable background out of which the music of the Ninth Symphony grew. But all this background (which cannot truthfully be divorced from the state in which Beethoven was when he was truly being a creator) is not to be found in the finished product—the musical score or its performance by a noted orchestra. Only the result is there. The fact that this background has been deleted from our present-day idea of Beethoven is the result of an intellectual trick which is played upon us by centuries of being indoctrinated by the cultural conserves. If we look upon the initial spontaneous creative phase in Beethoven's composition of the Ninth Symphony as a positive phase and not as a transition in the direction of the end-product, we can see in Beethoven's musical compositions his concepts of God, the universe, and the destiny of humanity, in the loves, joys, and griefs of his private life, and—especially—in the gestures and movements of his body, a united pattern from which a surface layer (the cultural conserve) can be lifted to satisfy certain pragmatic demands.

At the moment of composition, Beethoven's mind experienced these concepts, visions, and images in conjunction with the developing symphony. They were integral parts of a creative act—of a series of creative acts. He made a cross-section through them in such a way that only the material which could be fitted into the prospective conserve was included; the direction of the cross-section was determined by its frame. In this particular instance, the frame was that of musical notation; in another case, it might have been the frame of language notation; in still another, it might have been a mechanical invention.

It is exactly at this point that our theory of spontaneous creativity is able to take a stand against what Beethoven did—and probably was trying to do. If we imagine a Beethoven who would remain permanently in that initial, creative state—or at least, as long as the state lasted—and who would refuse to give birth to musical conserves, a Beethoven, however, who would be just as determined as ever in his efforts to create new musical worlds, then we can grasp the psychological meaning of pure spontaneous creativity on the psychodrama stage.

Experiments on the psychodramatic stage have confirmed by hundreds of tests the validity of the above conjectural analysis of the inner, initial processes experienced by creative geniuses. It was confirmed that spontaneous states are of short duration, extremely eventful, and sometimes crowded with inspiration.

These spontaneity tests opened up two avenues of experimentation. In the one case, spontaneity testing became the means whereby we could study the structure of spontaneity states and creative acts; in the other case, spontaneity tests enabled us to examine the readiness of any given subject to respond to a new situation. When it was discovered that a certain subject lacked in readiness--that his organism was unequal to the demands put upon it-- spontaneity training was applied. The difficulty encountered by the subject is that a motive may arise in him a fraction of a second earlier than the gesture which corresponds to it; hence the component portions of an act are diffused. Therefore, the organism of the subject must become like a reservoir of free spontaneity in order to have in constant readiness the ability to perform the greatest possible number of varied, swift, and practicable movements and acts.

From the point of view of systematic research in spontaneity, perhaps the most significant phase consisted in the measurement of spontaneity and the development of spontaneity scales. The earliest study in spontaneity scales concerned itself with calculating the quotient of spontaneity for any cultural conserve. For example, a motion picture at the moment of presentation had a

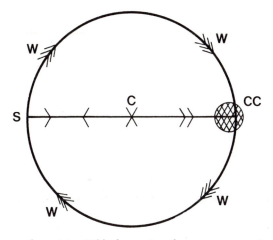

FIGURE 5-1 Canon of creativity. Field of operations between spontaneity, creativity, and cultural conserve. CC = cultural conserve; W = warming up, the operational expression of spontaneity; S = spontaneity; C = creativity.

Operation 1: Spontaneity arouses creativity.
Operation 2: Creativity is receptive to spontaneity.
Operation 3: From their interaction, cultural conserve results.
Operation 4: The catalyzer spontaneity revitalizes cultural conserve.

Spontaneity does not operate in a vacuum; it moves either towards creativity or cultural conserve.

zero spontaneity quotient; a puppet show has a certain small degree of spontaneity in a moment of presentation because the factor of spontaneity enters via the personality of the persons who activate the strings; a theatrical performance has a quotient still higher than the puppet show because the actors are there in the flesh. Another spontaneity scale attempted the reverse: it tried to determine the relative conserve quotient in various quasi-spontaneity patterns—the Commedia dell'Arte, for instance. Underlying its improvisatory character, this form had strong conserve components, types like "Harlequin," "Columbine," and "Pantaloon," and a dialogue which was, to a great extent, repeated at every performance.

Other spontaneity scales are based on the degree of readiness shown by various subjects in different impromptu situations or on their deviation from a statistically established normal response in standard life situations.

The first significant consequence of spontaneity work is a vitalization of the cultural conserves . . . . A prayer, for example, consists of four components: speech, thought content, feeling, and a pattern of action. The essence of prayer is true repetition; it would be sacrilegious to change the speech, thought, and gestures prescribed in the prayer. But when it comes to the feeling, the subject can transcend the conserve, actually nullifying its repetitiousness by introducing a spontaneous factor. Feeling is the wedge by which spontaneity training can enter a religious experience. By the introjection of a spontaneous factor, the variation and intensification of feeling with which the subject accompanies a prayer may bring a depth into a stereotype—literally the same for millions of others—which may differentiate him from all other people praying at that time.

Another illustration is the drama. The dialogue and the thoughts of the playwright are sacred and inviolate, but the actor trained along spontaneity lines becomes able to turn out a new play at every performance. Feeling and often gestures are here the vehicles for reinvigoration.

For still another illustration let us turn to the performance of musical compositions. Numerous techniques can be used in order to stimulate the fantasy of the players in an orchestra, for instance, as they play one of Beethoven's symphonies, so that they may attain a semblance of the spontaneity which was the composer's at the moment when he created the symphony. As a prelude to their performance, the musicians can be trained to undergo auxiliary experiences similar to those Beethoven underwent when he was creating.[2]

The more a cultural conserve is, in the moment of presentation, a total recapitulation of the same process, and the more a subject is conditioned to respond to it with the same feeling (in essence, the same feeling today as, let us say, ten years ago), the more the question arises as to what value the conserve has for the subject. It cannot be denied that the recall of a conserve is accompanied by a great satisfaction and even joy. The periodic recapitulation seems to whisper into the subject's ear that all is the same, all is well— the world has not changed. The cultural conserve renders to the individual a service similar to that which it renders as a historical category to culture at large—continuity of heritage—securing for him the preservation and the continuity of his ego. This provision is of aid as long as the individual lives in a comparatively still world; but what is he to do when the world around him is in a revolutionary change and when the quality of change is becoming more and more a permanent characteristic of the world in which he participates?

MENTAL CATHARSIS

A change may take place at any time in the life situation of an individual. A person may leave or a new person may enter his social atom, or he may be compelled to leave all members of his social atom behind and develop new relationships because he has migrated to a new country. A change may take place in this life situation because of certain developments in his cultural atom. He may, for instance, aspire to a new role—that of an aviator—which brings him, among other things, face to face with the problem of mastering a new machine. Or he is taken by surprise by new role in his son or his wife which did not seem to exist in them before. Illustrations of changes which might press upon him could easily be multiplied. Influences might threaten him from the economic, psychological, and social networks around him. It can well be said that, with the magnitude of change, the magnitude of spontaneity which an individual must summon in order to meet the change must increase in proportion. If the supply (the amount of spontaneity) can meet the demand (the amount of change), the individual's own relative equilibrium within his social and cultural atoms will be maintained. As long, however, as he is unable to summon the spontaneity necessary to meet the change, a disequilibrium will manifest itself which will find its greatest expression in his interpersonal and interrole relationships. This disequilibrium will increase in proportion to the falling off of spontaneity and will reach a relative maximum when his spontaneity reaches its maximum point. It is a peculiarity of these disequilibria that they have their reciprocal effects. They throw out of equilibrium other persons at the same time. The wider the range of disequilibrium, the greater becomes the need for catharsis. Numerous methods have been developed in the course of time which produce some degree of purification—catharsis. It may be interesting to review some of these catharsis-producing media from the point of view of our spontaneity theory.

Let us consider first the situation with which Aristotle introduced the concept of catharsis—spectators witnessing a Greek tragedy. What is it that makes the drama catharsis-producing in the spectator? Aristotle explained it by a brilliant analysis of the emotions of the spectators, and he was correct as far as he went. But from the point of view of spontaneity theory, however, he omitted the salient point: the spectator is witnessing and experiencing this human tragedy *for the first time*; these emotions, these roles, these conflicts, and this outcome are in this constellation a novelty for him. For the actors on the stage, however, the novelty has diminished more and more with each repetition. Their need for and their possibilities of mental catharsis were consummated equally in the course of their inspirational readings and rehearsals. The more the drama became a conserve for them, the less catharsis they could obtain from it.

It is different with the spectator, however. The effect upon him of the performance of the spectacle he happens to witness resembles the effect of the first reading upon the actor. The events in the drama may arouse in the spectator emotions which may have disquieted the spectator privately, but which are now magnified before him on the stage. However, it is the spontaneous factor of the first time which, on the one hand, arouses his disequilibrium to a high degree of articulation—a degree of which he would not have been capable by himself—and, on the other hand, makes him a wide-open target for the purge of his impure emotions—in other words, his mental catharsis.

A spectator, just as he may read a book a second or a third time, may be anxious to see a drama or a motion picture more than once. Every time he sees it he may experience portions of the spectacle which he overlooked earlier and which will act on him as another "first time," so to speak, operating as an irritating and catharsis-producing agent. But as soon as he is well acquainted with the entire spectacle, he will react to it as a conserve. By that time, moreover, his possibilities of and his need for catharsis will have become almost nil.

The spectators, as private persons, have no experience and no knowledge of the trials and pains through which the playwright, the director, and the actors have had to go in order to make possible a performance on the stage or in a film, or of the anxieties and strains the actors go through at the time the spectators are watching them. Comparatively speaking, the spectators are in a state of mind free of pain and fear. They are in an aesthetic situation, entirely inactive and quite willing to let their feelings follow the impressions which they receive from the stage, and to allow their ideas to develop in such a way that they may fit in with the pattern of the play. It is, in other words, the warming up process of the inactive subject. The more the spectator is able to accept the emotions, the role, and the developments on the stage as corresponding to his own private feelings, private roles, and private developments, the more thoroughly will his attentions and his fantasy be carried away by the performance. The paradox is, however, that he is identifying himself with something with which he is not identical. The spectator can sympathize with acts which take place on the stage just as if they were his own acts, but they are not his; he can experience with the actors all the pain and the torture, all the misery and joy which they go through—and still be free of them. The degree to which the spectator can enter into the life upon the stage, adjusting his own feelings to what is portrayed there, is the measure of the catharsis he is able to obtain on this occasion.

The written drama of today is the organized mental product of one particular person, the playwright. For him, the creative states and the roles which he had introjected into his drama may correspond, in some degree, to certain of his private notions and unactualized roles. From this point of view we may say that the process of writing the drama may have been accompanied by a catharsis—at least during the time of writing.

But for the actors, to whom this man's ideas are foreign, the situation is entirely different. If it should happen that an actor has a certain affinity for the part which is assigned to him—if the playwright has managed to express certain of his private emotions better than he could have expressed them— we may expect some degree of catharsis to take place in the private person of the actor. But one must not forget the effect made upon the actor by the great number of times he has to repeat his performance of this role in the course of rehearsing the role and, later, playing it night after night on the stage before an audience.

There are actors who give their best performances at their first reading of a role, and their performances grow more and more conserved from this point on. Apparently they are more spontaneous at the first reading, and if there is a tele relation between their own emotions and life roles and those expressed by the part to which they have been assigned, they are spontaneous in proportion to the novelty of the experience of acquaintance. The more often they have to rehearse and play a part, the more will they lose spontaneity, sincerity, and private interest. The amount of private interest an actor has in a part is a measure of the spontaneity he is able to display in it. The amount of spontaneity, in turn, is a measure of the amount of catharsis which the private personality of the actor will gain from the process of acting this part.

Aristotle and, with him, most later theorists of the drama, like Diderot, Lessing, and Goethe, were apparently influenced in their judgment of what mental catharsis is by their common frame of reference, the drama conserve.[3] Their views would have been vastly different if they had approached the problem from the point of view discussed in this paper, the point of view of spontaneous drama.

CATHARSIS IN THE PSYCHODRAMA

Historically there have been two avenues which led to the psychodramatic view of catharsis. The one avenue led from the Greek drama to the conventional drama of today, and with it went the universal acceptance of the Aristotelian concept of catharsis. The other avenue led from the religions of the East and the Near East. These religions held that a saint, in order to become a savior, had to make an effort; he had, first, to save himself. In other words, in the Greek situation the process of mental catharsis was conceived as being localized in the spectator—a passive catharsis. In the religious situation the process of catharsis was localized in the individual himself. This was an active catharsis. In the Greek concept the process of realization of a role took place in an object, in a symbolic person on the stage. In the religious concept the process of realization took place in the subject—the living person who was seeking the catharsis. One might say that passive catharsis is here face to face with active catharsis; aesthetic catharsis with ethical catharsis.

These two developments, which heretofore have moved along independent paths, have been brought to a synthesis by the psychodramatic concept of catharsis. From the ancient Greeks we have retained the drama and the stage, and we have accepted the Near East's view of catharsis, in which the actor has been made the locus for the catharsis. The old locus (the spectator) has become secondary. Furthermore, as actors on our stage we now have private persons with private tragedies, instead of the old Greek tragedians with their masks, their make-up, and their detachment from the theme of the drama.

These private tragedies may be caused by various disequilibrating experiences, one source of which may be the body. They may be caused by the relationship of the body to the mind, or by that of the mind to the body, and result in an inadequacy of performance at the moment. They may also be caused by an individual's thoughts and actions towards others, and by others' thoughts and actions towards him. Again, they may be caused by a design of living which is too complicated for the amount of spontaneity the individual is able to summon. Practically speaking, there is no sphere of the universe imaginable, whether physical, mental, social, or cultural, from which there may not emerge, at one time or another, some cause of disequilibrium in a person's life. It is almost a miracle that an individual can achieve and maintain any degree of balance, and man has continually been in search of devices which will enable him to attain or increase his equilibrium.

One of the most powerful media which can produce this effect is mental catharsis. It can take place and bring relief from grief or fear without any change being necessary in the external situation. Large amounts of energy are thus retained which otherwise would go into efforts to change reality. Every disequilibrium, however, has its matrix and its locus, and the catharsis-producing agent—in order to achieve the effect intended—has to be applied at the seat of the ailment.

Mental catharsis cannot be reproduced wholesale and on a symbolic plane to meet all the situations and relationships in which there may exist some cause for disequilibrium within a person.* It has to be applied concretely and specifically. The problem has been, therefore, to find a medium which can take care of the disequilibrating phenomena in the most realistic fashion, but still outside of reality; a medium which includes a realization as well as a catharsis for the body; a medium which makes catharsis as possible on the level of actions and gestures as it is on the level of speech; a medium which prepares the way for catharsis not only within an individual but also between two, three, or as many individuals as are interlocked in a life situation; a medium which opens up for a catharsis the world of fantasies and unreal roles and relationships. To all these and many other problems an answer has been found in one of the oldest inventions of man's creative mind—the drama.

---

*If "mental" catharsis seems an odd term for a process that describes emotional and physical release, Moreno's terminology can perhaps be best understood by remembering his historical epoch, in which "mental hygiene" was a new concept. As a psychiatrist director of a sanitarium for the "mentally" ill, he undoubtedly used terms that would make his work acceptable. (Ed.)

One of the problematic characteristics of human relationships as we live through them is their quality of looseness. A love relationship, for instance, takes time to develop. All worthwhile experiences in life take a long time to come to fruition. From the point of view of common sense, life appears full of tensions, disillusions, and dissatisfactions.

There is a pathological aspect to all life situations as they exist in our culture today—regardless of the mental conditions, normal or abnormal, of their constituents. Very few relationships are continuous and permanent, and even these few are often prematurely ended by the death of one of the partners. Most relationships are fragmentary and end in a most unsatisfactory fashion. In one case a life situation is distorted because partners spend too much time together; in another, because they spend too little time together; in another, because they have to exist side by side in one narrow room; while in another because they have too much freedom from any one locality. Such phenomena are not consequences of the economic structure of our society but, as we know from studies of such phenomena as the sociodynamic effect, they are inherent in the psychological currents which underlie all interhuman relationships.

Excepting rare instances, therefore, but few undertakings of any of us ever get so much as started . . . . Most of our roles remain in the "dream" stage. They are never attempted or begun, and any attempts at actualizing them (rare as they are) remain, like most of our relationships, fragmentary, inconclusive loose ends. The number of major and minor disequilibria rising from instances such as these is so large that even someone with superhuman moral resources might well be confused and at a loss. These phenomena have become associated in the mind of sociometric and psychodramatic workers with the concepts of the social and cultural atoms. It is these concepts which illustrate systematically and in the most dramatic fashion how impermanent and uncertain the organization and the trend of human lives can be.

In the course of studying the cultural atoms of individuals, we have most often encountered two groups of people in particular. In one group, the demands made upon them by the role and tele relationships of the group in which they live are so much greater than their resources or their interests that they would prefer being transferred, if possible, to a society whose total design is simpler and in which the number of roles in which they would have to function is reduced. A trend like this should not be compared with infantile behavior; the reason for this desire to live in fewer roles and relations may be that these people wish to live more thoroughly in a few roles, rather than less so in a greater number of them. The other group desires to develop and realize many more roles than the pattern of the society in which they live can afford them. They would prefer an expansion and not a reduction—an enrichment of design and not a simplification. In between these two extremes there fall groups of people who would prefer a reduction of some phases of life but an expansion of some others.

THE SIMPLIFIED WORLD OF THE PSYCHODRAMA STAGE

Let us see how the principle of reduction operates. The cultural atom of a monk—after he has joined the monastery—in comparison with his cultural atom during the time he lived in society, must show a drastic, well-nigh revolutionary change. As long as he was in the world outside, he acted, for instance, in the role of husband to his wife, father to his children, supporter to his parents, and employer to the hands on his farm. If he had desires for women other than his wife, then he may have acted in the role of a Don Juan; he may have been an adventurer, a gambler, a drinker. In other words, he acted in a number of roles which were suited to the pattern of society in which he lived. By entering the monastery he moved into a society which reduced the number of his roles to a minimum; the roles of husband, father, employer, et cetera, were cut off at one stroke. The greater the number of roles in which an individual operates in any society, the greater will be the number of conflicts in which he can become involved. The monastic community, by contrast, offers to the newcomer a culture of the simplest possible design. By reducing the number of roles, disequilibrium arising from suffering is also reduced—catharsis by reduction.

If we consider the monastery as a purely psychotherapeutic device, divorced from its religious trappings, it can be said that it takes its "patients" out of the society in which they have been living (and to which they are never to return) and places them in a society modeled after different principles but in better accord with the requirements of the "patients." The psychodramatic situation, based on a different philosophy and aimed at different ends, has utilized in modern form a similar point of view. It takes the patient away from the world in which he lives and places him in the center of a new world, separated from the rest of his experiences. This new world is a dramatic stage, equipped with all the devices which can throw him into a new pattern of society—a miniature society—in which living is different and much easier. At times it is simpler and at others it is much richer than the society from which the patient has come, but to him it is just as real as— sometimes more real than—the world outside. On the stage he continues to live his own life, but it is more compact because it has been reduced to its essentials. Husband and wife, after 25 years of marriage, go onto the psychodramatic stage and in a few hours exchange experiences of a depth which they have never known before. On the psychodramatic stage things are accomplished so much more quickly than in real life; time is so intensified. It is characteristic of the design of the psychodrama that in it things begin and end within the time and space allotted to them.

The subject (or patient) is allowed in the psychodramatic work to omit many scenes and details of his life—at least to begin with. This gives him at the start a freedom from the complexities and intricacies of his everyday life at home. Sometimes he is also allowed to emphasize certain key moments and situations of his life and to leave unmentioned what seems to him monotonous and insignificant. This also brings him relief.

A subject is put on the psychodramatic stage and given the opportunity to live his life just as he would wish to live it. A lifetime is condensed into an hour or two, and the fragmentary quality of existence outside the theatre is reduced to proportions in which we are able to express the essential experiences of our existence. Thus the psychodramatic stage is able to give one's own life a unity and completeness which a great dramatist presents to his public on a symbolic level only.

Some mental patients exhibit a strong tendency towards simplification of their life designs and a reduction of the number of roles they are called upon to play. As an illustration let us take the case of a woman who was suffering from a progressing form of manic-depressive psychosis. She showed a one-role pattern.[4] For, although she expressed agreement when asked to play the role of a princess on the psychodramatic stage, she did not act out the role when it came to the actual playing of the scene; instead she began to voice to her "suitor" in the scene her delusional plaint, which involved her desire to die and a compulsion to work and save money to send to her husband who was in South America. Placed in the role of a salesgirl, a housewife, a nurse, or a schoolteacher, although it apparently was her intention to act out these roles according to the proposed design, she did not make an attempt at any illusion but always acted her delusional role.

Accordingly, we tried to reduce the dimensions of the world around her, and on the stage as well, in order to be more in accord with her own spontaneity. When we had, to some degree, accomplished this we perceived that an open catharsis took place in the patient, followed by an increase in the coherence of her actions on the stage, although her behavior outside the theatre continued to show a high degree of incoherence and confusion. As she began to improve it was still characteristic of her performance on the psychodramatic stage that she mixed a certain number of private elements with the roles, but in lucid intervals which approached the normal she was finally able to carry out a symbolic role without too obvious reference to her private problems.

Many patients have come to my attention who, in the course of a paranoid form of dementia praecox, have brought to near extinction, one after another, the roles which normal life demanded of them—but not, apparently, because of any trend towards reduction. On the contrary, they seemed to have a frantic desire to make room for numerous other role aspirations which were impossible of expression within the bounds of their normal existence. An illustration of this phenomenon of expansion is the case of a mental patient whose conduct showed the presence of the seeds, at least, of many roles. At breakfast he claimed to be an aviator; at lunchtime he said he was a member of the British royal house; he spent the afternoon as a cowboy; and at the supper table he was a Chinese citizen. In a normal group these roles remained almost entirely on a verbal level since they received no support from the reality around him.[5] He confused the people round him, and he became more confused, himself, by their lack of response. To the growing vagueness and subjectivity of his paranoid conduct a stop was put when psychodramatic treatment was undertaken. The stage work showed that the action pattern of his delusional roles had a greater coherence than had been apparent in real life and that there was often more organization to them than mere verbal symbols. When the patient was supported by appropriate partners it was seen that these roles—unlivable in the outside world—could be given a semblance of reality for him in the psychodramatic stage. Since these roles were short-lived, he could live through many of them within a two-hour session in the theatre and derive satisfaction from the realization of all of them. For these completely hallucinatory roles and relations the psychodramatic stage was, indeed, the only possible vehicle. His optical and acoustic hallucinations found not only an expression through the aid of the partners, but in the audience in the theatre they also found a world which could give them a social reality—a world whose flexibility was able to accommodate the patient's trend towards expansion of his constellation of roles.

CATHARSIS AND ACTION

It has become an accepted fact in psychodramatic therapy that action patterns have a definite value in the process of catharsis. The climax in a patient's treatment usually takes place in the course of psychodramatic work on the stage and not during the interview preceding it or the analysis which comes after each scene. Interview, psychodrama, and postdramatic analysis form a continuous pattern, often so intertwined that it is difficult to tell where one leaves off and the other begins. But however relieving an analysis of situations may be for the patient, for a final test he must go back onto the stage in a real-life situation. There it may rapidly become clear that the equilibrium he had thought to have gained from the analysis is not adequate. What seems lacking is a "binder" between whatever analysis can give him in the way of equilibrium and the action in the moment of living. This binder is the spontaneity which the patient must be able to summon with split-second swiftness when a life situation calls for it. Retest after retest must be made in order to assure the patient that the necessary catharsis has been attained within him. It is spontaneity in its various expressions which at last crowns the efforts of the psychodrama and gives the patient the final certainty of an established equilibrium.

Theoretically speaking, the subject should be able rapidly to summon the spontaneity required for any given situation. Nevertheless, we often see a patient who puts up great resistance when asked to act out his problem. It may also happen that his mind is willing and he is able to make a start on the verbal level but the body lags behind; or, the body is brought into incomplete action which results in cramped gestures and movements and a disequilibrium of the function of speech as well; or undue haste and impulsiveness may throw the body into overheated action. In situations like these, the spontaneity associated with verbal and mental images does not have the power to carry the body along with it. Analysis does not help; action is required. The method is to warm the subject up by means of mental and physical starters, calling in another person to assist, if necessary. If this method is applied again and again, the subject learns through self-activation to get his organism ready for spontaneous action. It is a training in summoning spontaneity. In the course of overcoming the disequilibrium between the somatic and the mental processes, larger and larger portions of the organism are brought into play, pathological tensions and barriers are swept away, and a catharsis takes place. Disequilibrating experiences are often found between two or more persons in the roles and situations in which they are compelled to live. When they are placed upon the psychodramatic stage they seem to lack sufficient spontaneity in respect to one another to operate together in a common task. Psychodramatic methods can bring them to a point where they can reach one another at a depth-level which has been missing from their relationship. At this depth-level they can exchange thoughts and express emotions which will go far towards clarifying and easing the causes of their conflict.

Two persons may carry on a relationship for an indefinite time in harmony. All of a sudden they find themselves enemies. They do not know why. In the treatment of or interview with a single person it is impossible to find the true seat of the disequilibrium; both people are necessary, and they must be brought together in a situation which is crucial for them and in which they can act spontaneously. On the psychodramatic stage in one of these situations they will find themselves discarding evasions, reticences, and equivocations, and revealing their true, naked emotions and feelings. They remain essentially the same two individuals who, a moment ago, stepped upon the stage, but facets of their natures are revealed which each had forgotten in the other person—if, indeed, they had ever been apparent before. It is here, on this level, that the true point of conflict is revealed. The basic features of their interpersonal clash can be gradually brought to visualization and, finally, to their co-experience. If this depth-level had been ignored—if the essential core of their conflict had remained undiscovered and unexplored—no sound and permanent solution for their difficulty could have been reached. It required the stimulus of one personality upon the other in a spontaneous interaction to bring it to light.

SPECTATOR AND GROUP CATHARSIS

We have found that persons who witness a psychodramatic performance often become greatly disturbed. Sometimes, however, they leave the theatre very much relieved, almost as if it had been their own problems which they had just seen worked out upon the stage. Experiences such as these brought us back to the Aristotelian view of catharsis—as taking place in the spectator—but from a different angle and with a different perspective. The audience in a therapeutic theatre was originally limited to persons necessary to accomplish the treatment. This is still considered the classic approach.* At first we concerned ourselves with what this group meant to the actor-patients on the stage. It was soon discovered that they represented the world—public opinion. The amount and the kind of influence which the group exerted upon the conduct of a patient on the stage became an object of research, but in the course of time we made another discovery—the effect of psychodramatic work upon the spectator . . . .

By its own momentum the psychodramatic situation arouses people to act their problems out on a level on which the most intimate interindividual and interrole relationships find expression. This momentum is a dynamic factor which drives the subjects—once they have started—to act and talk things out in a way which takes them (and the spectators) by surprise.

There is a significant difference between the catharsis experienced by the spectator of a conventional drama and that experienced by the spectator of a psychodramatic performance. The question has been asked again and again: what factor produces the difference and in what does this difference consist? The persons on the psychodramatic stage do not really act in the conventional sense. They are presenting themselves, their own problems and conflicts, and—this must be emphasized—they make no attempt to make plays out of their problems. They are in dead earnest; they have been hounded by a conflict and they have come up against a blank wall in trying to escape. The spectator in the conventional theatre and the spectator of a psychodramatic performance can be compared to a man who sees the motion picture of a volcano in eruption and a man who watches the eruption from the foot

---

*Today the term "classical psychodrama" has come to refer to the nature of the protagonist's catharsis rather than the composition of the group. (Ed.)

of the mountain itself. It is the drama of life, in primary form, which, through the vehicle of the therapeutic theatre, comes to view; it never does, otherwise. Man protects such intimate relationships and situations from inspection with every possible means of concealment. The ultimate, private—yet anonymous—character of the psychodrama makes every spectator in the audience a silent accomplice of those on the stage, no matter what may be revealed there. More and more the whole meaning of his function as a spectator vanishes, and he becomes a part of and a silent partner in the psychodrama. This may explain the different character of the catharsis experienced by an onlooker in the therapeutic theatre compared with that which he attains from a conventional theatrical performance.

We are now about to consider the still deeper effect of psychodramatic work upon mental patients when they are spectators. It has been noticed here at Beacon Hill . . . that mental patients show a remarkable sensitivity for one another in daily life, a tele relation for one another's actions and words which is often surprising to the staff, and which amount to a high appreciation of their various ideological and emotional patterns. This heightened sensitivity was brought to a true test when we began to permit mental patients to witness a delusional, depressive, or paranoid experience of another patient reproduced on the psychodramatic stage.

From the psychodramatic point of view the behavior of mental patients can be divided into three categories: refusal to enter the theatre, willingness to enter the theatre but only as a spectator, and finally, willingness to take part in what is going on upon the stage. The gap between the first two categories is relatively wide, but sooner or later every patient can be persuaded to become a spectator, and once he has reached this phase, a therapeutic approach to his disorder is possible, even if he never goes onto the stage. The mental patient who, from his safe seat in the audience, witnesses a psychodrama—especially if the central person in it is a patient with whom he is acquainted—will show an interest and a curiosity for surpassing the normal and will reveal profound repercussions afterwards. The explanation of this effect is that the dramatization of psychiatric phenomena brings into three-dimensional expression for the spectator-patients patterns of experience which have not been permitted in the world outside the theatre. The mental patient in the audience thus comes into contact with the delusional or hallucinatory portion of another patient's world; he sees it worked out before his own eyes as if it were reality. There are hidden correspondences between the delusional portion of the scene he has seen acted out and his own delusions, many of which he had refrained from verbalizing. In addition, the reactions of the mental patient to what some other mental patient has acted out on the stage reveal relationships between his own delusions and those he had seen worked out which are suggestive both of his relations outside the theatre on the psychotic level with this particular patient and of the kind of catharsis he experienced in the theatre.

The discovery of a spectator-catharsis in mental patients opened up a prospect of treating them at the same time as the patient on the stage. The latter became more and more a prototype of pathological mental processes for the entire group of patients in the audience. Patients who suffered from similar complaints or who had similar patterns of delusion were selected to sit together in the audience. They then had similar cathartic experiences when a patient with a problem resembling their own was being treated on the stage.

The importance of this approach as a method of group psychotherapy is evident. At times, instead of using the mental patient as a prototype, specially trained psychodramatic assistants, so-called auxiliary egos, have been used with equally beneficial results.

Methodologically, the use of the auxiliary ego was an advantage because of the frequent difficulty of influencing more or less non-cooperative mental patients to choose situations or plots which were fruitful for the whole group and not merely for themselves. The employment of auxiliary egos who were under our own control and sufficiently sensitive to the experiences of the psychotic marked an important step forward in the technique of "group catharsis."

The return via psychodrama to the Aristotelian view of catharsis has vitalized the original conception. Large mental hospitals, mental hygiene clinics, child guidance bureaus, and community theatres may be able to make use of the following scheme which has the obvious goal of treating large numbers of people at the same time. It is, of course, a special experiment within the psychodramatic sphere. It has to be tried out under the direction of someone who is highly skilled along psychiatric, psychodramatic, and theatrical lines. It does not exclude the methods and techniques outlined in this paper and will never be able to replace them, but it may become an important auxiliary technique where individual or interpersonal treatment is practically impossible and where group catharsis is the method of choice.

The playwright of the conventional drama is, in this scheme, replaced by a more complicated mechanism. The community in which the subjects live— they may be mental patients or normal people—is explored, and by direct interviews or other means the dominating ideologies, emotions, or illusions of the community are determined. The more thorough this preliminary investigation is, the better. In addition, many of the subjects may have been able to supply pertinent material about themselves. All this material is then studied carefully by the auxiliary egos, and the design of one or more psychodramas is worked out. These psychodramas are so constructed that they may reach the depth levels of as large a portion of the subjects as possible. They may even be assisted in this process by some of the subjects themselves. The resultant psychodrama is preferably spontaneous, but a conserve drama can be visualized as possible in this situation. The actors of the conventional drama are replaced for this psychodrama by auxiliary egos. If the objective is to be the treatment of mental patients, the auxiliary egos will have been trained to portray delusions or hallucinations—or any psychotic processes which suit the purpose.

In contradistinction to the conventional theatre, the spectators of this psychodrama are then witnessing a performance which is expressly intended to relate (and which, in fact, does relate) to their specific individual problems. The reactions of the spectators during and immediately following the performance can be made the basis for individual psychodramatic treatments. Thus is Aristotle's concept of catharsis brought to its rightful, logical culmination.

The therapeutic aspect of psychodrama cannot be divorced from the aesthetic aspect, nor ultimately, from its ethical character. What the aesthetic drama has done for deities like Dionysius, Brahma, and Jehovah, and for representative characters like Hamlet, Macbeth, or Oedipus, the psychodrama can do for every man. In the therapeutic theatre an anonymous, average man becomes something approaching a work of art—not only for others but for himself. A tiny, insignificant existence is here elevated to a level of dignity and respect. Its private problems are projected onto a high plane of action before a special public . . . . The world in which we all live is imperfect, unjust, and amoral, but in the therapeutic theatre a little person can rise above our everyday world. Here his ego becomes an aesthetic prototype—he becomes representative of mankind. On the psychodramatic stage he is put into a state of inspiration—he is the dramatist himself . . . .

CHAPTER 6

The Role Concept, A Bridge Between Psychiatry and Sociology

1961

Editor's note: This article contains Moreno's concepts of the self and the unconscious as well as role. In his view all three are active and interactive in nature.

According to Zilboorg two psychiatric revolutions have taken place in the last three centuries.[1] Each psychiatric revolution was accompanied by a new body of theories and by new methods of clinical practice. The first psychiatric revolution was connected with the name of Philippe Pinel, his freeing of inmates from chains (1792); the second psychiatric revolution, with Sigmund Freud, his treatment on an individual basis through psychoanalysis (1893). In retrospect, Zilboorg's view requires basic correction. The second psychiatric revolution had at least two other highlights: Ivan P. Pavlov's conditioned reflex (1904) and Adolf Meyer's psychobiology (1906).

There is wide consensus that we are now in the midst of the "third" psychiatric revolution. Psychoanalysis faces its greatest crisis; it is in decline in the West and is rejected in the Communist countries of the East. The new

From *American Journal of Psychiatry* 118 (1961), 518-523.

era is one of multiple innovations which have set the pace for the new developments in psychiatry. It is characterized by the group psychiatric approach. The theories of interpersonal relations, microsociology, and sociometry—and the theories of the encounter, spontaneity, and creativity—have opened up vast areas of research in psychiatry, social psychology, and social anthropology. New methods of therapy—group psychotherapy, psychodrama, sociodrama, psychosomatic medicine, and psychopharmacology—have been introduced. The ideas of the therapeutic society, therapeutic community, the day hospital, and the "open door" of prisons and mental hospitals are beginning to replace the older coercive methods of the management of prisoners and mental patients . . . .

A new body of theory has developed in the last thirty years which aims to establish a bridge between psychiatry and the social sciences; it tries to transcend the limitations of psychoanalysis and behaviorism by a systematic investigation of social phenomena. One of the most significant concepts in this new theoretical framework is the role concept.

Current surveys of the origin and development of role theory and role concept emphasize the contributions made by sociologists and psychologists but neglect the contributions of psychiatrists. The reader gets the impression that psychiatrists had nothing to do with the development of role concepts. The authors of these surveys are often psychiatrists. Why do these authors look for the origin of new ideas in other sciences, neglecting their own, psychiatry? Psychiatrists are often given second place when it comes to theory; they react with inferiority feelings when they are accused by psychologists and sociologists of being less scientific. Sociologists, in contrast, suffer frequently from a superiority bias, writing, rather than observing and experimenting, being their favorite occupation. It is only fair to point out that besides non-medical authors, numerous psychiatrists have had a profound bearing upon the development of the role concept, influencing many sociological and psychological authors in their own, more academic formulations.

"Role," originally an Old French word, which penetrated into medieval French and English, is derived from the Latin "rotula." In Greece and also in ancient Rome, the parts of the theatre were written on the above-mentioned "rolls" and read by the prompters to the actors who tried to memorize their part by heart; this fixation of the word appears to have been lost in the more illiterate periods of the early and middle centuries of the Dark Ages. It was not until the sixteenth or seventeenth centuries, with the emergence of the modern stage, that the parts of the theatrical characters were read from paper fascicles, whence each scenic part becomes a "role."

Role is thus not a sociological concept; it came into the sociological vocabulary via the drama. It is often overlooked that modern role theory had its logical origin and its perspectives in the drama. It has a long history and tradition in the European theatre from which gradually developed the therapeutic and social direction of our time. It is from Europe that the seed of these ideas were transplanted to the U.S.A. in the middle of the 1920s. From the roles and counterroles, the role situations and role conserves developed naturally their modern extensions: role player, role playing, role expectation, acting out, and finally, psychodrama and sociodrama. Independently, the sociological concept of role taking by G. H. Mead took form (1934) and was further developed by R. Linton (1936); both of these men were apparently unaware of the basic dependence of the process of role taking upon the drama. Many American sociologists have monopolized the concept of role, especially T. Parsons, as if it were sociological property. But most terms and meanings which Parsons and associates present in their writings can be found in prior publications.[2]

DEFINITION OF ROLE

Role can be defined as the actual and tangible forms which the self takes. We thus define the role as the functioning form the individual assumes in the specific moment he reacts to a specific situation in which other persons or objects are involved. The symbolic representation of this functioning form, perceived by the individual and others, is called the role. The form is created by past experiences and the cultural patterns of the society in which the individual lives, and may be satisfied by the specific type of his productivity. Every role is a fusion of private and collective elements. Every role has two sides, a private and a collective side.

The role concept cuts across the sciences of man—physiology, psychology, sociology, anthropology—and binds them together on a new plane. The sociologists G. H. Mead and R. Linton limited the theory of roles to a single dimension, the social. The psychodramatic role theory operating with a psychiatric orientation is more inclusive. It carries the concept of role through all dimensions of life; it begins at birth and continues throughout the lifetime of the individual and the *socius*. It has constructed models in which the role begins to transact from birth on. We cannot start with the role process at the moment of language development, but in order to be consistent we must carry it through the non-verbal phases of living. Therefore, role theory cannot be limited to social roles; it must include the three dimensions—social roles, expressing the social dimensions; psychosomatic roles, expressing the physiological dimension; and psychodramatic roles, expressing the psychological dimension of the self.

Illustrations of psychosomatic roles are the role of the eater and the sexual role. Characteristic patterns of interaction between mother and infant in the process of eating produce role constellations of the eater which can be followed up throughout the different life periods. Psychodramatic forms of role playing, such as role reversal, role identification, double and mirror playing, contribute to the mental growth of the individual. The social roles develop at a later stage and lean upon psychosomatic and psychodramatic roles as earlier forms of experience.

The function of the role is to enter the unconscious from the social world and bring shape and order to it. The relationship of the roles to the situations in which the individual operates (status) and the relation of role as significantly related to ego have been emphasized [in *Who Shall Survive?*].

Everybody is expected to live up to his official role in life; a teacher is to act as a teacher, a pupil as a pupil, and so forth. But the individual craves to embody far more roles than those he is allowed to act out in life, and even within the same role, one or more varieties of it. Every individual is filled with different roles in which he wants to become active and that are present in him in different stages of development. It is from the active pressure which these multiple individual units exert upon the manifest official role that a feeling of anxiety is often produced.

Every individual—just as he has at all times a set of friends and a set of enemies—has a range of roles in which he sees himself and faces a range of counterroles in which he sees others around him. They are in various stages of development. The tangible aspects of what is know as "ego" are the roles in which he operates, the pattern of role relations that focus around an individual. We consider roles and the relationships between roles as the most significant development within any specific culture.

Role is the unit of culture; ego and role are in continuous interaction. Role perception is cognitive and anticipates forthcoming responses. Role enactment is a skill of performance. A high degree of role perception can be accompanied by a low skill for role enactment, and vice versa. Role playing is a function of both role perception and role enactment. Role training, in contrast to role playing, is an effort, through the rehearsal of roles, to perform adequately in future situations.

Regressive behavior is not a true regression but a form of role playing. In paranoiac behavior, the repertory of roles is reduced to distorted acting in a single role. The deviate is unable to carry out a role in situ. He either overplays or underplays the part; inadequate perception is combined with distorted enactment. Histrionic neurosis of actors is due to the intervention of role fragments "alien" to the role personality of the actor.

By means of role reversing one actor tries to identify with another, but reversal of roles cannot take place in a vacuum. Individuals who are intimately acquainted reverse roles more easily than individuals who are separated by a wide psychological or ethnic distance. The cause for these great variations is the development of co-conscious and co-unconscious states. Neither the concept of unconscious states (Freud) nor that of collective unconscious states (Jung) can be easily applied to these problems without

stretching the meaning of the terms. The free associations of A may be a path
to the unconscious states of A; the free associations of B may be a path to the
unconscious states of B; but can the unconscious material of A link naturally
and directly with the unconscious material of B unless they share in unconscious states? The concept of individual unconscious states becomes unsatisfactory for explaining both movements, from the present situation of A, and
in reverse to the present situation of B. We must look for a concept which is
so constructed that the objective indication for the existence of these two-
way processes does not come from a single psyche but from a still deeper
reality in which the unconscious states of two or several individuals are
interlocked with a system of co-unconscious states. They play a great role in
the life of people who live in intimate ensembles, like father and son, husband and wife, mother and daughter, siblings and twins, but also in other
intimate ensembles, such as in work teams, combat teams, persons in concentration camps, or charismatic religious groups. Marriage and family therapy, for instance, has to be so conducted that the "interpsyche" of the entire
group is reenacted, so that all their tele relations, the conscious and co-
unconscious states, are brought to life. Co-conscious and co-unconscious
states are, by definition, such states which the partners have experienced and
produced jointly and which can, therefore, be only jointly reproduced or reenacted. A co-conscious or a co-unconscious state can not be the property of
one individual only. It is always a common property and cannot be reproduced but by a combined effort. If a re-enactment of such a co-conscious or
co-unconscious state is desired or necessary, that re-enactment has to take
place with the help of all partners involved in the episode. The logical
method of such re-enactment a deux is psychodrama. However great a genius of perception one partner of the ensemble might have, he cannot produce that episode alone because the partners have in common their co-
conscious and co-unconscious states which are the matrix from which they
drew their inspiration and knowledge.

As a general rule, a role can be (1) rudimentarily developed, normally
developed, or overdeveloped; (2) almost or totally absent in a person (indifference); (3) perverted into a hostile function. A role in any of the above
categories can also be classified from the point of view of its development in
time: (1) it was never present; (2) it is present towards one person but not
present towards another; (3) it was once present towards a person but is
now extinguished.

A simple method of measuring roles is to use as a norm permanently
established processes which do not permit any change, role conserves like
Shakespeare's *Hamlet* or *Othello*, Goethe's *Faust*, or Byron's *Don Juan*. Another method of measurement uses as norms social roles which are rigidly
prescribed by social and legalistic customs and forms. Illustrations for this
are social roles as the policeman, the judge, the physician, and so forth.

Another method of measurement is to let a subject develop a role *in statu nascendi*, placing him into situations ranging from the little structured to the highly organized. The productions of different subjects will differ greatly and will provide us with a yardstick for role measurement. Another method of measurement is to place a number of subjects unacquainted with each other into a situation which they have to meet in common. Illustration: six men of equal military rank are camping. Suddenly they see an enemy parachutist landing in the nearby forest. They have to act on the spur of the moment. A jury watches to see how the group grows *in statu nascendi*; the jury may discern three things. (1) what relationships develop between the six men: who is taking the initiative in the first phase, in the intermediate phase, in the final phase of their interaction? Who emerges as the "leader"? (2) What action do they take towards the enemy? (3) How is the situation ended and by whom?

Another significant method of measurement is the analysis of role diagrams and sociograms of individuals and groups from the point of view of role interaction, role clustering, and prediction of future behavior.

A considerable amount of experimental and validation studies have been made in recent years with regard to role theory.

SUMMARY

The concept underlying this approach is the recognition that man is a role player, that every individual is characterized by a certain range of roles which dominate his behavior, and that every culture is characterized by a certain set of roles which it imposes with varying degrees of success upon its membership.

In contrast to the theories presented by psychologists and sociologists, "psychiatric role theory" developed largely out of clinical contexts, of methods of prevention, of treatment of psychoses and neuroses, of marriage and family groups, of interpersonal relations, of problems of industrial adjustment, of the fields of mental hygiene and education.

Role research and role therapy are still in their infancy. Psychodrama presents a valuable vehicle for experimental and control studies of roles. It permits the observation of individuals in live situations in which they are concretely involved.

CHAPTER 7

Notes on Indications and Contra-Indications for Acting Out in Psychodrama

1973

Editor's note: Though brief, this article shows the importance Moreno placed on accurate diagnosis and appropriate treatment.

The psychodramatic realizations of suicidal or homicidal fantasies may give courage and prepare a patient to carry out the suicide in life itself. Such a patient may be already warmed up to the near action point when the treatment begins. It is obvious that such a treatment process is contra-indicated unless the greatest precautions are taken to protect the patient against himself. First of all, he has to be in the supervised environment of a hospital community. It is contra-indicated in day hospitals, in doctors' offices, and in extra-mural clinics.

It is useful to differentiate between individuals who tend to be "tele-sensitive" and those who tend to be "transference-sensitive." Many so-called

From *Group Psychotherapy, Psychodrama & Sociometry*, 26 (1973), 23-25.

psychopathic personalities belong to the first class; for them a dynamic and open approach is indicated. The psychodramatist has to have, besides telic sensitivity, knowledge of the codes of alcoholics and drug addicts, as well as of prisoners in prison, in order to approach them effectively. Any kind of role playing on a fictitious level, unrelated to their actual dynamic problems, will not reach them. They need direct and realistic psychodrama. In order to meet the needs of extreme realism, we have gone . . . to the point where we have a bar and a bartender in the theatre, so that a group of alcoholics can act as freely as in a real bar room. They sit at the counter, order their drinks, and get them. They make conversation with neighbors, like in a bar. This is often the starting point of alcoholic psychodrama. This apparent extreme tolerance gives the psychodramatist unlimited opportunities for diagnosing and participating in the activities of the patients as if in situ, but still under the conditions of possible supervision and control.

Acting out is used in group sessions only when there is a clear indication for it. Frequently an entire session is spent in discussion of a previous session or preparatory to a psychodrama in the next session. It should be remembered that psychodrama and group psychotherapy are two independent developments. Contrary to unsophisticated opinion, psychodrama is the broader classification. Individual, "a deux," psychodrama is possible; it is an accepted and valuable form of psychotherapy, but obviously "individual" group psychotherapy is a contradiction. Individual psychodrama may be combined with psychodramatic group treatment in such cases where certain types of problems are not suitable for group revelation or when the patient feels the level of acceptance is not compatible . . . .

It should be remembered that verbal group psychotherapy is the audience portion of psychodrama without the action portion. However, due to the non-psychodramatic orientation of many group psychotherapists who have entered the field, the verbal portion has tended to rely largely on analysis and interpretation, or discussion and verbal confrontation. It is still the major contribution of psychodrama to have insisted that even verbal interchange should not be of this nature, but more on the basis of the encounter, with group members sharing revelations about themselves rather than analyzing and interpreting. This sharing has become one of the more important areas of practical application in group therapy and prepares the group members for the next step, that of going from the verbal to the acting dimension, wherever indicated and when the process can be guided by a skilled psychodramatist.

CHAPTER 8

Psychodramatic Treatment of Psychoses

1939

Editor's note: When Moreno wrote this article, his hospital in Beacon had been open for only three years. Psychodrama was still in a development stage. Nevertheless, the method worked. In the following report Moreno conveys his sense of the nature of mental disorder and the role of the psychotherapist in working with psychotic patients.

It has been established that psychoses can be treated by means of the psychodrama, but questions have been raised as to just how this treatment can be accomplished and what effect the psychodramatic treatment has upon the psychotic and his disorder.

Freud distinguished between those mental disorders in which a transference from the patient to the physician can take place and those of such narcissistic character that no transference is possible. He declared persistently that psychoanalytic treatment can be applied only to patients who can produce a transference to the analyst. Consequently, as soon as he discovered that a patient was suffering from a schizophrenia or similar narcissistic disor-

---

From *Sociometry* 3 (1940), 115-132.

der, he declined to treat the patient further, stating that psychoanalytic treatment would do no good.[1]

Now the fact that a patient is suffering from schizophrenia or a disorder of a predominantly narcissistic character does not in any way preclude psychodramatic treatment, for this treatment may proceed quite well when transference from the patient to the psychiatrist is negligible, or even absent. The psychotic experiences of the patient have been incapable of adequate expression in the world of reality, which is strange and unfitted to them. As long as the patient remains without psychodramatic treatment, his psychotic experiences remain in a vague and confused subjectivity, without any anchorage. The *psychodramatic principle* consists of providing a means for their objectification by means of the establishment of an imaginary reality. As a matter of fact, the narcissistic element in the ego of the patient causes him to welcome a sphere in which it can realize itself to an extent which far exceeds the bounds of the "reality" principle which has hitherto confined him. It is just such a sphere which is provided by the psychodrama and the psychodramatic stage. On this stage, the auxiliary egos assist the patient to realize the roles in which he sees himself and which he may never before have been able to actualize. By the very methodology of the psychodrama, the patient is enabled to project his psychosis as it radiates from his ego in the form of delusional, hallucinatory, or normal roles. The auxiliary egos do not restrict the narcissistic element in the patient's ego. In the first stages of the treatment, at least, they extend it and establish—in their various roles and on the level of these roles—a relationship to the roles of the patient.

The function which transference performs in the psychoanalytic treatment of psychoneuroses and which it fails to perform in narcissistic disorders is replaced, on the psychodramatic stage, by new factors which operate on the interpersonal and on the role-to-role level. (For important theoretical reasons—as has been discussed elsewhere—this interrole and interpersonal feeling has been called "tele" instead of "transference.") By means of this tele, a situation has been created in which an attempt to guide and to cure can be made in the case of mental disorders which psychoanalysis has openly eliminated from its therapeutic field.

On the basis of a considerable number of cases, a working hypothesis has been established which—notwithstanding variations between individuals treated—has certain general lines of psychodramatic procedure common to all psychotic patients. In the center of the treatment is the patient, always, and the task of developing the psychodramatic process is, as much as possible, in his hands. The psychiatric director and the staff of auxiliary egos act as prompters and foils for the patient as he acts out the various roles of his psychosis. The patient may be able to present only the fragments of an imaginary world, or he may have ready a complete system or plot, with definite characters and roles—or any degree of completeness between these two extremes. In each individual case it is the task of the auxiliary egos to assist the patient to round out his imaginary world fully and in accordance with his specific requirements. The psychodrama actually functions as a milieu which will reflect that patient's psychosis in such a way and on such a level that he can see his psychotic experiences objectified. As the treatment progresses, this objectification begins to interest the patient and continues to do so, more and more. For him the world of reality and of socialized action has become so unstable—so unreal—that a new and imaginary world is a necessity as an anchor for him if his experiences are not to be permanently reduced to the level of false signals and symbols.

THE PSYCHODRAMATIC PRINCIPLE

This imaginary reality is provided by the psychodramatic principle, which operates with psychotic patients in somewhat the same way that the "reality principle" operates with non-psychotic subjects. In this imaginary reality on the psychodramatic stage, the patient finds a concrete setting in which all his hallucinatory and delusional thoughts, feelings, and roles are valid and in which he finds the roles in other people which meet his own on a common footing. His social and cultural atoms become full and rich, instead of being empty and unsatisfying. He can live in a setting which is far more convincing and far truer than the reality in which he lived before and which he had "outgrown" in the early days of his delusion. This earlier reality had been uncomfortable for him because it no longer was fitted to him in his new roles—the roles introduced by his disorder. On the therapeutic stage, however, he finds a new "reality" which has been exactly tailored for him.

To the naive participant or spectator it may seem, on first sight, that the exhibitions permitted the patient must lead to a deeper confirmation of his delusions. However, it is soon perceived that the organization set up within and around the patient by the psychodrama—for the very reason that it is exactly fitted to him—acts as a much more effective restraint than the restrictions of the real world which he had been forced to burst asunder, with the result that they had ceased to exert any control whatsoever over his delusions. In his new, imaginary reality he feels comfortable and at home. This has the effect of channeling his delusions and his functions in life situations along a line which is integrated with the procedure on the psychodramatic stage. He no longer diffuses his efforts in vain attempts to realize some of his delusions. They are now the real stuff of life in this new reality. By supporting his hallucinations and delusions, the auxiliary egos can keep them within the bounds of the psychodramatic imaginary reality. This enables the psychodramatic staff to guide the patient in such a way that he actually restrains himself, and at the same time insures against any further deterioration into his psychosis. To maintain this position in regard to the psychotic patient requires constant watchfulness, and a particular lookout must be kept for any signs of new productivity on the part of the patient.

When the patient is in a productive phase, the psychodramatic treatment can keep pace with him and prevent him from going astray into an overrich delusional development. As can be observed, once the patient is warmed up to a new range of delusions, the process becomes very rapid, due to the infectiousness one association has for another. In order to catch up with the patient's new delusions and keep the process of guidance alive, very soon after a new delusional development begins, psychodramatic work must provide a reality—an anchor—for it. These anchors become—whenever the patient returns to the psychodramatic stage—rallying points for him around which he can develop his new delusions. The mental catharsis which takes place within the patient is not a momentary satisfaction, nor is it is merely a spontaneous release of pathological experiences (*abreagieren*). It is a full-fledged system of relationships, an auxiliary world to which the patient can return at later phases in his treatment. Hence, the pauses from one psychodramatic session to another must remain flexible, carefully timed to the patient's inner activities. In psychodramatic work, patients can just as easily be undertreated as overtreated.

In the course of our study of psychotic patients who have been living in the atmosphere of a psychodramatic imaginary reality for a longer period of time, we have often asked ourselves whether the presence and intrusion of common reality (which, naturally, can never be entirely prevented from influencing patients) does not weaken the effect of a great deal of the work which has been accomplished on the psychodramatic stage. In answer to this we have arrived at the opinion that the patients do not need to be continuously within the reality on the psychodramatic stage which has been tailored to fit them. It appears to be sufficient if they are placed within this imaginary world at certain crucial times, for the purpose of establishing certain points of coordination of the delusion to a corresponding reality. The length of the intervals between these points of coordination does not matter as long as they keep pace with the productivity of the patient. This situation has its parallel in the life of the normal and the near-normal person. We know from psychodramatic work that a normal person, in his interpersonal relationships, does not continuously participate in the realities of other persons and objects. A great part of a normal person's life is lived in the fantasies which are often as distant from the reality principle as the fantasies of reality of our psychotic patients are from the psychodramatic stage, its staff, and the whole method of psychodrama.

The concept of "points of coordination" has been found to be of significance in all the interpersonal and role-to-role relationships, as we have already remarked in our study of warming up processes as they flow between persons in any interpersonal performance. Its full meaning is that a relationship between two persons does not require a continuity of tele contact in order to be adequate. It is sufficient if this contact occurs at certain moments which we call the points of coordination. These points are a rhythmic expression of the fundamental pattern of interpersonal relationships. They make possible the great economy in the interpersonal exchange of emotions. For instance, in order to produce an adequate husband-wife relationship, it is not necessary that these roles be actuated continuously, but only at certain moments from which the illusion of continuity radiates into the intervals between them. The same is true, of course, in friendship relations, leader-follower relationships, and so forth.

THE CULTURAL ATOM IN MENTAL PATIENTS

One of the first steps to be taken with a psychotic patient is to discover how far he has been able to go by himself in the forming of an imaginary reality. We are, to be sure, to a certain extent interested in his social atom, but his cultural atom—the roles in which he sees himself and in which he sees others in relation to his roles—is of paramount importance to us, for it is from his cultural atom that we get our picture of his inner world. With this picture as a base, we can proceed to paint in the firm outlines of this world which we create for him, peopling it with the persons and the roles which his delusions demand, so that we can meet him on common ground. Let us consider how these roles begin, grow, and change.

Every role in which an individual operates has a certain duration, a certain lifetime. Each has a beginning, a ripening, and a fading out. A role, after it has served for a period in a certain function, may vanish from the manifest life of an individual, but it continues as a dynamic factor in his inner life. It becomes a matrix from which a new role may draw strengthening support—first by imitation and later by contrast, until the new role establishes itself within its own sphere and in its own right. There is, therefore, a dynamic interdependence between a certain series of roles in the dimension of time, but it is in discord with psychodramatic evidence to assume that a role acquired in early infancy operates like a compulsion and dominates subsequent roles, mastering them and submitting them to its own pattern—as psychoanalytic investigators, for instance, have declared. The evidence on the psychodramatic stage suggests that a new role—when it is in its infancy—*leans* upon an older role until the time comes when it is able to free itself and operate alone. It can well be said that, like a cell separating itself from the parent cell, a role, when it is just coming into its full and self-sufficient growth, is separating itself from the mother pattern. In the course of time, this new role may become the mother pattern for other new roles. An illustration of this is seen in artists like writers or painters who, in their first efforts religiously copy a certain form, leaning upon it, but later gradually develop their own forms.

At times, however, a new role may emerge instantly, without precedent and without leaning upon any mother pattern. This is occasioned by some situation which is to such a degree original and new to the subject that he is stimulated into summoning the spontaneity necessary for the particular performance.

We have seen that cultural atoms change swiftly in the temporal dimension and in the interpersonal (the role-counterrole) dimension. These changes do not necessarily mean that the configuration of the cultural atom at one time does not have a dynamic similarity—or even identity—with its configuration at another time. We have observed, in comparing the social atoms of a person at different times, that, although certain persons vanish from his social atom they are replaced by other persons who fulfill similar needs. It is probable that it is much the same with cultural atoms—that roles and counterroles vanish and are replaced by new roles and counterroles which go to make a role configuration of a similar equilibrium.

We have also noted that these changes seldom take place instantaneously and completely. There is in the evolution of the cultural atom a structural carryover from one temporal phase to the next which serves to bind together the cultural development of an individual.

PSYCHODRAMATIC TECHNIQUES

In the course of psychodramatic work with patients who are suffering from narcissistic mental disorders, we have developed a number of techniques which are of great help in forming, with and for the patient, this imaginary reality, this auxiliary world, which enables us to treat a psychosis of this sort. These techniques are of use not only at the start of the treatment, but later, too, when some channeling of the patient's hallucinations and delusions has been accomplished.

Our patient, when we first try to get him to act "himself" on the psychodramatic stage, may refuse to do so in any role which expresses a private capacity. He may be suspicious, and he may resent any intrusion on his privacy. This difficulty is overcome by a simple psychodramatic technique. The patient is asked to act out the role of his father or his brother, or that of any other person who is closely associated with him. In expressing their personalities and their attitudes as he sees them, he will betray a great deal of information about himself, and, at the same time, about what he feels towards the person he is portraying. If the patient refuses to act as any one of these persons on some such grounds as that "it is too private" or "too personal," this same technique is varied in that he is asked to act in some symbolic role which seems to him to be remote from this and his close associates. In most cases he can be prevailed upon to choose this role himself. If he does, the role will of course be one that appeals to him and, in all probability, we shall find that it is one of the roles in his cultural atom. Without being aware of it he will thus show us much of himself and his relationship to this role. This process of making one role act as an auxiliary to bring out a suppressed role is called the *substituting role* technique.

Another useful device in the psychodramatic treatment of a psychotic patient is the *mirror* technique. Sometimes a patient overacts when he is too eager to act as himself. In order that the patient may see himself from the proper perspective, an auxiliary ego acts in the role of the patient. The patient is then trained to see himself more objectively, much as in a mirror, and he learns, from watching the auxiliary ego, how to act in better relation to the realities. The mirror technique can also be used in another way. The patient may refuse to act at all, and therefore an auxiliary ego takes his place on the stage and portrays him in a series of life situations—if possible with someone who is closely associated with the patient. If the action on the stage and the portrayal of himself is repugnant to the patient, we may hear him making comments from his place in the audience, and he may even walk onto the stage and take over the role of "himself" from the auxiliary ego.

Another technique comes into play when a patient has projected his system of delusions into a plot which he wants to see acted out on the stage by the auxiliary egos, in order to create a psychodramatic reality for himself and the imaginary characters within his system of ideas. To illustrate: a patient suggested and directed a series of scenes in which auxiliary egos acted his father, his mother, and himself as a little boy. He, as a small boy, was present during a violent scene between the father and the mother; this scene led to his father's leaving the house and, eventually, to his parents' separation. The patient's parents had been brought together again by the illness of their son, and they were present in the audience when these scenes were played. All through the action the patient watched them to see how they were affected by the actions of their representatives on the stage. This recalls the scene in Hamlet where the player king and the player queen act out before the real king, Hamlet's uncle, and the queen, his mother, the action depicting the poisoning of Hamlet's father as Hamlet imagined it had taken place. This psychodramatic technique is known as the *projection* technique.

Objectification of himself by the patient can also be accomplished by means of the *reversal* technique. The patient is asked to place himself in the role of someone in his social atom, and an auxiliary ego—or the actual person whom the patient is to portray, if possible—is placed in the role of the patient. In this situation, the patient is not only made to objectify himself, as in the mirror technique, but he must react towards "himself" in the way he thinks the person whose role he is playing would react. An illustration of the operation of this technique is provided by the case of a boy who had disclosed to two psychiatrists and a number of auxiliary egos that he was laboring under the delusion that he might turn or be turned into a girl. At a strategic point in his treatment, he was placed in the role of one of the psychiatrists who had heard his disclosure. Acting in the role of the boy, the psychiatrist was to come to the boy—now in the role of the psychiatrist—for advice about his fears. In this way the patient was compelled to act in an advisory capacity toward another person who was exhibiting the same abnormal ideas as those with which he was obsessed. This gave him the opportunity to test for himself the degree of responsibility and stability he had reached in the course of our treatment, and it afforded us a chance to see what degree of maturity he had attained. He seemed to be acting both himself and the psychiatrist at the same time but, by the technique of reversal, he was forced to objectify his real self and his obsession from what he conceived to be a psychiatrist's point of view.

Psychodramatic treatment can be started with a role which is at a considerable distance from the role in which the patient actually lives, or the role to which we wish eventually to lead him. To begin with, the private roles of the patient are purposely eliminated from the focus of attention, just as in the technique of the substitute role. In this particular technique, however, the procedure is to progress gradually from the first far-distant role through a series of roles which increase in their semblance to reality, until we have arrived at the role in which we wish to see him. As an instance of the operation of this technique we have the case of a five year-old boy who had a compulsion to beat his mother. We began his treatment by putting him in the role of a young prince, because he was able to understand that a prince "surely would not beat his mother, the queen!" By gradually lowering the social status of the roles he was given, he was finally brought to the point where, when he played himself, he did not beat his mother, real though she was. This technique is called the *symbolic distance* technique.

In some cases the patient will be found to be suffering from a pair of opposite attitudes. One state of mind warms him up—for instance, to the idea of self-destruction. He may have almost reached the climax—or may even be parallel with this state—when a contrary state of mind begins to argue that life still has much to offer him. Continuously forced from one extreme to the other, he finds himself the scene of a permanent conflict, one portion of his ego combating the other portion. In obsessional neuroses and in some psychotic conditions which display symptom patterns of this sort, the following technique has been found to bring relief: the patient's two egos, so to speak, are portrayed on the stage. The surface ego—that face of himself which he manifests in ordinary life and with which he is commonly identified—is acted out by an auxiliary ego. The deeper ego, which is invisible, torturing, and trying to defeat the "official" ego, is acted out by the patient. The surface ego—played by the auxiliary ego—not only gives expression to the patient's ordinary superficial conduct, but fights back at the deeper ego as it is acted out by the patient. The result is an objectification of the violent fight going on between the two alternative factors in the patient's mind. This is known as the *double ego* technique.

In addition to their use in the treatment of psychotic patients with narcissistic trends, these techniques—as must be clear to any student of psychodramatic literature—have, with some modifications, proved useful in many cases of simple neurosis and generally in all types of mental disturbance to which suggestive therapy, psychoanalysis, and other forms of psychotherapy are usually applied.

In the course of the lives of all of us—indeed from the moment of birth on—we are surrounded or we surround ourselves with helpers (and opponents) of all sorts—parents, siblings, friends, rivals, competitors, et cetera. Unknown to them (since they are driven by the same kind of motives as we are) they operate as auxiliary egos, extensions of our egos—increasing (or decreasing) our power and welfare. With psychotic patients, the situation is, of course, the same, but the auxiliary egos in real life are, however, often incompetent and unsuccessful in bringing about the results the patient is attempting to achieve. This is probably so because in life these people are only accidentally in the role of auxiliary egos. Actually they have their own personalities, and are auxiliary egos only as a by-product, so to speak. They are seeking to take advantage of other people as auxiliary egos, just as the patient is doing with them. These interpersonal processes work out for some people in a satisfactory fashion, as is indicated in sociometric charts. These lucky people ascend to a position in the group which is adequate for their needs and find themselves surrounded by a sufficient number of helpers and followers—sometimes even by too many.

There is a group of individuals, however, who do not fare so well in their development. Apparently the reason for this does not lie in a lack of ability in these individuals, but it has to do with other factors . . . . We are here concerned only with what these individuals do—how they behave, how they try to help themselves when they find themselves in positions of this sort. On the one hand we have the individual who is able to command such a position in the group that he is, at all times, doing what he wants and getting what he desires, and on the other hand, we have the individual whose position is such that he gets little aid from the group and, in addition, rejects what little aid is offered him. The withdrawal symptoms of a patient of the latter sort are, therefore, a peripheral expression of a deeper process going on within him as well as between him and the members of the group. When the barriers between him and an ascendancy in the group become too great, and when many futile attempts at social recognition and power have disillusioned him (perhaps too rapidly), he decides to substitute . . . certain self-created and invented personality patterns, products of his imagination which are much more satisfying to him than the real people in the real world. The result is that he becomes indifferent or hostile to the real people of his social atom and quite naturally prefers his own inventions which, like people in a fairy tale, are at his command at any time and can be multiplied or changed whenever necessary and at a moment's notice. The fact that the patient cannot successfully exist without the help of real people—whether he likes it or not—produces a difficulty of which many of the paranoid patients we have studied were (at least in part) aware, at one time or another . . . .

When our paranoid patients are brought into a milieu in which professionally trained auxiliary egos are available and who are more adequately suited to their tasks than the friends or parents of the patients, the patients are aroused to reconsider their situation and to use the auxiliary egos in their attempt at establishing a new and imaginary world for themselves which is more fitting for them than the world of reality. These auxiliary egos seem to the patients to fit better into the mental creations which they have already developed than the auxiliary egos of real life, and these new ones offer the happy advantage that they provide a bridge to the world outside which the patients have abandoned or which they reject. The psychodramatic auxiliary ego plays a double role. In the therapeutic theatre he is an ideal extension of the patient's ego in his effort to establish a sort of psychotic hierarchy, a self-sufficient world, and outside of the theatre he is an interpreter between the patient and the people of the real world. Of course the patient's attempt at self-sufficiency is, at best, only partly successful. Most of his imaginary roles remain rudimentary and distorted. Here, again, the auxiliary ego can act as a valuable helper to the patient in the direction of his own aspirations.

THE AUXILIARY WORLD TECHNIQUE

The majority of patients can be treated in the therapeutic theatre by means of one technique or another. Only a very small number resist any participation whatever in the psychodrama. In the case of patients like these, however, there remains a further psychodramatic technique, the *auxiliary world*. In this technique, the patient's total milieu—wherever he may be at the time of the approach—is made the stage for this psychodrama. It may involve the assumption on the part of all persons with whom the patient comes into contact in and around the institution that they are the patient's vassals, his slaves, or whatever the roles may be which he assigns to them. The institution itself may become his castle or his tent on the field of battle. In other words, the auxiliary world technique consists of transforming the whole institution and every person in it into one great psychodramatic stage with auxiliary egos on it. This, of course, takes organization and requires great sympathy and understanding on the part of every member of the staff, including service help and maintenance staff. Once this transformation is achieved, however, the institution as a whole functions towards the patient just as the psychodramatic stage would. His stage is now the whole institution, and the treatment—the channeling, the guidance, and all the rest— proceeds just as it would if he were in the therapeutic theatre.

Here are presented three typical stages in the treatment of psychotic patients with a highly developed paranoid trend. Since, by the very structure of the psychodrama, the treatment is interlocked with continuous clinical exploration of the patients, we are able to give an idea of how the psychotic processes can be interpreted by psychodramatic and sociometric means simultaneously with a description of the treatment.

A boy of fourteen years of age was transferred to us for treatment with the diagnosis of schizophrenia. His dominant delusion was that he was changing into a girl, physically and mentally. A sociometric test revealed that at school he was an isolate, unchosen by the other boys, while he chose older men outside the school—his father, an uncle, et cetera. On the psychodramatic stage he preferred to act in roles of a warlike character or in those which expressed aggressive masculinity, like army officers and shrewd petty criminals. He rejected his mother, and women and girls in general. His partners in the situations were males. When an auxiliary ego in a female role was forced upon him on the stage, he did not like to come near her or touch her. Although his spontaneity in mature roles and complex situations was surprisingly great and expansive, when it came to roles and experiences on his own age level, his spontaneity was weak and immature—more like that of a boy far younger than he. At the beginning of his treatment he often refused to act in situations and roles on his own age level.

Sociometric studies indicate that, in groups of children between the ages of eight and twelve, a homosexual cleavage develops as a normal trend. Since it is the first time that boys join other boys and become male partners on the same age level in a common group action in roles of an aggressive character (as uncovered by psychodramatic tests), the tele sensitivity may tend to extremes and leave the boys open to pathological developments. From the point of view of the group process, this homosexual group cleavage seems of great significance for the development of psychotic processes. The treatment of this boy was successfully carried out by means of the psychodramatic techniques discussed above (especially the projection technique and the mirror technique). We succeeded in channeling the crucial roles in which he had been operating off and on for some years in fantasy, or in reality but hidden from everyone. In the first phase of the treatment these roles were transformed from vague experiences into actualizations in the psychodramatic stage. In the second phase, after these roles had become actualized by means of this objectification, they became open to correction, amplification, and guidance.

A second and later stage in the development of a psychotic process (which might very well, in time, have been that of the boy described above, had he not been treated while he was young) was illustrated by a patient 35 years of age. The case history suggested a similar situation during adolescence to that of the boy we have described above—a sociometric isolate when he was between the ages of eight and fourteen, attracted to roles which expressed a great male superiority, rejecting boys of his own age, admiring older men, and indifferent to the other sex. When he came to us, as was disclosed by various psychodramatic methods, he lived in a world of male roles, a world from which female roles were totally erased. This masculine world was organized along hierarchic lines—males expressing the greatest aggression and inspiring the greatest fear came first; males without weapons and power of any sort came last and were to be despised. The patient shifted from role to role, as required by his homicidal appetite and his craving to inspire fear; he assumed such roles as a member of a royal family, the commander of an air squadron, and a two-gunned cowboy of the wild West. He surrounded himself with the insignia of power—toy guns, toy airplanes, and pen knives which were never put to any real use. Symbolic short cuts to real power satisfied him completely. His family was entirely erased from his existence.

The technique applied in this case was largely the auxiliary world technique. When he was transferred to us with the diagnosis of dementia praecox, paranoid phase, his fantasies showed themselves to be rudimentary in many respects. In the first phase of the treatment, therefore, we allowed him not only to talk about his cowboy experiences, but to act and dress like a cowboy in his daily life in and around the institution. We allowed him not only to talk about revolvers and guns, but actually to go out and buy toy guns. And so, at least in the short cuts which seemed to satisfy him as abbreviations of reality, he was permitted to dress, talk, and act like an adventurer, a hunter, a two-gun man, a spy. He chose, as auxiliary egos, women and children, preferably, and others in weak roles, such as servants. He was also gentle to animals. The auxiliary egos who collaborated with him in appropriate counterroles were, for us, therapeutic agents, and, for him, real people who gave credence to his tales of his "experiences" and aided him in actualizing some of his infantile schemes. The auxiliary egos also acted as translators and interpreters of his ideas and schemes into our language and intentions and, in the same way, of our therapeutic plans and schemes into situations and scenes which fitted his roles and delusions.

In the second phase of the treatment, full advantage was taken by us of the established channels of relationships in his delusions. Our auxiliary egos, having been projected into his world and accepted within the realm of psychodrama by the patient, could now function in an attempt at returning him to more normal situations and roles. The goal of an approach like this was to bring his imaginary world, by means of the psychodramatic principle, into an equilibrium with the official reality so that he might be able to live in the open community without harm to anyone and without any frustration of his own aspirations.

The third stage in the development of a psychosis (and this also could be either of the two foregoing cases at a later date, provided that they had been left untreated) was shown by the case of a woman of 60. She had superimposed on her previous relationships (her social and her cultural atoms) a new system of relationships. This system was already highly organized when she was transferred to us with the diagnosis of paranoia. There was hardly anything rudimentary about her scheme. She based her scheme on her ability to "catch people thinking," and, finally, to hear voices. Her system was so efficiently organized that she could recall thoughts of other people "with the greatest accuracy." After she had lived with us for a short time she was able to hear the thoughts of the staff and the other patients. Whereas the patient described above, in the second stage of the psychotic development, showed uncertainty and doubt as well as fears and worries, this patient had reached a state of conviction of safety which penetrated all her relationships.

Her system was one of persecution. A ring of crooks, led by a black man, had threatened to rob her and attack her physically. She loved to come to the theatre and exhibit her ability to uncover the ring of people who were persecuting her and, finally, to disclose all the injustices which people in the institution attempted against her (which she had discovered by "catching them thinking.") Her case history indicated a sociometric isolate. Although she had been an attractive girl, she had persistently rejected the advances of men and had remained unmarried. As her treatment on the stage progressed, she gradually withdrew her delusions of persecution from the ring of gangsters in the district where she had made her home and focused her delusional field on the institution. We were therefore much better able to help her to objectify and treat her delusions than if they had been focused at a distance . . . .

CHAPTER 9

Psychodramatic Treatment of Marriage Problems

1940

> *Editor's note: Moreno wrote frequently about working with couples. This article explores in some detail the psychodramatic approach to a matrimonial triangle.*

Psychodrama projects actual processes, situations, roles, and conflicts into an experimental milieu, the therapeutic theatre—a milieu which can be as broad as the wings of imagination can make it, yet inclusive of every particle of our real worlds. Applied to the marriage problem, it opens up new vistas for research and treatment. A relationship which is initiated with affection and dignity breaks up all too often with an amount of distaste and disillusionment so disproportionate to the original intentions that a more carefully considered approach . . . seems necessary. If love must begin and marriage be entered upon, why should the relationship not begin in accord with all the maxims of genuine spontaneity from both sides, and if they must end, why should they not end in a manner which is as dignified as it is humane?

From *Psychodrama*, Vol. 1 (1946), 328-347. Another version appears in *Sociometry* 3 (1940).

The psychodrama offers such a method: those involved come together in a setting, apart from life, to find a better understanding of their interindividual conflicts and tensions . . . .

The theatre is an objective setting in which the subject can act out his problems or difficulties relatively free of the anxieties and pressures of the outside world. In order to accomplish this, the total situation of the subject in the outside world has to be duplicated, on a spontaneous level, in the experimental setting of the theatre and—even more than this—the hidden roles and invisible interhuman relationships he may have experienced have to find a visible expression. This means that certain functions—a stage, lights, a recording system, auxiliary egos, and a director—have to be introduced.

When a couple with marital difficulties comes for consultation and treatment, the procedure begins with independent interviews with each partner.

The purpose of the first interview is to get to the point rapidly and to find the clue to the crucial problem. From this clue, the first psychodramatic situation with which to begin the process of treatment can be constructed. No elaborate case record is started. The partners, instead of boldly setting forth the immediate difficulty, may drift into descriptions of situations which are remote in the past. At times the motive for a first situation may come from just such a side issue. It is extremely pertinent that the clues be volunteered and suggested by the subjects themselves. Since it is a reliable psychodramatic experience that, once the subjects are working on the therapeutic stage, they are carried by the momentum of psychodramatic dynamics from the surface to the deeper level of their relationship, a first situation can be built around any motive which comes spontaneously into the mind of a subject during the interview.

It is often the case that each partner puts forth a different set of complaints, each, as well, having formulated remedies for them. On other occasions, perhaps only one partner, the wife, for instance, is anxious for advice or treatment, while the other party, the husband, may be indifferent to professional intrusion or treatment. Other factors, such as economic problems, may enter into the marital situation, but most important are any other persons who are actually an integral part of the friction itself, such as another woman or man, a mother-in-law, a grown-up son, or children by a previous marriage. Such factors may force upon the psychodramatic consultant a shift in his strategic procedure. Before a first situation is set, he may need more preparatory material, or interviews with a third, fourth, or fifth participant in the conflict. Therefore, after the first interviews with the immediate partners, many preparatory steps may be needed before an adequate start on the stage is possible. When couples tend to use dilatory tactics in the interviews, it is often advisable to put them directly upon the stage. They are told to act as if they were at home, with the one difference that they may act and think out loud more freely. This device can usually be relied upon to produce a clue and set the procedure in motion.

It often happens that only one partner is interviewed, the other being either indifferent or ignorant that advice is being sought. In this event the procedure is to begin with this one person and gradually to break in the other person or persons involved. As a rule, before the first situation is acted out, it is possible to form a rough picture of the social atom of each of the persons involved; the details can be filled in gradually as the treatment proceeds. Similarly, a rough picture of the cultural roles of the participants may be obtained. These may be useful when the spontaneity of the subjects begins to diminish, and situations must be constructed for them.

By far the most conspicuous marriage conflict brought to the attention of the psychodramatic consultant is the triangle, or better, the psychological triangle of husband, wife, and a third party, man or woman. This situation is so delicate and can bring so much misery and bitterness that the slightest tactlessness in the course of action or during the analysis of the action may produce a deadlock. The director must take great care to make no suggestion as to what course of action might be preferable. The therapeutic theatre is not a court, the auxiliary egos who may be present are not jury, and the director is not a judge. Moreover, the therapeutic theatre is not a hospital where the subjects come to show their wounds and have them healed by skilled professionals. The initiative, the spontaneity, the decision must all arise within the subjects themselves. Indeed, they are stirred to a greater initiative and spontaneity than they can have experienced day by day in a drab home life. To the director, one solution appears to be just as desirable as another, provided only that it brings the maximum degree of equilibrium to the participants. In one case this may mean a reintegration of the husband-wife relation, and in another, a break-up of the relationship, a divorce catharsis.

There is one misunderstanding which must be carefully avoided. Psychodrama is not an "acting" cure, as an alternative to a "talking" cure. The idea is not that the subjects act out with one another everything on their minds— off guard, in a limitless exhibitionism—as if this sort of activity, in itself, could produce results. Indeed, it is here that the experience of the director in the art of the psychodrama will count most. Just as a surgeon who knows the physical state of his patient will limit an operation to the extent which the patient's condition can withstand, the psychodramatic director may leave many territories of his subjects' personalities unexpressed and unexplored if their energies are not, at the time, equal to the strain.

A PSYCHOLOGICAL TRIANGLE IN MARRIAGE

The First Session. The number of persons permitted in the theatre is limited to the auxiliary egos chosen by the subjects and such others as the director may deem necessary. The following case is a typical illustration. One particular couple, Mr. and Mrs. T, could not offer any satisfactory clue during the interviews. They were told to go upon the stage and to make their present situation in the therapeutic theatre the motive around which to build the action. Perhaps either Mr. or Mrs. T may have been the driving force in the coming to the theatre for treatment, or they may have disagreed about it for some reason. Whatever the case, they were to pick up the thread of thought and continue talking it over, just as if they were in their own home, but with one difference: they were to feel free to act more spontaneous, breaking some of the conventional regard for one another's feelings which they might have at home.

After a few seconds of hestitancy, they settled down to a quarrel about the expense of the treatment. Mrs. T argued that any expense would be worthwhile if it helped to make their marriage happy again. Here Mr. T burst out and told her for the first time that he had reached the end of his tether, anyway, because he was in love with another woman. A secret which had been carefully hidden was suddenly out. The psychodramatic stage had worked as a means for defining their situation precisely. It was, of course, a shock to the young woman. She cried: "Who is she?" The situation was interrupted and an auxiliary ego was picked to personify the other woman, whom we shall call Miss S. Mrs. T returned to the audience. Mr. T explained that he had a dinner appointment with Miss S for the next evening. It was this dinner situation which was the first to be projected on the therapeutic stage. Auxiliary ego B acted as a substitute for Miss S.

In the scene, as Mr. T projected it on the stage, he told Miss S (auxiliary B) that he had started a treatment in which the participants in a marriage conflict were made to act out the difficulties they have with one another. He went on the say that, when he was acting with Mrs. T yesterday, his feeling for her, Miss S, had come out. While acting, he had begun to realize that he was suffering from an immaturity, carrying two other people as well as himself into greater and greater difficulties, and that he must come to a decision, one way or another. Right there on the stage he had made the decision that what he truly wanted was a divorce from his wife, and marriage with her, Miss S. Auxiliary B acted in accordance with her instructions and the scene ended with the strengthening of the bond between Miss S and T.

The Second Session. Mr. T had met miss Miss S for dinner the day before, and when he and Mrs. T came to the therapeutic theatre for their next treatment, he was told to project the meeting on the stage as it actually took place. Auxiliary B again substituted for Miss S, and Mrs. T remained in the audience. The actual meeting had brought some surprises to T. Miss S had come to her own decision; returning to T a keepsake he had given her as a symbol that all was over between them. Mr. T seemed much less sure of himself than he had been in the problematic scene projected during the previous session. When Miss S told him that she did not want to rob another woman of her man, her feeling of guilt found an echo in him.

Mrs. T, who had not heard anything of what had taken place at their meeting, was pleasantly surprised and was glad to hear that T was to return to her. After the scene, Mr. T complemented auxiliary B for having portrayed Miss S's reaction so well. When he saw his wife elated he remarked that, although he might not marry Miss S, he nevertheless was going to separate from his wife. He said that he realized the cruelty of this course, in view of the sacrifices made by his wife during many years of marriage; he had kept silent about his attachment for Miss S because he feared his wife would break down if faced with the situation. But the psychodramatic treatment had brought the underlying feeling-relations to the surface.

The Third Session. Miss S was present for this session and Mrs. T stayed away. Mr. T and Miss S enacted a series of scenes beginning with their first meeting and showing, step by step, how their relationship had developed. Miss S had come unwillingly to the therapeutic theatre; she was determined to sacrifice her love for T and to retire from "the whole mess" with a heroic gesture, but these scenes brought a total change. The reminiscences, the dreams, and the plans which emerged in the course of the action brought their relationship on the stage to such a climax that their desire and decision to continue and get married was spontaneous and irrevocable. Two roles in which T showed a deep community of feeling with Miss S were those of the poet and the adventurer (in which he and he wife had no contact), but the crux of the matter was that Mr. T wanted to have a child (a boy) with Miss S. In the analysis which followed the scenes, Mr. T asserted that he now realized why he had persistently avoided having a child with his wife, although they were compatible as lovers and his wife was a fine homemaker. Miss S was the first woman with whom he had been able to visualize himself in a father-mother relationship.*

Later Sessions. These were devoted to bringing the relationship between Mr. and Mrs. T to an optimum equilibrium, in view of the probable outcome of the conflict. Mrs. T tried every approach which might bring T to consider a continuance of their marriage, scenes reproducing their early courtship, the suffering she had gone through in order to advance his career, their early childhood and their old age. It was to no avail. However, for her it had a cathartic value. It strengthened her ego and prepared her for a life along new lines. She lost her vindictiveness towards Miss S. T's gentleness and understanding increased, but his desire for a union with Miss S was not altered. A full catharsis for a separation and a divorce was attained.

---

*The adventurer role might be thought of as the antithesis of the parent role, yet both are frustrated in actuality and are simultaneously experienced as unfulfilled. (Ed.).

The entire material of this case cannot be presented here, as it would cover several hundred pages. Besides Mr. and Mrs. T and Miss S, two women and three men appeared on the stage as auxiliary egos. The treatment covered a period of three months. A total of 60 situations were acted out in which more than 100 roles were assumed.

INTERPRETATION

In the case of Mr. T, an unfulfilled role (the poet) became linked to the related role (adventurer). They later merged and aroused a deeper unfulfilled role (father). The chain of poet-adventurer-father roles awakened by Miss S in turn reawakened towards her his mate-lover role. The more inclusive the warming up process of a role is—the broader the territory of a specific personality it embraces—the more satisfying the role becomes and the more inspiring it is for the development of initiative and spontaneity in the subject's total life setting. It is this important interindividual mechanism which operated in the case of Mr. and Mrs. T and Miss S. As long as the poet and the adventurer roles alone were interacting with the complementary roles in Miss S, the situation was bearable. As soon as they combined with the father-baby-mother and lover roles, even the roles of lover and homemaker, which until then had been well-adjusted between Mr. and Mrs. T, began to break. Now these latter roles seemed flat and monotonous compared with the roles in his new experience. The narrower field, represented by the same roles up to the time of his meeting with Miss S, was now replaced by a wider field in which a complex of roles was operating.

In the course of the triangle study it was observed that a role required by one person may be absent in his or her partner in a close relationship and that the absence of a role can have serious consequences for a relationship . . . .

Let us take the mother roles of the two women in the above triangle—roles which played a very significant part in this conflict. In the case of Miss S, the mother role was highly developed (on the fantasy level) and, what was most important, closely linked with her roles of poetess and adventurer. The combination of all three roles made her an almost perfect complement for T with his unfulfilled roles. In Mrs. T, the mother role was developed only to a rudimentary degree (on the fantasy level). This coincides with experience in many other cases. The mother role is necessary if an actual physiological situation demands it—pregnancy, for instance. A total absence of this role (zero tele) during the period of gestation and after the child is born must be evaluated as being just as pathological as an overdevelopment of this role would be. To take another example, a married man who has not developed the husband role at all—or in whom it is lacking towards the woman he has married—is equally in a pathological situation. Many marital situations and conflicts have been treated by the psychodramatic method. In the majority of cases, an adjustment between husband and wife was reached. The duration of the treatment varies. In mild conflicts, a catharsis is obtained after a few sessions. In complicated cases in which one or the other partner suffers from a deep mental disturbance, more time may be necessary than in the case of Mr. and Mrs. T and Miss S.

THE AUXILIARY EGO TECHNIQUE IN MARRIAGE PROBLEMS

When a husband, for instance, comes alone for treatment, the absent wife has to be substituted for by an auxiliary ego. The husband is required to coach this auxiliary ego in the role of the wife. This phase in itself is a significant part of the procedure. In the course of a few minutes the subject must warm up to the auxiliary, show her how his wife acts and what sort of things she says. All this, of course, serves to inform the director how the subject feels about his wife and indicates which of her characteristics have most impressed themselves upon his mind. He is told that it is not an accurate portrayal which he should expect from the auxiliary ego, but a basis sufficiently suggestive to get him started. Often it is good strategy to let him work out his complaints and conflicts with an auxiliary "wife" and then have an alternate session in which the wife, in turn, works out her problems with an auxiliary "husband," before they begin to work face to face. The better trained an auxiliary ego is in the roles required and the more he or she meets the spontaneous affinities of the subject, the greater will be the success in getting the subject started.

The training of an auxiliary ego, especially in marriage problems, is of great importance. In the first place, the auxiliary ego must learn to detach himself entirely from anything in his own private life which might bias him toward one or the other of the marriage partners. Elaborate spontaneity training may be necessary before his own private conflicts cease to affect his function as an auxiliary in marriage problems. In some cases, only certain roles and situations may be permitted him. The auxiliary ego does not know the persons he is to represent. He is dependent upon the subject to direct his characterization of them. Even in symbolic roles (Satan, God, a judge, et cetera) he should act only as suggested by the subject, and interject his own personality as little as possible. Later in the course of the treatment the actual persons (the wife, or the other man or woman) may themselves act in the role in which the auxiliary has substituted. The resulting contrast, the amount of deviation, is an interesting phenomenon. The auxiliary ego may be seen to have simplified the wife too much; the husband may have had too easy a time getting along with her. In the course of the treatment, near-life

A

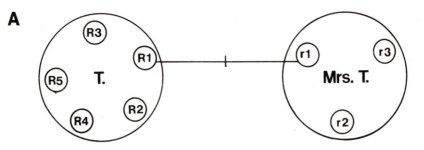

B

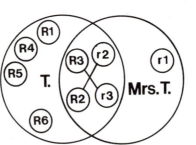

C

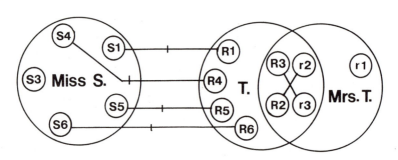

Figure 9-1 Development of the cultural atom, interrelation of roles in marriage.
A: Pre-marital state. R1, role of lover; R2, role of supporter; R3, role of husband; R4, role of poet; R5, role of adventurer; r1, role of lover; r2, role of homemaker; r3, role of wife. It is in the roles of lover that T and Mrs. T are attracted to one another. The other roles do not enter the relationship at this stage.
B: Marital state, initial phase. R6, role of father. The roles of husband and supporter in T are finding fulfillment in Mrs. T's roles of wife and homemaker. The roles of poet and adventurer are unfulfilled, and a new unfulfilled role has appeared, father. Both lover roles are in the background.
C: Marital state, later phase. A third person has entered the situation, Miss S. S1, role of lover; S2, role of wife; S3, role of poetess; S4, role of adventurer; S5, role of mother.

stimuli may be obtained if the subject coaches the auxiliary to interpolate into her presentation as many characteristics of the real wife as possible.

At times the husband may be hard to please: none of the auxiliary egos available is able to meet his demands, or all of them fall short of his image of the person for whom they are to substitute. The subject may criticize an auxiliary sharply and even insult her if he believes that she purposely tries to distort the character of the absentee. In such cases, the subject is asked to act as his own auxiliary ego. He can show how his wife acts and talks and, if necessary, pick one of the auxiliaries to substitute for him, the subject. For instance, the subject may play his own father-in-law in a quarrel scene, while an auxiliary substitutes for the subject. Technically, he is both absent and present at the same time. The use of the subject as his own auxiliary ego is a very useful technique for obtaining from him the impression which the different members of his social atom have made upon his mind.

It is obvious that the auxiliary ego can become a tool for testing psychodramatic behavior. From a therapeutic standpoint, he is a target for the subjects, and sometimes a guide. Since he is a permanent fixture, he becomes, from a research point of view, a reliable frame of reference. His personality equation, his range of roles, and his personal difficulties are known to the director; they have been carefully studied and are checked from time to time. Thus a basis for comparison—a frame of reference—has been established against which the subjects, as they come and go with their reverberations, inconsistencies, and extremes, can be measured. The methodological value of the auxiliary ego technique may be more fully appreciated when compared with the participant observer technique of studying the behavior of persons. A participant observer watches people, asks questions about them, and spies into their intimate lives, but he cannot reach beyond a certain point. In the auxiliary ego technique, however, the aspects of participant observer are only supplementary to its crucial functions and have their place when the auxiliary egos are seated in the audience, watching the process as they take place on the stage, or mingling with the subjects between sessions . . . .

THE CATHARSIS OF THE AUXILIARY EGO

The auxiliary ego who took the part of Miss S, the other woman in our typical illustration, behaved in a peculiar manner on the stage. At times she acted in a way which was in utter contrast with the instructions the subject had given her. She was apparently not aware of it. In the scene at the dinner table, when Mr. T told her how happy he had been the day when she told him that she loved him, she replied violently: "I never did and I never will!" Mr. T retorted: "But you did!" And then, in an aside to the auxiliary, he said

"What is the matter?" The auxiliary regained her poise and continued according to her instructions. When the situation ended, she burst out crying and continued to cry after she was back in her seat. After the session, she was called upon the stage and the director inquired what had happened to her. She said that she thought she had acted as required, but when harder pressed, admitted that she was at that time going through a similar experience; there was a man whom she loved and there was also a woman who was pulling him away from her. When the subject expected her to act the same way in the scene on the stage, she fell out of her role for a moment.

This process can be called the psychodramatic effect. It affects subjects and egos. This sort of experience was made the basis for treating the auxiliary as if she were a subject. Her own marital conflict was treated separately, from phase to phase, with the aid of two other auxiliary egos on the staff. Her experience on the stage is called the psychodramatic catharsis of an auxiliary ego. It has also happened that an auxiliary ego assisting in the treatment of another auxiliary betrayed personality difficulties of his own. Afterwards he, in turn, had to be given treatment.

A better way of treating an auxiliary ego takes place in the course of the psychodrama itself. When the auxiliary ego shows any odd conduct, the inquiry about it is made in front of the subject—in fact, in front of the whole group. The auxiliary may explain: "Yes, I am in a triangle situation myself." She may sketch her situation briefly, and then go on working with the subject, but keeping control of her actions and speech. In the course of working with a subject, a double analysis is always made, one of the subject and another of the auxiliary. The analysis of the auxiliary is made with special attention to the extent to which her actions toward the subject may have reflected her private problem. Compared to the other kind of procedure, this has many assets, and is therefore preferable to it. The subject is present when the auxiliary is caught in a trap, and as the problem is revealed and eventually enacted, the subject can get some sort of a picture of how he himself looks from a distance. He now gets the catharsis of a spectator as well as that of an actor. In addition, he may be asked to act as auxiliary ego to the auxiliary who has a problem. This creates what may seem to be a paradoxical situation—the psychiatrist becoming a patient and the patient a psychiatrist—but the subject has the advantage of having an opportunity to help, with his experience, someone who has just tried to help him. It is now he who is instructed how to portray the role of a certain man—perhaps a husband who is betraying his wife (the auxiliary ego). The subject is still a spectator, but one who is in action. He may thus experience a double catharsis—as a subject who has come for treatment, and as an auxiliary ego who is employed to aid another person.

Another asset of this procedure is that all other auxiliary egos who are present—and perhaps other subjects as well—undergo a process of experience which is important training for them. They are always midway between the spectator and the actor, and midway between being influenced as private persons and being stimulated as professional people.

As a net result, just as the psychodramatic subjects emerge from the treatment as people able to perform more adequately in the situations treated, so do the auxiliary egos grow wiser and more versatile in their own spheres of living.

The Problem of Guidance

The initiative and spontaneity of the director and the auxiliary egos during the action on the stage is one of the dominant features of the treatment. Many times a couple has to be prepared because they are not ready for the procedure. The preparation may take many forms. It may happen that the subjects are suffering from an interpersonal conflict which they have not been able to handle and which is in definite need of treatment. Perhaps they have been unaware that this sort of treatment is possible, or one of the partners was not willing to undergo treatment. Or their particular type of conflict may need some general preparation, such as a description of what the treatment is, what effect the treatment has had in other cases, and what effect or solution of their problem they can expect from the treatment. In one case it may be a relative of a friend who takes the first step in bringing them to the therapeutic theatre. This person functions, so to speak, as an auxiliary ego from their own milieu. In another case, it may be their lawyer who gives instructions in how to approach them.

Another technique of guidance becomes necessary in the phase preliminary to action on the stage. The two partners are on the stage, for instance, but refuse to enact any of the crucial situations which they have disclosed during the interviews. The director tries to get them started by shifting their attention rapidly from one plot to another. This may put their minds at comparative ease and make them willing to work. If this brings no result, he will suggest that they can pick any subject at random, or anything which they would like to tell one another at the moment. If this also is without effect, the director may suggest that they project upon the stage any of the more pleasant situations in which they may have found themselves in the past (when they were first in love), or any situation which would express how they would have wished their marriage to develop (perhaps having a baby or a large family), or a situation in the future which would express any change they might like to have in their life situation. If these do not bring any results, there still remains the choice of symbolic situations and symbolic roles for which they may have an affinity or which might be constructed for them. If all this does not have the effect of an actual start, the director does not plead or insist too strongly, but sends the subjects back to their seats. They are then allowed to participate in another session when other subjects are being treated for problems similar to theirs. To all appearances they are mere spectators. It may happen in the course of the treatment of another couple on the stage that one of them is asked to help out as an auxiliary ego. This technique of making an auxiliary ego out of a subject, for therapeutic reasons, may be used for a considerable time, both subjects being treated for their own problems in an indirect manner. It often happens, after the treatment is half-completed in this manner, that they spontaneously volunteer to act, not realizing that what they are doing is what the director wanted all the time.

Guidance can also be achieved when the auxiliary ego is being coached for a role. Here the auxiliary is the agent. In the illustration above, for instance, Mr. T had to explain to the auxiliary ego who was to portray Miss S how she acted when he met her for the first time. However, he appeared unusually inarticulate and hesitant in giving adequate information. The auxiliary then showed great enterprise and skill in gradually drawing him out. She discussed poetry with him and in other ways gave him the confidence to start a scene which he had been trying to evade for some time. This sort of guidance also strengthened his relationship to this particular auxiliary; he learned that he could rely upon her support (as an extension of his ego). Another form of guidance is illustrated by the following incident: Mr. T projected a dream upon the stage in which he and his wife were at the funeral of his mother-in-law. However, this fact seemed to be almost all he could remember of the dream. While he was endeavoring to enact the dream and while he and the auxiliary were walking side by side at the funeral procession, he suddenly stopped and said: "From the way the auxiliary walked, and looked at me, I now recall that when I reached the grave, it was my wife who was dead." The auxiliary showed such intensity of grief in her glance and carriage that it had warmed him up to the state of experience needed for recollection. At times the work on the stage may seem beyond the control of the partners. Then the director can send in another auxiliary to stimulate action. Or the work may lag or be barren of significant action. Then he stops the action and suggests a new start. At other times, the subject may persistently choose to exhibit the same situation. If repeated too often, this can have an adverse effect and the director may have to limit the territory of the treatment. He may prefer to leave certain aspects of the conflict unexplored and untreated, leaving their solution to the spontaneity of the subjects themselves. However, the correct use of such discretion is the most difficult task in guidance.

A FRAME OF REFERENCE FOR THE MEASUREMENT OF ROLES

The psychodrama presents a new method for studying roles. It provides an experimental milieu, free of boundaries of any particular community or culture. Here there is no need for an ultimate definition of roles (legal, social, and economic information is merely supplementary). They are studied *in statu nascendi*—they are not given, they emerge in the flesh, they are created before our very eyes. The poet is not hidden behind the work; indeed, he is assisting us through the processes of conception, from phase to phase, through all the processes of enactment. This not only opens the way for studying roles in vivo from the moment of their birth but also provides the possibility for a scientific form of reference and of measurable evidence. The roles do not need to be defined—they define themselves as they emerge from the *status nascendi* to full mature shape. Some roles are postulated by a legal situation (the lawyer, the criminal), some are postulated by a technological situation (such as a radio announcer), or some are postulated by a physiological situation (the eater), but it is only during psychodramatic work that we can study how they take form spontaneously.

We have shown above how the auxiliary ego is used for therapeutic ends. In our therapeutic theatre, we have a number of persons, men and women, who are trained to act in any role needed by a subject portraying a life situation. In the absence of a wife or a sweetheart, one of the female auxiliary egos can step in and portray her, after due coaching by the subject. From the point of view of treatment, this opens up three possibilities: on the one hand, to make the situation as concrete as possible for the husband—the subject; on the other hand, to guide him deftly though moments of indecision; and third, to determine the deficiencies in the personality of the auxiliary ego herself.

After studying auxiliary egos in hundreds of roles, it became possible to classify their ranges of roles and their patterns of presenting them. For instance, a certain auxiliary ego was extremely effective in two or three kinds of husband roles, but in one particular variety another member of the staff had to be used. After a period of years, it was learned to classify each auxiliary ego, not only in reference to the range of his roles, but also in reference to his psychodramatic behavior in them.

A test of auxiliary egos was constructed in order to establish a frame of reference for all the roles which might be portrayed by subjects on the therapeutic stage. Among many others, the following situation was evolved for testing of people for roles in marriage: "Show how you would act if your husband (wife) suddenly revealed to you that he (she) was in love with another woman (man) and wanted a divorce." An analysis of each performance was made in order to disclose which lines of conduct were followed by a majority of those tested, and the amount of deviations one from the other. The most important points of deviation were (a) the duration of the spontaneous state; and (b) the intensity of the spontaneous state, calculated from the dynamic interrelation between the acts and pauses. A larger number of words, phrases, gestures, and movements expressed together with short or few pauses observed per time-unit indicated a high degree of spontaneity of the subject. A group of observers sat in the audience during the tests. After the role of the husband (wife) in the above specific situation had been portrayed by several auxiliary egos, the performances were roughly classified in several categories: A, B, C, D, et cetera. Each of the observers was then asked to place himself into a category of performance. Thus a preliminary norm, indicating how most people would behave in that specific situation, was obtained. In this manner a frame of reference could be established for this and for other roles. Every subject who comes for treatment and acts in all the roles pertaining to him and his situation can be measured against the established norms which have been worked out with our auxiliary egos. The spontaneous deviations from the norm of a role which are shown by a subject can now be determined and measured in reference to the general direction of the role: the course of action, the duration of the spontaneous state, the amount of movement on the stage, the range of vocabulary and phraseology, and the character of voice and gestures used. In the course of experimentation of this kind, the preliminary frame of reference itself is continuously tested and retested in order to further refine and improve it. A project like this will produce a more precise answer to such questions as "How can a role be measured?" "Into what categories does a certain subject fall as a husband or a father?" "What kind of a wife or mother is a subject's best possible complement in life or on the therapeutic stage?" "How can we predict success or failure in marriage?"

STEPS IN THE DEVELOPMENT OF A TYPICAL MARRIAGE RELATIONSHIP

The following construction of a typical development of a marriage relationship can be made from psychodramatic case studies of marital conflicts.

Two persons, before they enter into marriage, have separate social atoms. These social atoms are either independent of one another or, at most, partially overlapping. A smaller or greater part of each social atom remains unknown to the other partner—i.e., some of the emotional acquaintances of the woman remain unknown to the man, and some of his, in turn, remain unknown to her.

A shift in behavior and in the organization of their social atoms takes place when the two partners pass from the premarital state into that of marriage.

They now act towards one another in roles which have not been fulfilled prior to this time—the roles of husband and wife, and of supporter and homemaker. They form a group of two persons, but the number of roles in which they interact is more than two. The change in behavior of the two partners towards one another can be ascribed to their new roles and to the relationship between these roles. The realization of a marriage situation not only precipitates new roles for the marriage partners but either enfeebles or intensifies roles already established between them—for instance, the role of the lover. The marriage situation and its consequent roles either bring forth new satisfactions for new frictions. Therefore, some of the imbalances which existed in the premarital state disappear and new imbalances emerge.

Every individual, just as he is the focus of numerous attractions and repulsions, appears, also, as the focus of numerous roles which are related to the roles of other individuals. Every individual, just as he has at all times a set of friends and a set of enemies, also has a range of roles and faces a range of counterroles. They are in various stages of development. The tangible aspects of what is known as "ego" are the roles in which he operates. The pattern of role relations around an individual as their focus is called his cultural atom . . . . Obviously, the term is selected as a correspondent to the term "social atom." The use here of the word "atom" can be justified if we consider a cultural atom as the smallest functional unit within a cultural pattern. The adjective "cultural" can be justified when we consider roles and relationships between roles as the most significant developments within any specific culture (regardless of what definition is given to culture by any school of thought). Just as sociometric procedures are the chief means of studying cultural atoms.

After marriage, two persons learn to know each other in many more roles than before marriage, and, in some of the premarital roles, they learn to know one another more intensively . . . . It is a peculiarity of the marriage situation that the participants are often inclined to think that they can fulfill *all* the substantial roles themselves. The degree to which all the roles of an individual may be satisfied by the marriage partner cannot be foreseen by the marriage partners themselves before marriage—unless they go through psychodramatic training, which appears to be the only way in which they may learn to anticipate or predict the stages in their marriage development.

Under ordinary circumstances, however, in order to live up to the official standard of marriage and the standard of fair play as well, they may actually resign from living in certain roles which they have been able to realize in the past, or they may even forbid themselves the development of new roles, fearing that the partner may not be able to accept or satisfy them. This often produces a typical conflict in the role structures of two marriage partners. As in the case of Mr. and Mrs. T, they are able to make a livable adjustment in two roles. The woman partner has a range which is limited to two roles, and she is perfectly satisfied and adjusted to the man. He, however, has several roles in which she is either a poor partner or no partner at all (see Figure 9-1B). In the course of time, as we saw, this produces a rift in their relationship. The unfulfilled roles in his cultural atom have been an open target for any other woman who is better able to satisfy them than the wife. Mr. T kept these roles hidden from his wife, or he never stressed them when he was with her. The conflict between them went on for years without producing anything but inarticulate irritation. Many married people lose their partners long before any open breach is manifest, just as in the case of Mr. and Mrs. T. The loss, in this case, was partial in one specific role (the father-baby-mother role) in which the marriage was not successful. This partial loss can remain, at times, without further consequences in the marriage situation if the roles which brought the partners into marriage are well-adjusted. However, this partial loss often becomes the entering wedge which may develop into a complete separation and divorce.

The change from what is purely the marriage situation (where there are not children) to the family situation brings about new shifts in the behavior of the two partners. The original group of two is augmented to, for instance, a group of five. While the partners can continue in their roles of husband and wife, on a strictly private level, they must also operate in new roles—those of father and mother. The incoming members of the family assume their roles of sons and daughters. Husband and wife have to act towards the children as father and mother. Moreover, when in the presence of the children, they have to interact in the latter roles. The roles of husband and wife are more and more restricted to situations which permit them the privacy of former times. The new distribution of roles covers up the fact that the family consists of two groups; the original group of two (husband and wife and their range of specific roles) on the one hand, and the group of five (husband and wife now in the roles of father and mother, and their children in the roles of sons and daughters) on the other. The duplicity of roles of the father (husband) and the mother (wife) account for the everlasting confusion in the minds of the children who fail to understand the existence of family roles and relationships in which they have no part.

On a different level, conflicts similar to those in the simple marriage situation crop up in the family situation. When a child is young, its limited range of roles can be easily satisfied by the parent in the various roles of nurse, educator, protector, and supporter. But as the child grows older, the range of roles which crave fulfillment expands. In formal situations such as are provided by the church or school, or in informal situations such as neighborhoods present, significant roles attached to individuals outside the family circle are introduced. These developments may bring about friction between the two parents, friction between the parents and the children, or friction between the children themselves. Such problems may not be solved until the children are fully grown, have separated themselves from the parents, and have begun to assume for themselves the roles which are essential to the grown-up world of adults.

CHAPTER 10

The Prediction and Planning of Success in Marriage

1941

> *Editor's note: In the previous chapter Moreno stresses the importance of ending a relationship well. Here he offers a plan, based on psychodramatic spontaneity tests, for couples beginning life together. Such topics suggest the usefulness of psychodrama for transitional periods in human experience.*

One of the greatest of the methodological difficulties which the social sciences have had to face has been the discrepancy between verbalized behavior (as expressed in interviews, free-associations tests, the answers to questionnaires, et cetera) and behavior in life situations (the action patterns of individuals), in which verbalized behavior is but a minor component, and the meaning of the verbal content itself undergoes a profound change due to the influence of the action pattern from which it springs. The more fundamental and central a situation or relationship may be in family and marriage relationships for the individuals concerned, the greater is the social tension if

---

From *Sociometry, Experimental Method & the Science of Society* (1951), 111-114 (under the heading in the original publication is affixed "1941," which indicates the year of the original draft).

such discrepancy arises. In premarital situations, a neglect of this discrepancy must account for grave errors in the analysis of the material, in the prediction of failure or success, and last but not least, in the rational planning of future relationships.

It seems to me that the most important major research in family and marriage problems must focus, in the next few years, upon the devising of theories, procedures, methods and tests which are able to bring this problem nearer to solution. The difficulty confronting the researcher in the field of interpersonal relationships has always been that there seemed to be but two main approaches available: studies based upon verbalized behavior and the observation of people in life situations by such means as participant observer techniques. Both methods have had their merits, but when it comes to actual planning of interpersonal relationships and the prediction of their development, these methods do not appear to be adequate. It is necessary, therefore, to find a middle way between these two extremes which is capable of coming closer to the action pattern of the interpersonal relationships themselves. In the course of dealing with many marriage problems by means of psychodramatic techniques, we have developed, I believe, a method which can diagnose with ease and accuracy the reasons for the failure of many marriage relationships as well as offer a means whereby future maladjustments may perhaps be prevented.

The psychodrama and its ally, sociometry, open up fields of action research which should make a great appeal to the young sociologist because of the almost unlimited possibilities of experiment in new devices which go far beyond the methods and tests worked out to date. Psychodramatic methods permit the researcher to observe interpersonal relationships *in action*. Sources of conflict, past, present, and future, come to light in a milieu where they can be diagnosed and treated, foreseen and dealt with, often with the result that, if and when they occur in a relationship, their importance is minimized, and they are viewed with the "proper" perspective. If conflicts in an interpersonal relationship can be prevented, it would follow that this relationship has a good expectation of success. It is therefore upon the prediction and prevention of interpersonal conflicts that the researcher should concentrate.

Psychodramatic procedure, in this field of research, deals first and foremost with actual life situations. The researcher can focus his attention upon the situation itself as well as the people in it. The psychodrama does not have to rely upon interviews, questionnaires, or reports. The subjects are studied, singly or in pairs, as they actually move and speak and act in a situation. The approach is a three-dimensional one and takes place in the present, not removed in point of time. In this way, the researcher can observe, simultaneously with the subjects, the spontaneous reaction of both partners in a relationship as they come face to face with the actual life situations.

The factor of spontaneity is a very important one. Confronted with a life situation which is often unexpected and provocative, the subject is called upon to react spontaneously. Observation will enable the researcher to arrive at the *spontaneity quotient* of the subjects. One partner, for instance, may be slow in his or her reactions, while the other, quicker one may grow increasingly impatient. A realization that the other's spontaneity quotient is greater or less than his own may help each partner to allow for this in the future, and an unconscious source of irritation may thus be mitigated. Based on the principle that each partner in a relationship is playing a role for the benefit of the other, and that everyone sees himself, at various times and on various occasions, in a variety of these roles, the psychodrama offers them an opportunity to play out these roles together. In the course of psychodramatic investigation of the structure of marriage relationships, we have been able to discern certain typical conflicts which appear in almost every marriage. Different solutions are arrived at by different couples: in fact, one might say that a great part of the success or failure of a marriage depends upon the solution arrived at and the ease and speed with which it is attained. Accordingly, psychodramatic procedure establishes a number of typical situations which are standardized for use in the various relationships which come under observation. These situations, of course, are based upon actual psychodramatic experience with many married couples. Each situation simulates an experience which could occur in almost any marriage relationship; it contains the seeds, at least, of a conflict and invariably leads up to some critical point at which one or both partners will be called upon to respond in some way which will work toward a resolution of the crisis which has materialized.

Thus, not only are the prospective bride and bridegroom warned, so to speak, of some of the difficult moments they will, in all probability, have to go through in the course of their married life, but their solutions for these difficult moments are analyzed with them and their mistakes and inadequacies pointed out. Not only do they see one another in the rosy glow usually prevalent in such premarital states, but they are forced to face some of the more unpleasant realities which are likely to come and of which they are as yet probably ignorant. Each partner is revealed to the other in a variety of roles: as a husband or wife, as a homemaker or provider, as a father or mother of a family which is still far in the future, as an errant husband or wife, the other reacting as jealous, complaisant, or in whatever spontaneous manner the action calls forth, and not solely as lovers anxious to show their best sides to the loved one. In the course of this procedure, hitherto hidden roles will emerge. Many undiscovered facets of both personalities will appear and are made use of in the education of the couple and the enlightenment of the researcher. The two are able, in a remarkably short time, to learn to know one another and to be prepared for similar situations in the course of the projected relationship.

Psychodramatic treatment of marriage problems has emphasized the importance of the part played by hidden roles in the personalities of the two partners. Many cases of failure have been noted in which the cause could be traced to the emergence of the role, say, of adventurer or poet, at a time which may be even years after the wedding. Had the other partner been aware at the outset of the presence of such potential but underdeveloped roles, these roles could have been allowed for, and some counterroles provided. In every case of failure through this kind of cause, it was the lack of the ability to satisfy a role of this sort which lay at the basis of the marriage's failure. The hidden role emerged, found no satisfaction in the marriage partner, and sought gratification elsewhere. How much happier would the outcome have been if the hidden role had been brought to the surface by psychodramatic means, then perhaps allowed to lie dormant until some later date when it could emerge to find satisfaction in the marriage partner rather than in someone else.

To set up the psychodramatic milieu in which an experiment of this sort can be conducted is an easy task. The results are two-fold and simultaneous: unlimited research material on a level of actuality and real life, together with practical preparation of and by prospective married couples for their life together.

CHAPTER 11

The Sociometric Test

1934

> *Editor's note: Moreno's development of the sociometric test was a major contribution towards understanding group dynamics. The dictum of "know thyself" could in fact apply to entire groups, but only by means of a process whereby each member becomes an active "experimenter" and the investigators themselves are carefully investigated.*

An instrument to measure the amount of organization shown by social groups is called the *sociometric test*. The sociometric test requires an individual to choose his associates for any group of which he is or might become a member. He is expected to make his choices without restraint and regardless of whether the individuals chosen are members of the present group or outsiders. The sociometric test is an instrument which examines social structures through the measurement of the attractions and repulsions which take place between the individuals within a group. In the area of interpersonal relations we often use more narrow designations, as "choice" and "rejection." The more comprehensive terms, attraction and repulsion, go beyond the

From *Who Shall Survive?* (1953), 93-110. A version of this article is also to be found in the first edition of *Who Shall Survive?* (1934); as well as *Sociometry, Experimental Method and the Science of Society* (1951), and *Group Psychotherapy, Psychodrama & Sociometry* 26 (1973).

human group and indicate that there are analogous social configurations in nonhuman groups.

To date, this test has been made in respect to home groups, work groups, and school groups. It determined the position of each individual in a group in which he has a function. It revealed that the underlying psychological structure of a group differs widely from its social manifestations; that group structures vary directly in relation to the age level of the members; that different criteria may produce different groupings of the same persons or they may produce the same groupings; that groups of different function, as for instance, home groups and work groups, tend towards diverse structures; that people would group themselves differently if they could; that these spontaneous groups and the function that the individuals act or intend to act within them have a definite bearing upon the conduct of each individual and upon the group as a whole; and that spontaneous groupings and forms of groupings which are superimposed upon the former by some authority provide a potential source of conflict. It was found that chosen relations and actual relations often differ and that the position of an individual cannot be fully realized if not all the individuals and groups to which he is emotionally related are included. It disclosed that the organization of a group cannot be fully studied if all related groups or individuals are not included, that individuals and groups are often to such an extent interlocked that the whole community to which they belong has to become the scope of the sociometric test . . . .

THE SOCIOGRAM

The responses received in the course of sociometric procedure from each individual, however spontaneous and essential they may appear, are materials only and not yet sociometric facts in themselves. We have first to visualize and represent how these responses hang together. A process of charting has been devised by the sociometrist, the sociogram, which is more than merely a method of presentation. It is first of all a method of exploration. It makes possible the exploration of sociometric facts. The proper placement of every individual and of all interrelations of individuals can be shown on a sociogram. It is at present the only available scheme which makes structural analysis of a community possible.

As the pattern of the social universe is not visible to us, it is made visible through charting. Therefore the sociometric chart is the more useful the more accurately and realistically it portrays the relations discovered. As every detail is important, the most accurate presentation is the most appropriate. The problem is not only to present knowledge in the simplest and shortest manner, but to present the relations so that they can be studied. The matrix of a sociogram may consist in its simplest form of choice, rejection, and neutrality structures. It may be further broken up into the emotional and ideological currents crisscrossing these attraction and rejection patterns.

Numerous types of sociograms have been devised. They have in common that they portray the pattern of the social structure as a whole and the position of every individual within it. One type shows the social configurations as they grow in time and as they spread in space. Other types of sociograms present momentary and transitory pictures of a group. As the technique of charting is a method of exploration, the sociograms are so devised that one can pick from the primary map of a community small parts, redraw them, and study them, as it were, under the microscope. Another type of derivative or secondary sociogram results if we pick from the map of a community large structures because of their functional significance, such as psychological networks. The mapping of networks indicates that on the basis of primary sociograms we may devise forms of charting which enable us to explore large geographical areas.

What gives every sociometrically defined group its momentum is the criterion, the common motive which draws individuals together spontaneously, for a certain end. That criterion may be at one time as fundamental as a search for home and shelter, food and sleep, love and companionship, or as casual as a game of cards. The number of criteria on which groupings are continuously forming go into many millions. They give to the overt and tangible human society a deeply unconscious and complicated infra-structure, difficult to uncover because of its remoteness from immediate experience and because there is not strict separation between the infra and the overt structures. One is interwoven with the other. At times genuine interpersonal structures can be perceived on the surface; at other times they require extensive sociomicroscopic study before they can be discovered.

Sociometric work has centered from the beginning upon testing all the basic collectives of which a community consists. Sociometrists have been particularly interested in groups which are built around strong criteria; formal and institutional groups were the first and most rewarding targets— home groups, work groups, school groups, cultural groups. Sociometry started out to enter into every social situation of which a community consists, from the simplest to the most complex, from the most formal to the most informal . . . .

In the course of the construction of sociometric tests it was recognized early that there are for every particular group certain values, goals, standards, or norms for the sake of which, apparently, groups are formed or which gradually emerge in the course of group formation. It is easy to spot these values in the case of official, institutional organizations, but they are the harder to define the more informal, casual, and marginal the groupings are. Therefore, instead of fixing our eye upon the social values and standards as they are given on the surface, we tried to enter a wedge at a level which is as universal as possible and as free of a cultural bias as possible. By taking, for instance, the sociogram of the official structure of an institution, of a family, a school, a religious or government hierarchy, and by replacing it by the socio-grams of the unofficial structures, the result was an ever-changing variety of social profiles, a wealth of expanding and spontaneous, infinitely small and infinitely protean social structures, invisible to the naked eye, but of the greatest significance for the macroscopic social structure surrounding them . . . .

"With whom do you live in proximity?" and "With whom do you wish to live in proximity?" are two of the earliest sociometric questions used. These criteria are so universally constructed that they can be applied to groups of any culture, sex, race, or age, whether the household is a Christian family, a harem, a family of the Jibaro Indian Tribe,[1] a couple living out of wedlock, or any number of individuals choosing to live together and sharing daily tasks for a reasonable period of time. Other criteria were "working in proximity" and "visiting each other." Such criteria as these three we found in all communities surveyed. Then there are criteria which are found in some communities but not in others, such as going hunting, fishing, boating, playing cards, playing baseball. The number of criteria increases with the complexity of the society in which they emerge. Criteria must be kept apart from the "motivations" and usefulness they have for the members of the group. In one culture the members may live in proximity because they like each other, in another culture because members of both sexes are present, in another culture because all members are of the same sex. Criteria questions are of exploratory value if they are significant to the members of the group at the time of the test; for instance, the questions, "With whom do you visit?" or "Whom do you invite for a meal?" imply that the individuals mentioned have had and still have a special value for the respondent or otherwise they would not have been selected. All criteria have this in common: that the respondents have some actual experience in reference to them, whether ex post facto or present; in sociometric language, they are still "warmed up" to them, otherwise the questions would not arouse a significant response.

Another consideration which may be useful would be to differentiate between diagnostic and action criteria. An illustration of a diagnostic criterion is "Whom do you invite to have meals in your house?" It is specific but it does not provide the subjects with the opportunity to get into immediate action and it does not justify the sociometric director to prompt the subject to act; in other words, the test provides only for information but not for action. An action criterion involves a different situation. It prompts the subjects to a different warming up process. It requires different instructions than a diagnostic test. An illustration of an action criterion in application is the sociometric planning of a new settlement. The settlers come to a town meeting and they are addressed by the sociometric counselor as a group: "You are preparing to move into the new settlement. Whom do you want there as a neighbor?" This is obviously a situation which is different from the diagnostic case. The people have an immediate goal to which they are warmed up. The choices they make are very real things: they are not only wishes, for the individuals are prompted to act at present and in the presence of the group. In the diagnostic case the reference is to the past, however crucial; the diagnostic approach can easily be changed into an actional one. Choices are then decisions for action, not reports of actions. The theory of sociometric testing requires (a) that the participants in the situation are drawn to one another by one or more criteria; (b) that a criterion is selected to which the participants are bound to respond, at the moment of the test, with a high degree of spontaneity; (c) that the subjects are adequately motivated so that their responses may be sincere; and (d) that the criterion selected for testing is strong, enduring, and definite, not weak, transitory, and indefinite.

SOCIOMETRIC ORIENTATIONS

We have studied group formation in three ways. The first way may be called observational and interpretative. We watched children as, free of supervision, they ran out of school to the playgrounds, noting the manner in which they grouped themselves spontaneously. We noted a regularity in their spontaneous groupings—one particular girl followed by a bunch of others, many who paired themselves off, and two or three, often more, walking alone. Similar patterns were formed when they played about the grounds undirected. A rough classification of the position of the individuals in the groups was possible—the isolates, the pairs, and the bunch that clung to the leader—but this did not reach beyond surface judgments in understanding the organization of the groups.

We then approached the task from a different angle. Instead of observing the formation of groups from without we entered into the group, became part of it, and registered its intimate developments. We ourselves experienced the polarity of relations among members, the development of gangs within the group, the pressure upon one individual or another. However, the larger the group under study was, the more we ourselves became a victim of such pressure, the more attached we found ourselves to some of its sections and the more blindfolded to other parts. Through this method of "partnership" we arrived at a somewhat finer classification of each individual than we were able to through observation. Or we selected a member of the group who was in a position to know its underlying relations—for instance, in a family group we consulted the mother; in a school class, the teacher; in a cottage group of an institution, the housemother; in a work unity, the foreman, et cetera. The selected informer, due to the mechanism of partnership, often had an inaccurate insight into the workings of the group. We cannot adequately comprehend the central direction of an individual in his development either through observation or through partnership. We must make him an experimenter. Considering group formation, we must make the members of the prospective groups themselves the authors of the groups to which they belong. To reach a more accurate knowledge of group organization the sociometric test is used. It consists in an individual choosing his associates for any group of which he is or might become a member. As these choices are initiated by the persons themselves, each individual is taken into partnership. This is true not only for himself but also for each individual towards every other individual. Thus we win an insight into how group structures of their own look compared with group structures imposed from without. This method is experimental and synthetic.

In school groups the test had the following form. The tester entered the classroom and addressed the pupils: "You are seated according to the directions your teacher has given you. The neighbor who sits beside you is not chosen by you. You are now given the opportunity to choose the boy or girl whom you would like to have sit on either side of you. Write down whom you would like first best; then, whom you would like second best. Look around and make up your mind. Remember that next term the friends you choose now may sit beside you." One minute was allowed for deciding upon choices before pupils were to write. The tester tried to get into rapport with the pupils and to transfer clearly the particular significance of the decisions.

For home groups the test had to be varied. The tester called the whole population of a given [institutional] community together and addressed them: "You live in a certain house with certain other persons according to the directions the administration has given you. The persons who live with you in the same house are not chosen by you and you are not chosen by them, although you might have chosen each other. You are now given the opportunity to choose the persons whom you would like to live with in the same house. You can choose without restraint any individuals of this community whether they happen to live in the same house with you or not. Write down whom you would like first best, second best, third best, fourth best, and fifth best. Look around and make up your mind. Remember that the ones you choose will probably be assigned to live with you in the same house."

Three points are of methodological significance. First, every individual is included as a center of emotional response. Second, this is not an academic reaction. The individual is caught by an emotional interest in a certain practical end which the tester has the authority to put into practice. Third, the choice is always related to a definite criterion. In the first instance, the criterion is of studying in proximity, actually sitting beside the pupils chosen.

In the second, the criterion is of living in proximity, actually within the same house. When this test was applied to work groups, the criterion was working in proximity, actually within the same unit and collaborating in the function to be performed. Other criteria must be used according to the special function of any group under study.

The test has been carried out in three phases: (1) spontaneous choice; (2) motivation of these choices; and (3) causation of these choices. Spontaneous choice reveals how many members of his own group, whatever the criterion of the group, are desired by an individual as associates in the activity of this group. The motivations, as they are secured through interview of each individual, reveal further the number of attractions and repulsions to which an individual is exposed in a group activity. The underlying causations for these attractions and repulsions are studied through spontaneity and role playing tests adapted to sociometric aims. The spontaneity test places an individual in a standard life situation which calls for definite fundamental emotional reactions, called spontaneity states, such as fear, anger, et cetera. If permitted to expand, they turn into role playing. The range of mimic and verbal expression during the plays is recorded and offers characteristic clues to the make-up of the personality acting, to his relation to the life situation acted, and to the persons or persons who act opposite him in the test.

CONSTRUCTION OF THE SOCIOMETRIC TEST

The problem was to construct the test in such a manner that it was itself a motive, an incentive, a purpose, primarily for the *subject* instead of the tester. If the test procedure is identical with a life goal of the subject, he can never feel himself to have been victimized or abused, even though the same series of acts may be a "test" in the mind of the tester. We have developed two tests in which the subject is in action for his own ends. One is the sociometric test. From the point of view of the subject it is not a test at all and this is as it should be. It is merely an opportunity for him to become an active agent in matters concerning his life situation. But to the sociometric tester, the test reveals his actual position in the community in relation to the actual position of others. The second test meeting this demand is the spontaneity and role playing test. Here is a standard life situation which the subject improvises to his own satisfaction. But to the tester it releases a source of information in respect to the character, intelligence, conduct, and social relations of the subject.

Psychometric tests and psychoanalysis of the child and adolescent, however contrasting in procedure, have one thing in common. They throw the subject into a passive state, the subject being a role of submission. The situation is not motivated for him. This tends to produce an attitude of suspicion and tension on the part of the subject towards the tester and to attribute to him ulterior motives in inducing the subject to submit to the test. This situational fact has to be considered irrelevant to how valuable and significant the revelations may be which come from the psychometric testing and from psychoanalysis. This aspect of the testing becomes especially conspicuous if the findings are used for the purpose of determining some change in the life situation of the subject, such as, for instance, his transfer to an institution for the feeble-minded. Through sociometric, spontaneity, and role playing tests the artificial setting of the psychoanalytic situation and of the Binet intelligence tests can be substituted for by natural life settings.

A point which deserves emphasis is the accurate giving of the sociometric test. Only such a test can be correctly called sociometric which attempts to determine the feelings of individuals towards each other and, second, to determine these in respect to the same criterion. For instance, if we demand that the inhabitants of a given community choose the individuals with whom they want to live together in the same house and motivate these choices, this is a sociometric procedure. If, on the other hand, the inhabitants of a community are asked whom they like or dislike irrespective of any criterion, this should be called near-sociometric. Being unrelated to a criterion, these preferences are not analytically differentiated; they may relate to sexual liking, to the liking of working together, or whatever. Secondly, the individuals will have no interest in expressing their likes and dislikes truthfully, as no practical consequences for themselves are derivable from these responses. It is similar if children in a classroom are asked whom they like or dislike among their class mates, irrespective of any criterion and without immediate purpose for them. Even if such a form of inquiry may at some age level produce similar results as the results gained through our procedure, it should not be called sociometric testing. It does not provide a systematic basis for sociometric research . . . .

Sociometry in communities and the psychodrama in experimental situations make a deliberate attempt to bring the subjects into an experimental state which will make them sensitive to the realization of their own experiences and action patterns. In this spontaneity state they are able to contribute revealing material concerning the web of social networks in which they move and the life situations through which they pass. This conditioning of the subjects for a more total knowledge of their social situation is accomplished by means of the processes of warming up and by learning to summon the degree of spontaneity necessary for a given situation.

THE SOCIAL INVESTIGATOR

A second fundamental aspect of the problem concerns the investigator himself. In the social sciences, the problem of the investigator and the situation in which the experiment of study is to be carried out have been of the gravest concern. However, the methods for dealing with this fundamental difficulty have been most unsatisfactory to date.

The participant observer, in the course of his exploration, enters into contact with various individuals and situations, but he, himself—with his biases and prejudices, his personality equation and his own position in the group— remains unexamined and therefore is an unmeasured quantity. The displacement in the situation to be investigated, which is partly produced by his own social pattern, does not appear as an integral part of the findings. Indeed, we have to take the inviolability of his own judgments and opinions for granted. Thus the uninvestigated investigator constitutes an ever-present error. Of course this is only true for social studies in which the investigators are, as individuals, essential parts of the investigation. It is different in social studies which investigate finished products—processes which have become stereotyped and stationary, lending themselves to actuarial study and the development of scales. Social measurements of such processes are, of course, a part of sociometry in its broader sense, but they have a limited practical meaning without the frontal approach—the direct measurement of interpersonal phenomena.

In order to overcome the grave errors which may arise in and from the investigator himself, we resort to a sociometric approach which is especially adapted to the microscopic study of social phenomena. The participant observer—in one particular form of this work--does not remain "objective" or at a distance from the persons to be studied: he becomes their friend. He identifies himself with their own situations; he becomes an extension of their own egos. In other words, the "objective" participant becomes a "subjective" one. As a subjective participant he can enter successfully or simultaneously into the lives of several individuals, and then function as a medium of equilibration between them. This is the first step.

If we consider the investigator who gives out questionnaires as being in a situation of maximum formal objectivity, then the investigator who identifies himself successfully with every individual participating in the situation approaches a maximum of subjectivity. A professional worker acting in this fashion produces excellent therapeutic effects, but the method does not improve upon the intended objectification of the investigator himself.

A step beyond this is the psychodramatic method, a situation which provides an experimental and a therapeutic setting simultaneously. Here, the director of the theatre is present, but outside of the exploratory situation itself. The investigators to be tested are placed in life situations and roles which may occur in the community or in their own private lives until their range of roles and their patterns of behavior in these life situations have been adequately gauged. This procedure is carried on until every one of the investigators is thoroughly objectified. Retests are made from time to time in order to keep pace with any changes which may have taken place in their various behavior patterns.

In the course of such work, the expansiveness and the range of roles of each investigator become clearly defined, and the stimulus which he may be to the subjects of his investigations becomes a known quantity. Thus, the psychodramatic procedure provides a yardstick by which we can measure and evaluate an indefinitely large number of subjects in specific life situations and in specific roles. The paradox is that the investigator, although he has become objectified by this process—a "controlled participant observer"—still continues to be what he originally started out to be: a subjective participant.

The process of objectifying the investigator takes many forms in accord with the situation which he is to explore. An ideal situation of this kind is obtained with a psychodramatic group in the experimental setting of the therapeutic theatre. For the members of a psychodramatic group, a range of spontaneity is permitted in roles and situations which far surpasses that of any actual community and yet may include all the roles and situations which exist there. At the same time, the behavior of every member of the community—however spontaneous it may be—is recorded in addition to the interaction between the members of the group both on the stage and off it. Thus the ideal background is constructed for the task assigned to the testers within the psychodramatic group itself.

When the investigator has been tested in this manner, we are able to use him as a tool for testing any group of subjects in typical situations, as described above. In addition to this, he can be used for the treatment of subjects in his new qualification as a subjective participant who is objectified to a point where he can be considered a known quantity in the procedure. He has become an auxiliary ego whose behavior in the process of guidance on the psychodramatic stage is within some degree of control.

This method can be used to advantage as an improvement upon the participant observer technique of investigation. As a result of careful gauging of the personalities of the investigators who are to be employed as sociometrists or observers in the community at large, a frame of reference is established at the research center to which the investigators return with their data and findings. The use of this frame of reference provides a more objective basis than has heretofore existed for evaluating the reflection of the investigators' own behavior characteristics upon their findings in the community. Thus the social investigation of any community, when based upon sociometric principles, is equipped with two complementary frames of reference. The one is the objectified investigator, so prepared and evaluated that his own personality is no longer an unknown factor in the findings. The other frame of reference consists of the members of the community who are brought to a high degree of spontaneous participation in the investigation by means of sociometric methods, and therefore contribute genuine and reliable data. Thus, the social structures which actually exist in the community at the moment of investigation are brought to our knowledge with a minimum of error on the part of both the investigators and the investigated.

CHAPTER 12

Authoritative and Democratic Methods of Grouping

1953

Editor's note: This article contains a description of sociometry as applied at the Hudson School for Girls. It reports on research with table and housing assignments. It stimulated other social scientists to pursue research in the field of group leadership.

A simple illustration of sociometric technique is the grouping of children in a dining room.

In a particular cottage of our training school live 28 girls. In their dining room are seven tables. The technique of placing them around these tables can take different forms. We may let them place themselves as they wish, and watch the result. Girl A seats herself at Table One; eight girls who are drawn to her try to place themselves at the same table. But Table One can only hold three more. The result is a struggle and somebody has to interfere and arrange them in some arbitrary manner. Girl B runs to Table Two, but nobody attempts to join her; thus three places at the table remain unused.

From *Who Shall Survive?* (1953), 652-673. Another version appears in *Sociometry, Experimental Method & the Science of Society* (1951).

We find that the technique of letting girls place themselves works out to be impracticable. It brings forth difficulties which enforce arbitrary, authoritative interference with their wishes, the opposite principle from the one which was intended—a free, democratic, individualistic process.

Another technique of placement is the one applied strictly from the point of view of the authoritative supervisor of the dining room. She places them in such a fashion that they produce the least trouble to her without regard to the way in which the girls themselves feel about placements. Or she picks for each of the seven tables a leader around whom she groups the rest without regard to the leader's feelings about them and without consideration of whether the "leader" is regarded by the girls as a leader.

SOCIOMETRIC METHOD OF GROUPING

A more satisfactory technique of placement is to ask the girls with whom they want to sit at the same table, and if every table seats at least four, to give every girl three choices; to tell them that every effort will be made that each may have at her table at least one of her choices, and if possible, her first choice. Every girl writes down first whom she wants as a first choice; next, whom she wants as a second choice if she cannot receive her first choice; and last, whom she wants as a third choice if she cannot have her first or second choice. The slips are collected and analyzed. The structure of affinities one for another is charted. The best possible relationship available within the structure of interrelations defines the *optimum of placement*. This is the highest reciprocated choice from the point of view of the girl. The order is as follows: a subject's first choice is reciprocated by a first choice, 1:1; a subject's first choice is reciprocated by a second choice, 1:2; a subject's first choice is reciprocated by a third choice, 1:3; a subject's second choice is reciprocated by a first choice, 2:1; and so forth, 2:2; 2:3; 3:1; 3:2; 3:3. Where there is no choice that meets with a mutual response, the first choice of the girl (1:0) becomes her optimum; that is from her point of view the best placement for her available within the structure.

These simple rules guide each placement. They can be called into effect with a high degree of efficiency. Even in instances in which a number of girls do not receive their optimum, they can receive their second very often. This procedure has two phases: analysis of the choices and analysis of placement. The analysis of choices discloses the structure of the group and the position of every girl within it. It discloses how many girls are wanted spontaneously by all three partners whom they want at their table, how many are wanted by two of the three partners whom they want at their table, how many are wanted by one of the three only, and how many by none of the three. It discloses the high percentage of girls who have to make some adjustment to the group because they cannot get what they want.

A technique of placement has been worked out to help the girls as far as possible where their spontaneous position in the group stops them in a blind alley. Their crisscross affinities as charted in a sociogram are simple, direct guides which a technique of placement can intelligently use. The attempt is made to give every girl of the group an optimum of satisfaction. We consider as the optimum of satisfaction the duplication for a girl of such a position in the placement as is revealed to be the most desired by her in accordance with the actual structure presented in the sociogram.

The tabulation of placement is figured out. It indicates the seating which has been calculated for every cottage. We find that sometimes it is possible to be efficient up to 100%; on the average we are able to give an optimum of satisfaction to more than 80% of the girls. Considering that the percentage of girls who would reach this optimum if left to their own devices is on the average not higher than 25 to 30%, the help coming from sociometric technique of placement is substantial.

It is a matter of principle with us to give every girl the best possible placement regardless of what her record may be or what experience the housemother may have had in regard to any two girls who want to sit at the same table. We do not begin with prejudice but wait to see how their conduct turns out.

Occasionally we see that two or more girls who have affinities for each other do not behave to advantage for themselves or for others. Then a different placement may be more desirable for them.

We have noted that the girls' own spontaneous choice may deadlock them in a certain position, and we can well visualize that they may be forced in actual life to make an adjustment which is very arbitrary and deeply against their wishes. These deadlocks are not something which every individual outgrows spontaneously, but are something which works like a social destiny for the majority of individuals. It was therefore of great interest not only from a practical but also from a theoretical point of view to study whether the technique of placement would have for the girls a significance beyond the temporary aid it gives them. If, through our intermediation, they can mix during their meal time with girls who appeal to them and learn to choose better the next time, if the technique helps them to facilitate and train and improve their social spontaneity and to break the deadlock more rapidly than if left to their own devices, then the service of such a procedure may find many applications.

The sociometric test in regard to table choice is repeated every eight weeks. To estimate accurately the progress, regression, or stand still of social interrelations, we have calculated the findings and made a comparative study of the test in 3 successive testings 8 weeks apart, a period of 24 weeks. In the first test, of the 327 girls who participated, 23.9% succeeded in having their first choice reciprocated by a first choice (1:1); 11.9% succeeded in having their first choice reciprocated by a second choice (1:2); and 10.4% succeeded in having their first choice reciprocated by a third choice (1:3). In the second test, of the 317 girls who participated, 27.1% succeeded in having their first choice reciprocated by a first choice; 15.1% succeeded in having their first choice reciprocated by a second choice; and 11.4% succeeded in having their first choice reciprocated by a third choice. The total success in the first test in getting a mutual choice of any sort in response to the first choice was for that population 46.2%. The success rate in the second test was 53.6% The difference of 7.4% represents the increase in the efficiency of the girls from the first to the second test in finding their first choices reciprocated without outside aid. The increase in efficiency from the first to the second test in regard to 1:1 mutual choices was 3.2%; in regard to 1:2 mutual choice, also 3.2%; and in regard to 1:3 mutual choices, 1%. In other words, the increase in efficiency shows up most in the 1:1 and 1:2 choices but is less noticeable in the 1:3 choices. In regard to second choices, the increase in efficiency was 10.6%, and for the third choices, 1.4%. The total increase in mutual choices is 19.4% from the first test to the second test.

In consequence of this increase in responses to first choices, there is a corresponding decrease from the first to the second test in outgoing choices which remain unreciprocated—19.4%. When we examine the findings of the third testing, we see the amount of mutuality of first choices still increasing (2.6% more than in the second test), but a falling off for second and third choices. What this means is the accumulation of benefit going to the first choices, as we see when we examine the number of unreciprocated first choices in the first testing, 53.8%, and number in the third testing, 43.8%, a difference of 10%.

To see whether these choices are being more broadly spread throughout the various cottage groups we calculated the percentage of isolated girls in each group for each period. For the first period the isolated girls were 17.6% of the total number, and for the third period, 14.8%, a decrease of 2.8%.

The question is whether the findings in this period of 24 weeks presents a significant trend. This question cannot be answered except through further testing. It appears reasonable to assume that the placement technique should increase the spontaneous efficiency of choosing. The procedure brings a number of isolated girls into contact with wanted girls who under normal circumstances might not pay any attention to them. The unchosen girl sitting beside her favorite has an opportunity to show herself to better advantage and to win the person she wants as a friend. Similar relationships of all sorts develop through our "shuffle," which lays the ground open for potential clickings to take place. Without the use of the placement technique the girls who know each other well get to know each other still better and the newcomers tend to be excluded. A control series of tests was given at intervals of 6 weeks over a period of 18 weeks to one cottage, with a population of 22 girls at the time of the first testing and 23 at the time of the third testing.

The placement procedure was not allowed to go into effect during this period. The findings indicate a continuous fall in the mutuality of choices—for first choices a decrease of 10.3%; for second choices, 14.2%; and for third choices, 31.9%—together with a continuous rise in unreciprocated choices amounting to 56.4%. While this is a very small group, it suggests the needs for sociometric placement technique and supports the trends mentioned above.

Since these sociometric control studies were made in 1935 a growing number of similar studies have been undertaken by various investigators. They corroborate my original hypothesis that *sociometric choices and decisions, when carried into action by the participants, (1) benefit the material inquiry—that is, the truth value of the responses obtained; and (2) increase the social cohesion, morale, and power of their groups.*

It must be added that what is a criterion of choice for the participants in one culture may not be a criterion in another. Criteria, to be comparable, must have an equivalent power of motivation, and when the choices are consummated in action, the social catharsis must be equally deep and strong . . . .

HOUSING ASSIGNMENTS

It happened during 1934, in part due to an influx of population beyond the capacity of our little community, that 16 new girls had been placed in one or another cottage without going through the usual sociometric process. These 16 girls represented an unselected group. As it is a rare occasion in Hudson that girls are placed in a haphazard, hit-or-miss fashion, we felt that this material might answer some questions that we have had in the back of our mind since the beginning of our work here.

The group position development of these 16 non-tested girls was studied according to our routine for the whole community, continuously every eight weeks. Here are presented the first 32 weeks of their social evolution in whatever cottage they were placed. We tabulated the number of girls who were unchosen or isolated, the number of girls who were chosen but who did not reciprocate any choice, and the number of girls who had one or more mutual choices.

For several years at Hudson the assignment of newcomers to a cottage had been made upon a sociometric basis. The factors entering into sociometric assignment are numerous—the psychological organization of every cottage, the sociometric saturation point for minority groups within them, the social history of the new girl, to mention a few. But the most important single factor is the factor of spontaneous choice. The affinity of a girl for a certain house-mother and of that housemother for her, and the affinity of the newcomer for a key girl of a particular cottage, and of that key girl for her, have been crucial in our consideration of adequate assignment.

The simple procedure of inviting the housemothers and the key girls to visit the newcomers in the Receiving Cottage soon after their arrival fur-nished us with ample information concerning the spontaneous immediate attraction they may feel for each other. In the early routine of this procedure we were compelled to give the findings some ranking, however arbitrary. We gave preference, for instance, to the strong affinity (first choice) over the weaker affinity (second or third choice). We gave a mutual choice preference over a one-sided choice. We gave a mutual first choice preference over a mutual second or third choice. We gave a mutual first choice of the new girl with the housemother and the key girl of that cottage preference over another new girl's mutual first choice which was only with the housemother or only with the key girl. We used this ranking as a working hypothesis, meanwhile gathering the data and awaiting an opportune moment to determine its valid-ity. It is for this purpose that this control study was made.

For the sake of comparison with the 16 non-tested girls we took an unselected group of 32 girls who had arrived in Hudson afterward . . . Sixteen of them had a mutual first choice with a housemother and her key girl and had accordingly been placed in the cottage thus selected. The other 16 had affinities of lesser rank and had been placed accordingly. As a matter of routine the group position development of these two groups of tested girls had also been followed up every 8 weeks. A like stretch of time, the first 32 weeks of their stay in Hudson, is represented in their group positions. The tabulation of the positions to which these girls laid claim, compared with those of the non-tested girls, is given in Table 12-1.

The findings show that the girls who were placed on the basis of the test (Group A) find a better position in the group from the start. The non-tested control group starts with 4 isolated; the tested Group A, which had some degree of affinities, though less than maximum, starts with 3 isolated; and for Group B, which had maximum affinities, the number of isolates at the start falls to zero. The control group starts with 8 of the girls being chosen but without any mutual choice. Finally, in regard to the most important factor, the mutuality of choice, only 4 of the control group receive from the start one or more mutual choices, while for Group A, the number is 5, and for Group B, the number is 11.

The tested girls undergo a quicker social evolution and integration than the girls who had been placed in a cottage without a test. At the end of the 32-week period, of the 16 girls in each group, the control group shows 4 isolated girls; the tested Group A, only 2, and the tested Group B, zero. The

TABLE 12-1 Psychological Positions of Girls Placed Sociometrically Compared with Girls Placed Hit-or-Miss

| | Elapsed time (in weeks) | | | |
	8	16	24	32
Control Group:				
(16 non-tested girls assigned to cottages without socio-metric procedure—i.e., hit-or-miss)				
Isolated	4	6	6	4
Chosen, but without any mutual choices	8	4	6	4
One or more mutual choices	4	6	4	8
Group A				
(16 tested girls assigned to cottages on the basis of socio-metric procedure; some degree of affinity with house-mother and key girl)				
Isolated	3	4	3	2
Chosen, but without any mutual choices	8	5	3	1
One or more mutual choices	5	7	10	13
Group B				
(16 tested girls assigned to cottages on the basis of socio-metric procedure; maximum affinity—mutual first choices—with housemother and key girl)				
Isolated	0	1	1	0
Chosen, but without any mutual choices	5	3	1	0
One or more mutual choices	11	12	14	16

control group shows only 8 girls receiving mutual choices, but Group A shows 13 girls, and Group B, all 16 girls receiving one or more mutual choices. The findings also show a marked difference between groups of tested girls, A and B. The girls who had a mutual first choice with house-mother and with key girl in the sociometric test given to them in the receiv-ing cottage and who had been placed in the chosen cottage with them made a far better showing in the positions attained by them in their respective cottages than did the tested girls of Group A, who had been placed on lesser degrees of affinity for their housemother and key girls. A certain number of isolates persisted tenaciously in Group A: at the end of 8 weeks, 3 isolates, at the end of 16 weeks, 4 isolates; at the end of 24 weeks, 3 isolates; and at the end of 32 weeks, 2 isolates. In contrast, the tested Group B had at the end of 8 weeks, no isolates; at the end of 16 weeks, 1 isolate (due to paroling of her mutual choice); after 24 weeks, 1 isolate (the same girl who lost her friend through parole); and after 32 weeks, no isolates. Accordingly, Group B showed from the start a rapidly increasing growth of mutual choices.

CONCLUSIONS AND COMMENT

- The greater the original affinity between the newcomer and the prominent members of the group (in this case housemother and key girl) the better will the newcomer be accepted by the whole group.
- Sociometric assignment protects the newcomer against social blocking at an early stage.
- Hit-or-miss assignment appears to facilitate social blocking and often firmly establishes an isolated position.
- It appears desirable that only the fewest possible individuals should be compelled to make an adjustment—and even they as little as possible . . . .

A problem which often recurs is that sometimes girls remain over to whom no satisfaction can be given in the placement. In placing a population of 412 girls on the basis of the first testing reported here, only 7 girls (or 1.7% of the population) received none of their three choices. (In the second testing, 1.7%, and in the third testing, 1% of the population received none of their three choices.) To such girls an individual explanation is given that to give them any one of their choices would block the choices of a great many other girls in the cottage; they are asked to accept the situation with the understanding that at the next choosing (8 weeks later), if it is necessary that any girl go without her choices for the sake of the majority of the girls, other girls than they will be asked to do so. The girls are told who these girls are who want to sit with them but whom they did not choose. They are glad to find themselves thus chosen, and take with a good spirit the placement they are asked to accept. They render a service to less well-adjusted and little chosen or isolated girls who choose them.

The argument may be raised that it matters very little with whom a girl sits at the table. The question whom one has at his table during meal time may rightly seem so very insignificant to a person who lives in a great city and has the opportunity to mix freely with everyone and has plenty of time at his disposal. But in an institutional community where the number of acquaintances one can make is strictly limited, and where a certain amount of routine is necessary, free association during meal time with the person you desire to be with is of great social value. We have made similar observations in the dining rooms and dormitories of colleges.

Another argument may be raised that for most people what they eat is more important than with whom they eat. This is partial truth which is valueless as long as it remains unqualified by quantitative analysis. Our social atom studies showed that there are people in whom the preferential feelings toward other *persons* are especially articulate and that there are people in whom the preferential feelings towards *things* are especially articulate . . . .

Another argument may be raised that a wanted and perhaps superior girl, although she may have received one or two of her choices, may have to tolerate as a third partner an isolated girl who chose her but whom she violently rejects. In reply to this it can be said that the wanted girl, exposed to chance, may not have received even the two friends whom she wanted; also it may be an important part of her training to expand her emotional experience also toward people who do not appeal to her so much as others. An increase in emotional flexibility should not decrease her preferential sensibility.

CHAPTER 13

Thoughts on Genetics

1953

Editor's note: In this article, relevant as much for its questions as its answers, Moreno speculates on the biological basis for sociometry. He implies that sociometrists, geneticists, and others who assume responsibility for guiding the process of natural selection would do well to count nobody out. Ultimately, he opts for a description of the world that he finds in religious thinking, where a "father has created the universe for all . . . and made its spaces so immense that all may be born and so that all may live."

It helped us in the beginning of the investigation to think of mankind as a social and organic unity. Once we had chosen this principle as our guide, another idea developed of necessity. If this whole of mankind is a unity, then tendencies must emerge between the different parts of this unity, drawing them at one time apart and at another time together; these tendencies may be sometimes advantageous for the parts and disadvantageous for the whole, or advantageous for some parts and disadvantageous for other parts; these tendencies may become apparent on the surface in the relation of individuals or of groups of individuals as affinities or disaffinities, as attractions and repulsions; these social and psychological facts, and this index, must be detectable; these attractions and repulsions or their derivatives may have a near or

---

From Nature's Planning and the Planning of Society, *Who Shall Survive?* (1953), 611-614.

distant effect not only upon the immediate participants in the relation but also upon all other parts of that unity which we call mankind; the relations which exist between the different parts may disclose an order of relationships as highly differentiated as any order found in the rest of the universe.

Whether in the end this guide will be proved to be a universal axiom or a fiction, it has aided us in the discovery and demonstration of tele, the social atom, the sociodynamic effect, and the sociometric network of communication. It may be permissible to let the fantasy run ahead of demonstrable proof and derive another necessity which seems to follow logically from the conception of mankind as a correlated unity. Just as we have seen the individual in the sociometric domain as the crossing point of numerous attractions and repulsions which at various times shrink and expand and which are not necessarily identical with the relations within the groups in which he actually lives but break through group life lines, it may be that also in the eugenic domain an individual cannot be classified but as a crossing point of numerous morphological affinities and disaffinities which are not necessarily related to the individuals with whom he actually propagates the race, but that they break through racial lines and the different levels of social organization. It may be that certain individuals belong to the same eugenic group, due to selective affinities for which an index of eugenic facts must exist, and that they do not belong to all other groups, at least not with the same degree of selectivity. It may be also that the balances and imbalances we have found within the social atom exist in some fashion also in the gene-atoms and that once such an evidence is secured a basis for a relation of eugenic classification with our sociometric classification will be won.

Since Linnaeus advanced the theory of the origin of the species by hybridization and Mendel discovered the laws of inheritance, it has been assumed that the bringing together of many diverse genes by hybridization and their various interactions are largely responsible for the increase of complexity found in the evolution of organisms. But the causes for successful and unsuccessful hybridization are in doubt. The beneficial and the dysgenic result of the meeting of differently constituted germ plasmas may be due to morphological affinities and disaffinities operating among the genes themselves or among complexes of them. And upon these affinities and disaffinities may depend the pooling of appropriate or inappropriate hereditary factors contributed to the offspring by the two parents. As long as the nature of eugenic affinities is not established by biogenetic research, we shall assume two practical rules: that psychological nearness or distance is indicative of eugenic nearness or distance and that clinical studies of crossings lead to a preliminary classification of eugenic affinity. We may have to consider not only changes in the genes but changes *between* the genes—whatever mutation may have taken place in a gene and for whatever reason, mechanical, chemical, et cetera. If this mutation should be favorable the genes must be attractive to one another, that is, must correspond to changes in some other genes. In other words, the genes must be able to produce a functional relation; morphological affinities and disaffinities between them may exist.

It can be doubted whether the attraction of one individual towards another and pairing inclinations are a fair index of morphological affinity, and conversely, whether repulsion of one individual for another and disinclination to mate are an index of sterility or reflective of a dysgenic factor. Our opinion is that as long as no better knowledge is available, affinities of individuals for one another should be considered a practical index. It is not known to us if a thorough investigation of the relationships existing between sociometric affinities and disaffinities and the eugenic reflections of them has ever been made. The more one considers sociometric processes as a fair index for bodily and social changes and the more one considers them as an index, not only for the needs of the individual but also for the needs of the kind, the more will one be inclined to expect that the factor of spontaneous choice and spontaneous clicking is not a random experience but an inherent expression of the whole organism. A definite relation may exist between gene effect (if we call a "gene effect" the reflection of one gene upon another and upon the individual characters) and tele effect.

The scant clinical evidence as far as is available today appears to give support to the hypothesis. We have the one extreme, a point of view held by many eugenic writers, that the physically and mentally abler members elevate the race through propagation and that the physically and mentally inferior cause the race to regress through their propagation, and the other extreme, that members of the superior class in general produce better offspring with members of the inferior class (and members of one race with members of another race) than when they remain within their own sphere; both extremes appear to find a point of coincidence in the hypothesis of eugenic groups, micro-biological relations which are not identical with the macro-biological groups as they appear on the surface.

From the point of view of such a biometric or eugenic classification the constructive approach of biological planning comes into a new light. Similar to therapeutic assignment in social groups, eugenic assignment to eugenic groups now looms as a possibility. Thus the notion of the unfit, at least for a large number of those who are now considered in this category, becomes relative, as numerous groups of varying eugenic value are uncovered. Some groups among those today classified as unfit for propagation may be found unfit when in relation to certain groups, but fit in relation to other groups, just as we have found in respect to populations that some groups which foster disintegration and decline in certain communities aid in the fruitful development of others. It is a forgone conclusion that if this be the case our present palliative measures such as sterilization will be discarded or undergo modification.

We may have gone too far with our disrespect for nature's wisdom, just as in times past we went too far in our respect for it. It may be demonstrated in the end that the slow and "blind" methods of nature's planning, however wise they have appeared at one stage in our knowledge and however deficient in parts at another stage of our knowledge, are true, taken as a totality. A new appreciation may then arise of the sense of the old myth which all great religions have brought forth in remarkable unison, the myth of the father who has created the universe for all, who has made its spaces so immense that all may be born and so that all may live.

PART III: Protocols

"But this mad passion, this unfoldment of life in the domain of illusion, does not work like a renewal of suffering. Rather it confirms the rule: every true second time is the liberation from the first . . . . One gains towards one's own life, towards all one has done and does, the point of view of the creator . . .The first time brings the second time to laughter."

(From *Theatre of Spontaneity,* 91)

CHAPTER 14

Psychodramatic Production Techniques

1952

Editor's note: Here is Moreno in action, conducting a public session that consists primarily of nursing students. He makes use of the occasion to explicate his theory of child development and discuss the basic psychodramatic techniques of the double, the mirror, and role reversal. The session also illustrates how the psychodramatist uses action techniques for diagnosis.

. . . MORENO: Now, ladies and gentlemen, before I begin to work with you this evening, I would like to bring to your attention three techniques which are used today in psychodramatic work: the double technique, the mirror technique, and the reversal technique. These techniques in psychodrama can be significantly compared to three stages in the development of the infant: (a) the stage of identity (or the stage of the double); (b) the stage of the recognition of the self (the stage of the mirror); (c) stage of the recognition of the other (stage of reversal).

What do you see on a psychodramatic stage? You may, for example see a certain person who is a mental patient. This person is mentally in such a condition that communication is extremely difficult. A nurse cannot talk to her, a

From *Group Psychotherapy, Psychodrama & Sociometry* 4 (1952), 273-303.

doctor cannot relate to her. And then you use psychodrama in the following way: You will take a certain person, Mary, and you say to Mary: "Now, you may have lost any kind of contact with your father, with your mother, with your sister, with your brother. You may have lost contact with your husband, or your fellow human beings, but if you could only talk to yourself. If you could only talk to that person who is closest to you, with whom you are best acquainted. If we could produce for you the double of yourself, then you would have somebody with whom you could speak, with whom you could act together, because you belong together.

Now this idea of the double is as old as civilization. It is found in the great religions. It has always been my idea that God created us twice. One time for us to live in this world and the other time for himself. So what you see on the stage is such a production . . . you see two people who are really the same person. One person puts his arm this way. (*MORENO demonstrates*) And the other does the same. If one bows his head, the other does the same. The double is a trained person, trained to produce the same patterns of activity, the same patterns of feeling, the same patterns of thought, the same patterns of verbal communication which the patient produces. Now, of course, we don't want to put this double there merely as an aesthetic agent, but in order to enter into this person's mind, to influence this person. What theoretical concepts are involved in constructing the double as an instrument of therapy? First, in the metaphoric sense we envision that after conception the embryo and the mother are enjoined in the sharing of food and locus until the child is born. Now, we do not know anything about the "mental" state of infants except that the mother has that infant, as a physical and psychological baby, on and on, within her, and that she, although not being in communication with it, exercises a tremendous influence upon the child. After the child parts from the mother at birth there are a few weeks of a particular kind of an existence. We call this particular phase in the growth of the child the *matrix of identity*. This term involves a hypothesis of the socialization process. Nobody has ever talked with an infant immediately after it is born because the child has no means of communicating with anyone in a way which makes logical sense. But if we could talk with the infants, I believe that they would agree with my description of the matrix of identity . . . The child experiences, if you want to call it experiencing, an identity of herself and all the persons and objects of her surroundings, with the mother agent—whether it is the breast, the bottle, or any other kind of immediate contact which is established with the infant. In other words, the body and the self of the infant don't as yet exist for the infant. There is no self, no person separated from the infant. There is an identity. I want to emphasize the fact that by identity we don't mean identification. Identification is an entirely different concept and it is important that this difference be clear to you. Identification presupposes that there is an established self trying to find identity with another established self. Now, identification cannot take place until long after the child is grown and has developed an ability to separate itself, to set itself apart from another person. So we say "identity," and we mean it. It is the state of the infant, in which mother and infant and all objects are a single whole. However, it is then and there that for all movements, perceptions, actions, and interactions the phenomenon of the double is activated for the first time. You may say that it is there that an experiment of nature is in progress which I have called the double. Whatever happens later on during the growth of that infant, this primary conflict foreshadows its destiny. It emerges from it, grows and differentiates further, and develops gradually into a complicated universe in which persons and objects are separated from one another. The matrix of identity suggests that unity and integration come first before there is differentiation.

Now we enter the mental hospital, and when we meet a person who has deteriorated considerably along a psychotic line of experience, unable to communicate, the double technique can be applied with the aid of a specially trained auxiliary ego, the double ego. They often achieve valuable results with schizophrenic patients. I don't want to give you the idea that this double therapy needs a theatrical stage. It usually takes place in life itself.

Let me explain to you why the double technique is so important in the course of the production, particularly for the nurse, the attendant, and of course the therapist. Many have the idea that in order to start a therapeutic session the therapist and the patient have to sit down on a chair or relax on a couch—you know, the traditional "therapeutic chair" and the traditional "therapeutic couch." There are other ways of doing it. Therapy can take place in open space, on a therapeutic stage, in the fullness of reality, and in full action. Nurses have always known that. Nurses have always known that you may have to go to the patient, go to his bedside, take his hand. Perhaps if we could grasp all that the nurses know operationally from their concrete contact with patients, we would have a wonderful kind of practical text book for psychotherapy.

Let us now go to the second technique, which is also so important for the therapist. This is the mirror technique. You've often seen the great experience of children looking into a mirror—infants, you know—and then you hear that surprised laughter, that astonished look! And then they stretch out their tongues and turn up their noses. All this is a great experience for them. When the child realizes that the picture in the mirror is a mirror of him, that is the turning point in his growth—an important turning point in his concept of self. There have been other psychologists of the young child who have developed theories of the growing self, but it has been the particular opportunity of psychodrama to develop techniques which can be specifically related to these infantile stages.

When we use the mirror technique in psychodramatic sessions we are drawing on the fundamental relations which the infant develops to his mirror companion early in life. The first time that they look into water or into a mirror and don't recognize themselves, they think it is a stranger and they are frightened. Then there is a gradual, insidious change in expression and gesture. How many times have you seen children go to a mirror, see their image, touch it, and maybe break it? And so all this, of course, has a great deal to do with why the mirror technique can be used so effectively by nurses in their hospital work.

The reversal technique is the third stage, at a still later development of the infant. Now, in the mirror stage, we presuppose that the infant gradually learns to recognize himself as an individual separated from others. The reversal presupposes, in addition, that you can move out of your own position into the position of the other and act his part. And so we may say that the double, the mirror, and the reversal are like three stages in the development of the infant which have their counterpart in the therapeutic techniques which we can use in the treatment of all human relations problems. When you practice these methods, I hope you'll realize that they did not spring out of role playing in a sort of naive way, but that they are profoundly related to the dynamics of human growth, and the reason for their profound effectiveness is due to the kind of relationship that they have. Thus the utilization of these techniques has helped to further a theory of the infantile self and a basis for its empirical verification.

Now let me see. This gentleman rather provokes me. (*MORENO speaks to a couple in the front row*) Are you with him?

AUDIENCE MEMBER: Sure am!

MORENO: How long do you know him?

AUDIENCE MEMBER: A long time!

(*This young man had been to a previous session with another young lady*)

MORENO: Do you know him longer than the other one did?

(*Audience laughter*)

MORENO: Or don't you know about the other one?

AUDIENCE MEMBER: What other one?

MORENO: Oh, you don't know!

(*Audience laughter*)

MORENO: How long have you known him?

AUDIENCE MEMBER: Five years.

MORENO: You always bring such a sweet girl along; she is very charming! What's the matter with you? I think you just bring them here so you can get our approval. (*Audience laughter*)

MORENO: What's your name?

AUDIENCE MEMBER: Helen.

MORENO: Will you come up for a minute?

(*MORENO takes her by the hand and leads her up in front of the audience . . .*)

MORENO: What was the name of the other girl you brought along?

GEORGE: Barbara.

MORENO: Do you know about Barbara, Helen?

HELEN: I don't. Apparently you do! (*Audience laughter and applause*) We've sort of been together for a long time.

MORENO: What do you do together?

HELEN: All kinds of things.

(*Audience laughter*)

MORENO: How did you meet him?

HELEN: We went to school together.

MORENO: That's a nice old fashioned way to meet someone.

(*Audience laughter*)

MORENO: Do you know what we mean by the double, the reversal, and the mirror technique? Do you understand it?

HELEN: (*Rather hesitantly*) Yes . . .

MORENO: All right, explain it then.

HELEN: He didn't tell me anything about this before we came. I came completely unprepared.

MORENO: So that's how you bring your girlfriends up here? (*Audience laughter*) I'd like to explain in action these various concepts. (*Speaking to the instructor who brought the [nursing] group*) Is this what you had in mind, Miss Frank?

INSTRUCTOR: Yes.

MORENO: Now I'd like to show this to the group.

HELEN: I'm not a nurse.

MORENO: Student nurse?

HELEN: No.

MORENO: All right, I'll tell you what we'll do. We'll start demonstrating with the double technique. Now you must understand that you are really one person, even though there are actually two people on the stage. Do you ever talk to yourself?

HELEN: No.

MORENO: I don't mean talk loudly but think about yourself? About George?

HELEN: No.

MORENO: Do you put him completely out of your mind?

HELEN: (*With certainty*) Completely.

MORENO: Who is on your mind, anybody?

HELEN: Various people, my mother, my father, my boss . . .

MORENO: Now where are you most frequently by yourself?

HELEN: In my room.

MORENO: What kind of room is it?

HELEN: It's a studio.

MORENO: What have you got in it?

HELEN: I have two studio couches.

MORENO: Two! Why two?

(*Audience laughter*)

HELEN: Well, it sometimes happens that somebody has to stay over.

MORENO: Oh, I see, who is the somebody?

(*Audience laughter*)

HELEN: Oh, relatives or some girlfriend.

MORENO: I see, that makes it legal. All right now, you're alone in your room . . . and what are you doing?

HELEN: Combing my hair.

(*MORENO motions to an auxiliary ego who comes up on the stage; he whispers to her that she is to act as HELEN'S double. HELEN combs her hair and the double does exactly the same thing.*)

MORENO: (*Explaining to the audience*) The double always follows suit.

DOUBLE: Do I have to do this? Really? (*Combs hair*)

HELEN: (*Seemingly confused*) Should I let her talk or what?

MORENO: The double is you. You continue her thought or contradict, whatever you want.

DOUBLE: I wish I could get it cut.

HELEN: Definitely!

DOUBLE: Why don't I do it?

HELEN: Oh, it looks more charming long, and everybody has their hair short; so this is a bit different.

DOUBLE: The only trouble is that other people don't have to take care of it.

HELEN: And it takes so much time in the morning when I have to go to work.

DOUBLE: Why do I do it anyway?

HELEN: Well, I guess mostly to please other people.

DOUBLE: Why do I have to always try to please other people? Why don't I try pleasing myself for a change?

HELEN: Well it pays off in most cases to please other people. That's how we live, to please other people and have others please us.

MORENO: (*To audience*) Do you see the warm up to the double?

HELEN: Well it's all set now. Let's go to bed.

(*Audience laughter. Helen and the double proceed to go to bed*)

MORENO: Hold it a minute. I'd like to make one point clear to you. You see how the double technique works. Intuitively she falls into line. She gradually responds to the double's movements, words, and actions; and you see how significantly she moves into line. Now any response Helen 1 makes, Helen 2 falls in with, and they begin to weave together their thoughts, their feelings, and their actions as if they were one person. The matrix of identity (*the process of growing identity*) is at work. Now I wonder if you have seen a mother talk to her baby. She pinches it and kisses it. When the baby laughs or makes all kinds of noises, she talks to it even more. Now of course, the baby enjoys it but doesn't understand a word that she is saying, but that doesn't concern the mother. She talks for the baby *and* for herself, and has a wonderful time doing it. (*Audience laughter*) It's really the double technique applied in an unprofessional way to a natural situation. These operations of a mother cannot be easily replaced by any psychiatry or by any therapy. What we are trying to do in a modest way is to translate into scientific terms these precious dynamic experiences of a mother. If a double can arouse in a person such an experience, she has produced that level of communication, and before you know it they are like one person. You may think that the double communicates through empathy, but it is not only that. It is not only an empathy from one side, but it goes both ways. It is a two-way empathy which takes place almost simultaneously. It is something which is going from one to the other and back to the other again. It is a peculiar sort of interweaving of feelings. It is not only that the double enters the mind of the patient (*into his actions and movements, however bizarre*), but the patient begins to enter into the mind of the double, and they then begin to influence one another. It is this interaction process which I have called the tele phenomenon (*like a "tele-"phone, it has two ends*). Empathy is a one-way feeling. Tele is a two-way feeling.

DOUBLE: (*In bed*) You know, I'm getting sick of my job.

HELEN: I like mine!

(*Audience laughter*)

DOUBLE: I've always really wanted something much more exciting.

MORENO: Now, just a moment. You see, the double may say something which is not quite so. That is like a provocation to the self to contradict, which is often very helpful and good to know. Now, don't think for a moment that the double must always be permissive. If such absolute permissiveness doesn't exist in the psyche—that is, the subject towards herself--why should the double be permissive? Why should the double be more permissive than the patient (*unless there is some good reason because of profound feelings of guilt with which the subject tortures herself*)? The concept of "permissiveness" can be stretched to the point where it theoretically becomes harmful. So always remember that often a double opposes in order to impart. This is often the door to important information. For instance, as you have just heard, the double (*Helen 2*) said: "I'm getting sick of my job," and the other, the real self (*Helen 1*) answered: "I like mine." That is exactly the kind of information that we would like to get. All right now, go ahead.

HELEN: I have a very nice job. It's really a pleasure to get up and go to work. I know that's unusual.

DOUBLE: Oh, I'm an unusual girl.

HELEN: Well, naturally I have an unusual background. Where else could you meet people and have a chance to express yourself when you can?

DOUBLE: I'm sure lucky, but I still want more.

HELEN: Not just yet.

DOUBLE: Telephone rings.

HELEN: Not at this hour. Who on earth could be calling me at this hour?

DOUBLE: They should know better.

(*Both get up to answer phone. Both pick up phone*)

HELEN: It's my brother. (*Audience laughter*) Well, how's the family doing? Everybody here is all right; you don't have to call after ten o'clock to find out. You coming to supper this week?

DOUBLE: Somebody is knocking at the door.

HELEN: In the middle of the night? Oh my God! (*Walks toward door*) What a night! Hiya, Nelly.

DOUBLE: Come on in.

HELEN: It's a heck of a time to start calling. (*Listens to Nelly*) No, I'm sorry, you can't watch the television set.

DOUBLE: Somebody is coming down the stairs.

HELEN: I can't hear the stairs from here. (*Audience laughter*) Besides this time I really don't care. I'm so tired. I've got to get up in the morning.

DOUBLE: I don't have to get up at six in the morning! Eight hours of rest isn't necessary. I don't see why I have to be so fussy about people phoning after ten .
. .

HELEN: But I'll never know when I'll fall asleep with all this racket.

MORENO: Where does your mother sleep? What floor?

HELEN: Same floor. It's an apartment.

MORENO: Where is the room where your mother sleeps?

HELEN: (*Pointing*) That a way. (*Laughing*)

MORENO: Does she sleep all alone?

HELEN: No, I have a father too.

MORENO: Does he sleep with her?

HELEN: I should hope so!

(*Audience laughter*)

MORENO: Now you are returning to your mother's bed. You are your mother and you (*points to auxiliary ego*) are the double. You (*to HELEN*) in the role of mother are sleeping with your father in that bed.

HELEN: No, separate beds.

MORENO: Oh, twin beds. All right now, you are your mother. What is your name?

HELEN AS MOTHER: Paula.

MORENO: How old are you?

HELEN AS MOTHER: Forty.

MORENO: How many children do you have?

HELEN AS MOTHER: Two.

MORENO: What is the name of the other one?

HELEN AS MOTHER: Ronald.

MORENO: Paula, you are in bed now, are you? (*These questions are asked in rapid succession and are answered just as quickly*)

DOUBLE AS PAULA 2: (*looking at her husband*) Is he sleeping?

HELEN AS PAULA: Yeah, fast asleep.

DOUBLE: He snores.

HELEN AS PAULA: (*With great emphasis*) Sure does!

DOUBLE: That's one of the reasons I can't fall asleep . . . I wish Ronald had called during the day instead of at night.

HELEN AS PAULA: Yeah. I wonder what we should have for supper this week. Let's see now, what should we have for supper?

DOUBLE: Oh, never mind about what we should have for supper. I don't care.

HELEN AS PAULA: Now, what should I make Helen for lunch tomorrow?

DOUBLE: Why doesn't she get her own lunch? I'm pretty sick of always having to get her lunch for her.

HELEN AS PAULA: She's getting to be a pretty lazy thing.

DOUBLE: She certainly is. I've told her that many times.

HELEN AS PAULA: Oh well, I have to go shopping tomorrow.

DOUBLE: I'm worried about Helen.

HELEN AS PAULA: Well, if she thinks that she's capable of taking care of herself, then let her. Let her get herself straightened out.

DOUBLE: Let her move out and find a place of her own.

HELEN AS PAULA: (*More tenderly*) I wouldn't like to take the chance of her moving out. She probably wouldn't know how to take care of herself.

DOUBLE: Oh, that wouldn't be so bad. She'll learn.

HELEN AS PAULA: (*With emphasis*) Well no, I'm not so sure. After all she is my responsibility.

DOUBLE: I don't know about that! She doesn't seem to think so.

HELEN AS PAULA: (*Decisively*) Just because she does not think so, that doesn't mean a thing. I'm older than she is and I know better.

DOUBLE: I think I do, but I really don't know with that one.

HELEN AS PAULA: Things usually work themselves out right. They generally do.

DOUBLE: They didn't seem to with Ronald.

HELEN AS PAULA: Well . . .

DOUBLE: He's still a problem.

HELEN AS PAULA: Well, he's on his own two feet now and he'll just have to take care of himself. I'm not going to meddle anymore. (*Yawns*) Maybe I'll try this side to sleep on. (*Turns over on this other side*)

MORENO: And now you are both falling asleep. Paula, what is your husband's name?

HELEN AS PAULA: Lou.

MORENO: Lou is now getting up and he's standing around. You are now Lou and his double is also there. You are now falling asleep again and beginning to snore. Then you wake up again. All right?

HELEN AS FATHER: (*Wearily*) Mmm.

DOUBLE: What woke me up?

HELEN AS FATHER: Must have been that mystery book I read before going to sleep.

DOUBLE: Maybe I just snored so loud that I woke up, like Paula says I do.

HELEN AS FATHER: Well, I guess everybody snores. What difference does it make anyway? It doesn't keep me awake most of the time. (*Stretching*) Let's see what the devil was that book about anyhow?

DOUBLE: I shouldn't read mysteries before going to bed, really.

HELEN AS FATHER: Well, I like to watch television, I guess.

DOUBLE: It gets kind of dull.

HELEN AS FATHER: (*With great zest*) But golly, that French wrestler. He's terrific! Just remarkable. Boy, he's just got a body full of muscles! But on the other hand, I don't know, either. He's got a bad leg.

DOUBLE: I got a bad leg too, sometimes. And I'm not a wrestler.

HELEN AS FATHER: Boy, do they clean up, wrestling on television. What a farce that is!

DOUBLE: Yeah, I wish I was in that racket!

HELEN AS FATHER: Well, I guess I just ended up in the wrong line. (*Yawns*) Ah, ah, television! Thank goodness for television! It gives me something to do at night.

DOUBLE: But what about the children? Don't they give me something to do at night?

HELEN AS FATHER: Ah, let's see. The children are rarely home.

DOUBLE: That's the trouble.

HELEN AS FATHER: (*Quickly*) That Helen. She gets home kind of late.

DOUBLE: I don't know what's happening to this family. It's just falling apart.

HELEN AS FATHER: Yeah, with Ronald moving out and now she's of age.

DOUBLE: It's a long time since I've talked to her . . .

HELEN AS FATHER: (*Interrupting*) She won't listen to me! So what's the difference? All I want to do is watch television.

DOUBLE: What about the boys she goes out with? They're pretty silly.

HELEN AS FATHER: Nice fellows, only thing is that they don't have enough money.

DOUBLE: Oh, money, that isn't so important. As long as she is happy.

HELEN AS FATHER: Ah, she'll be happy with money. Anybody is happy with money. Money is a pretty terrific thing. I know, and boy, I'll bet a bottom dollar on it. (*Audience laughter*) Yeah, I'll say again. It's a pretty terrific thing.

MORENO: And now you fall asleep and snore. (*Audience laughter*) Go ahead, snore!

HELEN AS FATHER: (*Snores very loudly, interjecting whistles and all kinds of grunts and noises. Audience laughter*)

MORENO: (*Very loudly*) And now I am taking you far away from this house and I'm taking you into the house of your boss. He's with whom?

HELEN: His wife, I hope.

(*Audience laughter*)

MORENO: What's her name?

HELEN: Ruth. (*Lets out a joyous, musical kind of laughter*)

MORENO: All right you are your boss and you are his double. What's his name did you say?

HELEN: Mike.

MORENO: So Mike. Get yourself ready, Mike. How do you sleep?

HELEN: God knows! (*Giggles*)

MORENO: You mean you never saw him sleeping?

HELEN: (*Laughing loudly, with the audience joining her*) No.

MORENO: How old is Mike?

HELEN: Oh, about 46 or 47.

MORENO: All right, Mike, go to bed! What position do you have in bed?

HELEN: (*Whispering*) I don't know. (*There is a bit of confusion at this point.*)

MORENO: You just had a dream.

HELEN AS MIKE: Oh boy! I wish they'd come through with . . . Oh gee . . .

MORENO: Mike, Mike, Mike. Come on there!

HELEN AS MIKE: Yeah. We're going to come through with that lawsuit. You must wait and see.

DOUBLE: It's a mess too, I don't know how I'm going to come out with it.

HELEN AS MIKE: The third one this year! Oh I'll be glad when I get out on the road selling. I don't like this being in New York in the office. That office can take care of itself. It's got a good staff.

DOUBLE: I don't know about that.

HELEN AS MIKE: I feel better out there. I have a better time out on the road.

DOUBLE: I might have a better time, but I'm not so sure that the office is being taken care of. My God, there sure are a lot of scatterbrains around. Think of that Helen!

HELEN AS MIKE: Ah, what do you mean? She's the only good possibility in that office. (*Laughs. The audience laughs, too.*) Well, I don't know, but I think that girl is getting up in the world.

DOUBLE: But she's so young and so scatterbrained!

HELEN AS MIKE: Ah, I think she's a pretty shrewd kid. She's going to start shoving a few people around out there. She's shoving already.

DOUBLE: But that's not what I want. I want her to get shoved once in a while.

HELEN AS MIKE: (*Not seeming to listen*) Boy, she certainly is learning fast how to shove. She certainly has learned how to handle those people. Gets along fine with them too. She'll make a terrific saleswoman. She's always got a smile ready. That's it, she knows how to enjoy herself. They're a bunch of old maids in the office.

DOUBLE: Well, what's the difference. She'll probably get married and then I'll lose her anyway.

HELEN AS MIKE: The difference between her and those girls is that they think they can tell me what to do. And they usually do. Boy, that Kay! She really runs the show. In fact I think she wishes that I' wouldn't be there most of the time. Well, I'm not going to be there.

DOUBLE: Kay won't be there either.

HELEN AS MIKE: Yeah, I think I'd like to see someone else shove her around for awhile.

DOUBLE: Maybe Helen will be the one to do it.

HELEN AS MIKE: Yeah, maybe she'll be the one. She'd be a darn sight better to look at than that girl. And above all, she would listen to me.

(*Audience laughter*)

DOUBLE: Yeah, maybe I can shove her around a bit.

HELEN AS MIKE: But then again, a girl like that probably wouldn't stay as long as Kay did.

HELEN AS MIKE: True, it has possibilities.

MORENO: And so, Helen, you return back to your own room and you are again in your own bed and you are again back with your double and you are again falling asleep. (*HELEN turns over, making herself comfortable; she is absolutely relaxed*)

HELEN: Oh boy.

MORENO: Helen, you are both falling deep asleep, both of you. When you fall asleep you dream, don't you, Helen? You had a dream just the other day, didn't you?

HELEN: I don't remember.

MORENO: Well, why don't you try to remember? You had a dream. It was a beautiful dream which you had.

HELEN: Oh, Gee . . .

MORENO: A long time ago.

HELEN: Oh yeah, a long time ago.

MORENO: You remember that dream don't you?

HELEN: Oh, it was in technicolor. I just couldn't forget it.

MORENO: Well! A dream in technicolor! What does it mean?

(*Hearty audience laughter*)

HELEN: Well, it was like this . . .

MORENO: Let's not talk about it. Let's see it. (*Instructs auxiliary ego to leave. She returns to her seat in the auditorium*) All right now, close your eyes! Close your eyes! And try to concentrate on that dream! Concentrate . . . Do you have a perception of it? All right. Now how do you sleep in bed? What position do you have?

HELEN: Usually on my right side.

MORENO: How are you dressed in bed? What do you wear?

HELEN: Pajamas.

MORENO: What kind of pajamas do you wear?

HELEN: Flannel pajamas in the winter time and shantung in the summer time.

MORENO: What is it now, summer or winter?

HELEN: Winter.

MORENO: So what do you have on?

HELEN: The flannels.

MORENO: Are they comfortable?

HELEN: Oh, they are wonderful!

(*Audience laughter*)

MORENO: And so you are very comfortable now. Right? Do you stretch your legs in bed? What do you do?

HELEN: (*Her voice very high*) Ohhhh! Folded up slightly.

MORENO: All right, fold them up slightly.

HELEN: (*She sighs contentedly*) Mmm.

MORENO: And so here we are and you are trying to fall asleep. Try to fall asleep, deep asleep. And here she is. And she is concentrating. Can you see the dream? And before we fall asleep we usually think of something or other. We have all kinds of images.

HELEN: (*Shakes head dubiously*) Well . . .

MORENO: Nothing goes through your head as you fall asleep?

HELEN: No.

MORENO: All right now, you are falling asleep, deep asleep and you are concentrating on that dream which you had on that winter evening. Concentrate! (*Very loudly*) Concentrate on that dream. What is the first thing which you see before your eyes when you have that dream?

HELEN: Blue sky.

MORENO: (*Loudly*) Blue sky! And you? What are you doing? Sitting down, standing up?

HELEN: I . . . don't . . . (*slight hesitancy*) I'm watching.

MORENO: You're watching. Can you see yourself standing or sitting?

HELEN: Just walking.

MORENO: Then get up and walk. Walk, just as you walked in the dream! (*HELEN gets up to walk*)

MORENO: Is this how you walk in the dream? In that direction?

HELEN: No not in this way, but this way. (*Reverses direction*)

MORENO: Do you see yourself?

HELEN: Yes, I see myself moving.

MORENO: Then move! Move on! (*HELEN moves around the stage*)

MORENO: Do you see anything?

HELEN: Very tall, dark green trees.

MORENO: Where are these trees?

HELEN: On both sides.

MORENO: Which side?

HELEN: Both sides.

MORENO: Green trees, what kind of trees are they?

HELEN: They're very tall and very green. They seem to be sycamore trees.

MORENO: Very tall and green. And you don't see yourself?

HELEN: (*Shakes head in the negative*)

MORENO: Do you see anything else aside from the trees?

HELEN: I see benches . . . Benches of white marble.

MORENO: Where are they? Touch them!

HELEN: (*HELEN touches them*)

MORENO: How high are they?

HELEN: About two feet high.

MORENO: How big are the trees? How high?

HELEN: Oh very high, about fifteen feet.

MORENO: And are they different from one another?

HELEN: No they are all exactly alike.

MORENO: How are they placed? Show us.

HELEN: (*Demonstrates to the audience*) They are lined on both sides. Making a sort of path. (*Moves her hands along her sides, swings them from the rear to the front of the stage*)

MORENO: Lined on both sides. How many of them are there? Count them!

HELEN: One, two, three—eight on each side. (*She has her eyes half closed in concentration*)

MORENO: How far are you from them?

HELEN: I'm far back.

MORENO: Back! Back!

HELEN: I'm, I'm standing here. Back! And they're all down there about five feet away. And I'm looking at all of this.

MORENO: You are looking at all the benches and the trees. And what are you doing? Are you moving?

HELEN: I'm standing in the middle; but back, not in it.

MORENO: And how do you feel about it?

HELEN: I feel I'd like to go . . . it's so peaceful and so quiet and I feel that I'd like to go right into it.

MORENO: Do you go into it?

HELEN: (*Very high voice*) No, I'm walking toward it.

MORENO: Then walk to it. Then go . . . (*HELEN walks, suddenly stops*)

HELEN: (*Interrupting*) But, but I don't get in.

MORENO: What happens then?

HELEN: (*In a low voice*) Someone is calling me back.

MORENO: (*Almost whispering*) Someone is calling you back. Once, twice.

HELEN: Several times.

MORENO: Go back and take the part of that voice. (*HELEN does so*)

HELEN AS VOICE: I am the voice.

MORENO: Are you a man or a woman?

HELEN AS VOICE: I am a woman.

MORENO: Do you hear the voice?

HELEN: No, I mean, I heard the voice.

MORENO: You mean you hear the voice. Let's hear the voice!

HELEN: It's melodious. It's like music and it calls me back.

(*MORENO calls an auxiliary ego, who comes upon the stage to present the voice in a different version*)

VOICE: Helen. Come back, Helen come back.

MORENO: Is that the way the voice sounds?

HELEN: No. It doesn't use those words. It says, "Come on back, come on back. Come on back; here we are. Don't go out there!"

VOICE: Come on back, here we are. Come on back.

HELEN: It's not pleading.

MORENO: It's what?

HELEN: It's just telling me.

VOICE: Come back. Come on back; come on back where we are. Don't go out there.

HELEN: This is the voice repeating the same words.

(*The audience all participate in calling her, imitating the voice*)

ALL: Come back, come back, here we are!

MORENO: And what do you do?

HELEN: (*Simply*) I go back!

MORENO: And then you go back?

HELEN: Yeah.

MORENO: Do you see anybody?

HELEN: No.

MORENO: Do you still hear the voice as before?

HELEN: No.

MORENO: And what do you do now?

HELEN: I want to go back and try to go back. (*HELEN suddenly stops near stage door*)

MORENO: You try to go back.

HELEN: But I just can't.

MORENO: (*Walking up to her and taking her hand*)

If you would have had the power to continue the dream, how would you have continued it? We will give you the privilege here to experience the dream the way you want it. We give you the poetic license to continue it, to end it the way you would have liked to end it. Go back to bed now! You're going to continue the dream. Go on dreaming! The last thing in the dream which you see are the trees. Is that right? Beautiful, tall trees, right? What goes on next?

HELEN: I don't know.

MORENO: All right, take the position which you have in the dream, now. Is this the position which you have in the dream? (*HELEN gets back to bed*) All right, you are still dreaming. You have not awakened yet. So what do you do now?

HELEN: I go back to the voice.

VOICE: Come back, Helen. Don't go there. Come back to us!

HELEN: I go back of my own free will.

MORENO: So you go back.

VOICE: Come on back. Don't go. That's it, Helen. That's the girl!

MORENO: Whose voice is it that talks to you?

HELEN: My mother's, I think. I wasn't sure when I dreamed it, but now I know.

MORENO: Does it sound like your mother's voice?

HELEN: No, I feel that it is.

MORENO: Why don't you change parts now. (*To auxiliary ego*) You take the part of Helen. (*To HELEN*) You take the part of the voice. (*They reverse roles*) Say it again now, and see for sure whose voice it is. You know how it should be spoken. All right, Helen.

HELEN AS VOICE: Come back, Helen! Helen, come back! Come on back, Helen! Helen, come back!

MORENO: (*Ending role reversal*) You are back now. Feel better, now that you are back?

HELEN: Yeah, I guess so. It is my mother's voice, I am sure.

MORENO: That is what you want to do. You want to go to Mamma.

HELEN: (*A surprised laugh*) Gee, I never thought of it that way!

MORENO: You didn't think of it that way. But that is what you are doing. (*Auxiliary ego returns to her own seat*) As the double operates we can imagine the profound implications which it has because we saw how we moved the double and how it is related to these different role processes—how we moved the double from the mother to the father to [the employer] till we had the total configuration. We saw all the people in her mind, the people with whom she lives. We thus see the perception that she has of her social world. So we became acquainted with her world. We saw how the double moves from its earliest moment of living. We don't really know what happens in the baby's mind during the nine months of pregnancy. Of course all this is in the realm of theory. We know what happens physiologically and anatomically. We know the great thing which happens at birth. The decision to go out from the dark world into a beautiful world of colors and lights, in technicolor. This is how it started for you 21 years ago. And that is the first relationship that we have to anyone which is within the matrix of identity, to that other which is a part of you, of which you are a part, and that is what we call the double. And that of course has been exemplified and developed into a method of treating people who have lost their contacts. You are returning to the most intimate, to the most exclusive, and to the most sensitive relationship which we have: the first thing to which we belong, the matrix of identity. When we work with so-called catatonic patients or when we work with so-called schizophrenic patients and suddenly they make a grimace, then the auxiliary ego makes a grimace too. We thus give them an experience which is that of someone understanding what goes on in the patient's mind. Maybe the patient has a tic, or a way of moving her head or shaking it. Now, as you do it in the double technique you begin to come closer to that person and then as you do it, maybe she will also begin to shake her head. Now, for instance, you see the doubles eating together. Many situations can be doubled up in the life of the patient in order to understand the patient's feeling. Often you don't know what they are. As you are moving into her action matrix you begin to experience the same thing that the patient experiences. Now, of course, this double technique must be studied with a great deal of care. Double research and double therapy are important developments which we need for certain types of patients whom we cannot analyze, with whom we can only work in action. These techniques are action techniques!

And now after we have seen the double we go to the mirror technique, which relates to an infant in a far later stage of development.

The next step is for the infant to look and to see something in the water or in a mirror. It sees another baby. The baby smiles when you smile and moves when you move. And when you cry, Mommy comes in to bring you the bottle. This happens to you—it happens also in the mirror.

Now, Helen, you sit down. You look very sweet in the mirror, as I look at you. You have fixed yourself up very nicely. She has earrings on and all the things that belong to a pretty girl. How do you know that you have earrings on? Can you see them?

HELEN: I can feel them!

MORENO: Well, and so here you are now and you look into the mirror. You see, to have a double is one thing. There you are in the matrix of identity. Then in the course of time you begin to pay more attention to certain things. That there are certain things which are nearer to you and things which are more separated from you. When they are hurt, you are not hurt. You hurt them. They hurt you. You see, when you have a double and you hurt it, you hurt yourself. But when you begin to hurt somebody and the pain exists and is felt outside of yourself, then of course there is a separation between you and that object.

Helen, let me explain to you what we are trying to do. You see, we are studying a person who cannot act herself. We are studying how she gets up in the morning, how she acts towards her mother, towards her father. Now she herself can't show us because she is too sick to act for herself. She is in a stupor, so we take someone, an auxiliary ego, a nurse, who enacts it for her, like a mirror while she herself is sitting in the audience. You understand?

(*GEORGE raises his hand*)

MORENO: Yes?

GEORGE: I have a request to make. Would you let me make a telephone call to Helen on stage? I think it will be very significant.

MORENO: Now you see this young man here wants to act.

GEORGE: It's all for her benefit.

MORENO: Yes, yes of course! You will have your turn. (*Audience laughter*) It's a very interesting thing, and a very interesting phenomenon about audiences but people come, and they have an idea and a desire to act for themselves. And that's a very wonderful thing because it shows how infectious psychodramatic sessions are. They have an enormous amount of action in them which must have some kind of an outlet.

Now after the patient has been observed, then of course that particular individual will then produce particular activities which she has observed in the course of time. The patient will then see himself or herself in action. All right now, here comes Helen. Helen, you are the client. Let's hear the situation which you want to have portrayed.

HELEN: I'm not satisfied with the raise I got for Christmas.

(*The real HELEN seats herself in the audience and the "MIRROR HELEN," an auxiliary ego, steps upon the stage to take HELEN'S part, after a short talk with HELEN*)

MIRROR HELEN: Well, how do you like that? A three dollar raise. What nerve he had! Boy, is he cheap! Giving me a three dollar raise. I'm certainly worth more than that! What a cheapskate. I ask for a ten dollar raise and I get—

MORENO: (*Interrupting*) You see the ego portraying a client sitting in front of her with a problem the client actually has. This is not just "playing." Do you understand why we do it, Helen? (*HELEN, in audience, shakes head*) Well, I'll tell you. When a person looks at himself and sees himself looking ugly, he may try to do something about it. We want him to become provoked by the mirror. That is one reason we use this technique. The mirror portrays you in a distorted way. You may become angry with it because it does not appear to be you. We often notice about patients (*as well as with non-patients*) that they have a false perception of themselves. The technique has achieved its aim if the patient realizes that a mirror of him is attempted. If some part seems distorted or misrepresented, they step in and interfere with the mirror. They tell the portraying ego that he is an imposter! That is exactly what we want from a person who has been mute and uncooperative and non-active, in order to get him going. And so, we would like to get you active. So let's do it all over again. Now you get into action yourself.

HELEN: But I don't know if that is the way I really am because I don't see myself.

MORENO: But you see Helen!!

HELEN: (*Interrupting*) My reaction?

MORENO: Yes, I want to show these nurses here how the mirror technique is used. You will show it to them, as we are here to help each other, and you help me to demonstrate. Have you ever been in a mental hospital, Helen?

HELEN: (*Shakes head*) No.

MORENO: No, well some patients are difficult to handle. Many of them don't know that they are sick. (*Audience laughter*) So like a patient, it is true that you are now rather cynical, after having been coaxed and having people try to make you cooperate.

HELEN: (*Pointing to auxiliary ego*) Should I contradict her right away?

MORENO: When you feel that is not just quite the way that you would do it.

MIRROR HELEN: Boy, some nerve. Just a three dollar raise. I better go and talk to him. But what am I going to say? Gee, I'm scared in a way. Three dollars! I'm not going to let them do that to me. Who do they think I am? If he thinks he can step all over me, he'll be sorry. He'll find out soon enough that he's knocking at the wrong door. I got to talk to him. What if he refuses me? What will I do then?

MORENO: Here's the boss.

(*Motions to GEORGE to come on the stage and take the boss role*)

MIRROR HELEN: Mr. Calbata, Mr. Calbata, you know three dollars, you know, I'm very surprised. (*Hesitating*) I . . . I . . . thought that you were more satisfied with me. (*Seemingly embarrassed*) Wouldn't you . . .

REAL HELEN: (*Interrupting*) No, no, she's not . . . No! That's not like me. She's showing him that she's scared.

MIRROR HELEN: (*Coyly*) Hello Mr. Calbata, I guess you know why I'm here.

MR. CALBATA: Why, no. I had no idea.

MIRROR HELEN: Well I thought you were satisfied with me. I was surprised when I got my pay last week. You've put me in the showroom so I was very surprised when I received my pay last week. A three dollar . . . Don't you think that I deserve a bit more?

MR. CALBATA: Well, business isn't too good at present, you know and I don't think the firm could stand an added burden on its pay roll.

MIRROR HELEN: Considering the fact that you've given me added responsibility I really feel . . .

MR. CALBATA: Well perhaps if you stay a little longer and business improves we'll be able to take better care of you. In the meantime . . .

(*Real HELEN is looking rather anxious and displeased with the course of events*)

MORENO: All right, Helen, go ahead if you're not satisfied.

HELEN: (*Hesitating*) Well, I wouldn't. I . . .

MORENO: Go ahead! Contradict her! It's your act.

(*Real Helen goes on stage and pushes MIRROR HELEN away*)

HELEN: I'm sure you must be pleased because you wouldn't have given me a job in the showroom. You said yourself that you were surprised at the leaps and bounds that I've jumped. I've only been here a year. I didn't ask to be put in the showroom. I really deserve a raise and I can't wait till Christmas for another raise.

MR. CALBATA: You wanted the work in the showroom, didn't you?

(*HELEN shakes her head in disapproval*)

MORENO: Does your real boss act the same way?

HELEN: Oh no!

MORENO: All right then, reverse roles.

HELEN: Well, first he would offer me a chair. (*She pulls out a chair and has ego, in the part of HELEN, sit down*)

MORENO: (*To HELEN*) What's your name?

HELEN: Mr. Calbata.

MORENO: (*To ego*) What's your name?

AUXILIARY EGO: Helen.

(*Audience laughter*)

HELEN AS MR. CALBATA: Well when you came here you already had a five dollar raise. After all . . . You know, Dr. Moreno, he doesn't know this so, I'll answer for him.

MORENO: Oh no you don't! He knows all right.

HELEN AS MR. CALBATA: True, when you came you said you expected $45 and we said we would start you off with $40 on trial. Well, when I discussed it with the rest of the people, the accountant and the secretary, they said that you already had a five dollar raise and they all felt that would be sufficient. You know, Helen, how satisfied I am with you and how I appreciate the fine job that you have been doing. But I'll tell you what. When I come back from the road about May or so, I'll have you put in the showroom and get someone else to take charge of your secretarial duties. Then I'll give you a really substantial raise. Don't let these few dollars bother you. You can trust me to take care of you. You're doing an excellent job. And who knows . . . maybe someday you'll fill in Miss Kay's place.

MORENO: What's the matter with you, George?

(*GEORGE in the part of HELEN, has been sitting, mouth open, throughout this whole dialogue. Audience laughter*)

MORENO: Why have you been sitting about? She, or rather he, hypnotized you?

HELEN AS MR. CALBATA: A few dollars can't mean that much to you, Helen. I can give you those few dollars, you know, Helen. But personally I think you will be better off if you wait till May.

MORENO: Go on, there (*to GEORGE, who still can't utter a word. Audience laughter*)

HELEN AS MR. CALBATA: Well, I know things will be all right and that they will work out and when I come back in May then you'll really be able to see how satisfied I am with you. Don't let it bother you. Now, Helen, let me tell you a bit about selling in that showroom—and off on a tangent we go.

(*Audience applause*)

MORENO: Fine. Well, look at George. He's hypnotized now. Does he always act like that when you're around?

HELEN: It's Mr. Calbata's effect upon him. He's a very hypnotizing person.

MORENO: Are you still working for him?

HELEN: Sure am!

MORENO: What happened to the raise?

HELEN: He came over to me the following day and said, "If it'll make you happier, here."

MORENO: You saw that even when the mirror is used on a person who is as regular as Helen, there is a violent response when things aren't done correctly. She couldn't sit there quietly when she saw her own self and her own life misrepresented. Now misrepresentation is at times often very subjective. I don't know if I've ever told you that the mirror is frequently used in mental hospitals. At one time a doctor at one of the mental hospitals had very great difficulties with the treatment of a non-cooperative homicidal patient. Eventually he manipulated the patient, Bill, into a psychodramatic session. Using the mirror technique, he reconstructed a situation during the war in which Bill was involved. His platoon was decimated, but he came out of it without any physical injury. It was in connection with this military action that Bill was decorated for bravery. Shortly afterwards, however, he became mentally ill, was a very sick boy, and was sent to a mental hospital. Now, as the action progressed on the stage he looked up somewhat bewildered—he did not hear his name mentioned in connection with the battle, although it was obviously his story. The mirror for Bill was portrayed by an auxiliary ego, an aide who had been in close contact with Bill for several weeks. He heard instead another name mentioned—the name of his closest buddy, Jack (*an auxiliary ego acting for Jack*). It was Jack who was running there. Jack was fighting. Jack was a hero. Jack received the medal. The patient got up, pushed Jack aside, and said, "It's all a lie! It's me! I did it—not him! This is how it happened!" And then the real psychodrama began.

So you see how the mirror warmed him up and got him into the production. And that is where therapy in the form of the mirror is useful (*because it is a real problem to the person for whom it is portrayed*).

It was a slight change in pattern which provoked and aroused the warm up, and not simple recapitulation. At times simple recapitulation of a traumatic situation is sufficient. Often a slight change in the story is needed to motivate the warm up. But if the distortion is too great nothing happens. Of course, in a mental hospital there are hundreds of situations which can be portrayed. A large group of veterans with similar problems can be brought together as a group. You can see how the mirror can be applied on the group level. It isn't only Bill and Jack; there are others who have gone through similar situations.

Now, let us show them the technique of role reversal.

HELEN: (*Laughing and with a slight moan*) Oh, no!

MORENO: The technique of role reversal is a far more mature technique. We've discussed the behavior of infants. In order to experience the reversal properly they must be able to separate themselves from their surrounding individuals. Now the matrix of identity has been broken up, and the mirror has established itself. The child can move now into the mirror and take the part of the mirror child; the mirror child can move out of the mirror and take the part of the real child. This is really the next step in the genesis of the technique. First comes the matrix of identity, with the double, then the mirror, with the self. And now the reversal, with the other self. The reversal, of course, is often used in matrimonial problems. I imagine you will be married soon; right Helen?

HELEN: We're friends, that's all. Very good friends.

MORENO: She's a very smart girl. She just says "we're friends." By the way, how many friends do you have? (*Audience laughter*) Not many? What's the matter with you, George. She says "not many." Why don't you take over from here? (*GEORGE shakes his head. He doesn't quite know what to say*) Give us a little insight into the present dilemma of you two? What is going on between the two of you?

HELEN: We have a very good friendship. If I find something that he would like I take him there, and if he finds something that I would like he takes me there.

MORENO: All right then, now let's start with that. You create any situation.

(*HELEN laughs and giggles*)

GEORGE: All right . . . (*takes the initiative*) I'm making a phone call.

MORENO: Go ahead, make your call. By the way, how old are you?

GEORGE: I'm 22.

MORENO: And you, Helen?

HELEN: 21.

MORENO: Together you are how old?

HELEN: 43.

MORENO: That's good enough.

(*Audience laughter*)

MORENO: Are you still living with your parents?

GEORGE: Yes.

MORENO: Brother?

GEORGE: Yes.

MORENO: Sister?

GEORGE: She's married. She just moved away.

MORENO: Helen, do you know his family?

HELEN: No.

MORENO: Do you know her family, George?

GEORGE: Yes.

MORENO: Whom do you know in her family?

GEORGE: I know her mother, father, and brother. (*Audience laughter*)

MORENO: He always knows everything on her side. Why doesn't he introduce you to his people?

HELEN: He comes to my apartment. I don't go to his.

GEORGE: She came to my store once but they weren't there.

MORENO: Was it an empty store?

GEORGE: No, one of the men was there.

MORENO: Oh I see. You fixed it that way?

(*Audience laughter*)

MORENO: And so you are here and you're making a telephone call?

GEORGE: I'm in the the store making a phone call.

MORENO: All right, go ahead. Where's the store?

GEORGE: In New York City.

MORENO: And where is she?

GEORGE: In her apartment.

MORENO: (*To HELEN*) Then go to your apartment. That's it! (*HELEN goes over to the left of the stage*) How many times do you call her?

GEORGE: Mmm. Once in a while she calls me and once in a while I call her. I would say about once every month.

MORENO: All right, call her.

GEORGE: (*Dials the number*) Hello, Helen?

HELEN: Yes?

GEORGE: How are you?

HELEN: How are you today?

GEORGE: O.K. Boy, our last meeting was pretty swell.

HELEN: Yeah, it certainly was. We really have to talk about that. I got notes all over the program.

GEORGE: Well, I don't know when we could talk about it.

HELEN: Oh, don't you want to go to the next meeting with me?

GEORGE: No, I wasn't thinking about that. It was, oh well . . . Whenever I've asked you to go out with me sort of on a Friday or Saturday night you've always hesitated. I've always wanted . . .

(*HELEN interrupts with a giggle*)

MORENO: Change parts, now you have the reversal technique. Try always to use a strategic moment for the reversal. Go ahead!

HELEN: Shall I do it just the way he did?

MORENO: Absolutely. You start from the point where he left off. Go ahead. (*MORENO claps his hand. To* GEORGE) And you start from the point where she left off.

HELEN AS GEORGE: You are always sort of hesitant about it. Are you getting married or something? Just wondering. You're willing to go to meetings with me but you don't seem to want to make it more social. Is there anything wrong?

GEORGE AS HELEN: (*Pausing*) No, not exactly. I'm not going steady. It's just that I'd like to see you on a friendship basis. (*Pause*) More or less.

HELEN AS GEORGE: That's fine. Let's make a friendship out of it. I want to go out with you. Let's make it Friday night.

GEORGE AS HELEN: No parking or stuff like that.

HELEN AS GEORGE: Parking is not a prerequisite of going out. It's just a matter of . . . you feel its expected of you, so you park. You react . . . well, you're afraid that maybe a girl will think that there's something wrong with her if you don't.

GEORGE AS HELEN: (*Hesitating*) Well . . .

(*Audience laughter*)

MORENO: (*Interrupting*) Change parts!

GEORGE: Well, after all, if you go out with a girl it isn't as though you were checking your hat. Of course it depends on how you feel about the girl.

HELEN: I'm just telling you the facts. (*Pauses*) I don't want you to feel that you're wasting your time. If you want to keep it company and just company, fine, you're welcome anytime. I thoroughly enjoy your company. But if you feel that going out on a Friday or Saturday night means necking or the general thing . . . that goes with Friday or Saturday nights, then . . . (*Audience laughter*) I'll go to meetings with you.

GEORGE: Of course you have a point there. Girls do have a problem. Because after all if a girl does go out with a boy she doesn't know why he is going with her. Whether it's for her or whether it's because of what he'd like to do. Of course there is one solution, you could say, well, O.K. I won't do anything with any boy and as a result if a boy goes with me then I'll really know that he likes me. That could be one solution.

HELEN: I don't think I have to find out whether you like me or not. I like your company, we have a fine time together. I thoroughly enjoy speaking to you and well . . . (*pause*) I enjoy speaking to you. (*Audience laughter*) I have a very interesting evening of it, but I just want you to know that there is nothing else, and I don't want you to feel that I led you to expect something.

GEORGE: What makes you think that it's like hammering against a stone wall, for instance?

HELEN: (*Whispers*) What stone wall? Oh, now I'm beginning to know!

(*Audience laughter*)

MORENO: Change parts!

GEORGE AS HELEN: I like our friendship the way it is, and I think we should keep it this way.

HELEN AS GEORGE: Fine, I didn't say I wanted to keep it any other way. It's just that I thought you'd like me to take you out on a Saturday night and most of the time all I see you at is meetings and then all we talk about is politics. I thought you might want to talk about something else and go for a drive. And just because . . . Oh, what do you expect to find, something separate in each person, a conversationalist, a tennis player?

GEORGE AS HELEN: Of course you know I told this to other boys and they don't like it at all. They won't go out with me anymore. And I think people can be very diversified and you can find some things in some individuals and you can find something else in others.

HELEN AS GEORGE: (*Very sophisticated tone*) What I would like to know is . . . (*Short pause*)

MORENO: How much did this telephone call cost?

(*Audience laughter*)

GEORGE: My father pays for it. He doesn't know yet how much it was.

HELEN AS GEORGE: What I would like to know is, if this holds true for everyone, or do things run differently with other people? Its just a question of curiosity.

GEORGE AS HELEN: Of course, naturally the same things don't apply to everybody. But there could be a difference that applies to different people.

HELEN: (*In own role, laughing*) It doesn't sound like George but me! (*Back in GEORGE's role*) I just wanted to bring out the fact.

MORENO: (*Interrupting*) Finish the phone call! Change parts.

GEORGE: Of course, you know when a boy goes out with a girl it sort of makes him feel peculiar to know that she is going out with other fellows and that different things happen with them. But look, how about Friday night; we're going down to see Dr. Moreno. I think I mentioned him to you before.

HELEN: Well, O.K., pick me up Friday night.

GEORGE: About 8:30?

HELEN: No, 8 o'clock.

GEORGE: O.K., I'll be there. On time.

MORENO: Thank you very much, both of you. You were very helpful. Well, now. Helen is very lovely, Come on back; don't go away yet. (*Laughter*) Well, these techniques were demonstrated so that you may be able to apply them in your professional work. Moreover, in the meantime something happened which is very significant for psychodramatic sessions. We became acquainted with what is called in technical language a dyad. A dyad is a pair, a couple of people in a group. And you see there how they are interwoven in their feelings. However, at the same time we became acquainted with two very fine people (*To HELEN and GEORGE*): I think that you did very well. You certainly have been a great service to us. You gave us a very vivid illustration with your native spontaneity of what we wanted you to do. I'm sure that all of us are very appreciative. If your mother had been here, Helen, what would she have thought of it?

HELEN: I think she would have been a little disturbed.

MORENO: Because mothers don't like to see their girls grow up so fast as you.

HELEN: I don't think she would like to see me on the stage in front of all these people.

MORENO: But these people are the world. You see that is exactly what we need. These people are a part of you and me. They are just people like you, and you give them a lot of your youth and of your warmth. I think your mother would say, deep down inside her heart, "She is really very good."

HELEN: She probably would.

MORENO: (*Laughing*) Thank you very much.

(*Applause*)

AUDIENCE MEMBER: Doctor, why did you pick Helen at the beginning? Was there anything about her which make you do it?

MORENO: Well, of course this is one of the frequent questions. Why do I pick certain people to go up on the stage? I started once to systematize it. Now this is an open group. I don't know who is coming. Of course, a good director has the responsibility of choosing a protagonist which will on the whole represent the group. Now, this was not so in Helen's case. I had no intention of running a regular session. I was asked to demonstrate and to introduce to a group of nurses some of the principles of psychodramatic procedures and to give what is called a didactic session. And so I thought anyone whom I might pick to illustrate the technique was good enough. You ask why I picked Helen. Well, of course, I'm always attracted to young women. I often pick girls anywhere between 18 and 75. (*Audience laughter*) To come back to Helen—well, she sat in the first row and

. . .

GEORGE: That was my fault.

MORENO: You put her there! (*Audience laughter*) He really did 90% of the job. He brought her here. He had all kinds of reasons for coming here tonight. Now here you come to a very dynamic element of why I picked Helen . . . From the point of view of microsociology, George set the stage. He wanted to treat her. I was merely a victim. (*Audience laughter*) The kind of session I run always differs with the type of group I have to deal with. Now, if you were all—let's say, psychiatrists—the usual procedure would be to have a presentation of psychological or psychotic problems. Now, I always try to fit the subject to the requirement of the group. In this particular group we had a group of nurses who specifically wanted to observe the various psychodramatic techniques in action. So any member of the group would have been sufficiently adequate to fulfill this purpose. We were very fortunate in having as talented and spontaneous a protagonist as Helen has been.

Now, every session has a period in which you warm up your audience, either by lecture or by questions. Then comes the second part of the sessions—the production. Of course, this was a didactic session and so you haven't seen an intensive psychodramatic procedure. Now, I invite you to participate and to respond to whatever has happened on the stage. Is there anyone who has something on his mind which affected him particularly about what he has just seen? Again, a true group participation cannot be confined to a discussion of other people. It always involves a giving and taking. It is not a discussion of general principles. That is not the point. On the group psychodramatic level you don't discuss Helen and George. You just participate with them and someone might join in and tell what happened to him five years ago. Someone else might say: "This could have happened to me," or "That is how my sister is." But let us not intellectualize at this point—to give analyses and points of view, et cetera. That is degrading. In other words: They have given much and they have a right to expect something from us. Remember that it is the function of group members to return the love which the protagonist has given. If you do that, then the group session will become very, very real instead of being flat and meaningless.

CHAPTER 15

An Experiment with Sociodrama and Sociometry in Industry

1951

> *Editor's note: This public session is of particular interest because it shows Moreno combining action methods with written sociometry. It also suggests the applicability of his approach in community settings, such as schools and business organizations.*

The problems of industry are not merely those of machines, of technological processes, or of scientific engineering. These are a part of the formal structure of the industrial concern. The best machines, the best scientific engineering, and the most carefully conceived technological processes are, however, meaningless without the adequate organization of personnel to implement the processes. Again, on the formal level, industrial concerns (and other types of organizations as well) devise tables of organization and designate the division of labor according to assigned formal statuses. The formal status is a title of office, and each status has associated with it certain expectations and norms of behavior. The table of organization usually takes a pyramidal form, there being few executive statuses at the top, and many worker statuses at

From *Sociometry* 14 (1951), 71-103. Co-authored with Edgar F. Borgatta.

the bottom. In the table of organization are visible the formal channels of communication. Such depiction of statuses is inadequate, however, to describe the operation of the industrial concern. The table of organization describes formal statuses, and there is no understanding implicit in such a formal structure of the changes and conditions which are set when personnel is placed to occupy the status positions. The table of organization is impersonal, and each status position may be filled by a score of different persons. The person is considered expendable, the status position is not.

The workers do not consider themselves as expendable items, replaceable at the whim of the person in the proper status position in the hierarchy of the industrial concern. They have expectations of their own, and these are by no means coincidental with those of the industrial concern.

In the overall view, two sets of interests may be seen to operate in the industrial concern. One set is associated with efficiency and the production of goods for a competitive market. The other set is associated with maintaining a standard of both living and working conditions. Historically, both these sets of interests have been considered as problem foci. On the one hand, plant operators and managers have attempted to find best organizations of men and machines towards the ideal of high efficiency, the latter frequently being measured in terms of cheapness of production, irrespective of whether this is achieved by reducing the cost of production method, of labor, or of materials. Associated with this, aside from the propaganda techniques and political and police methods used for this purpose, there grew up a branch of "science" which may be called "management psychology and sociology." In the class of management psychology we have such things as time-motion studies, organization studies, incentive studies, et cetera, where the avowed purpose is to find optimum production conditions rather than optimum working conditions. On the other hand, the public, the workers themselves, and groups of reformers from many sources have been interested in fostering the other set of interests. Laws controlling the work of women and children, hours of work, and working conditions stem from the pressures of public sentiment. The public sentiment may be activated by reformers; we recognize the work of writers, for example, and we do not underestimate the force of a play such as Hauptmann's The Weavers.*

One problem in the resolving of industrial conflicts of various sorts is to be found merely in the definition of the dichotomous interests. Thorstein Veblen is the man who has probably done most to popularize the dichotomy, and economists, however they regard his work, have given heed to his perceptive and penetrating books. The dichotomy of interests, given impetus in definition by Veblen and other writers, and finding its way into the general

*Naturalistic play by Gerhart Hauptmann (1862-1946) about Silesian weavers who revolted and were savagely suppressed. (Ed.)

thinking patterns of the public, is manifest in a particular condition. Management and workers have tended to find their interest as diametrically opposed rather than in any way congruent. These points of view, when accepted by the two parties, have tended to emphasize conflict, and in some ways have removed possibilities for resolving differences. Just as the classical economists thought of "economic man" (a hodgepodge of psychological tendencies which are a part of each and every man and which make him predictable in behavior), the groups allying themselves with the two sets of interests have tended to build stereotypes of each other. On the one hand, management interests have tended to stereotype the "worker," and conversely, the worker interests have tended to stereotype "management." The limitations of this procedure, which have frequently been given impetus by sociologists and psychologists, as well as economists during the last half century, are that the "worker" is not a uniform commodity, and that workers cannot be stereotyped and dealt with routinely as predictable in their behavior. Again, management is not always the bugaboo which it is generally made to be in the stereotype. The union may set itself up in opposition to "management," but the union is not synonymous with the "workers." The union itself may intrinsically provide additional situations for industrial problems, such as where the union becomes a vested interest in itself and apart from its membership. The interest of the union may become that of self-perpetuation in the existent form.

Such an introduction is not to disparage work which is done by the engineers who are concerned with the development of technological processes, nor those persons who deal with the formal structure of the industrial concern. What is obvious is that the human element, probably the most important, has been dismissed in the consideration of industrial problems, or has been relegated to the level of stereotypes of the cliches. The problem is one of human relationships—the focus of attention must be on interpersonal relationships. It is for this reason that sociometry, which has grown out of clinical practice on human relationships, is so well adapted to needs of the scientists and clinicians working in the industrial situation.

The interest in human relationships in industry on a large scale is rather recent. While economists wrote on the problem generations ago, while industrial psychologists have claimed a discipline for a generation, and while sociologists have been interested in group structure for half a century, the focus of attention by many disciplines in any concerted way has come about only in the last seventeen years, with the appearance of *Who Shall Survive? A New Approach to the Problem of Human Interrelations* by J. L. Moreno. In this volume, which may be said to be sociological and psychological in its approach, we have two great discoveries. The first is that people, surprisingly enough, do not necessarily respond to the stimuli to which they are expected to respond, and the second is that inside the formal structure of a community or of a plant there are to be found a myriad of informal structures. This book has served a great purpose in stirring up interest in many problem areas including the industrial one and stimulated Roethlisberger and Dickson, along with others like Wilbert E. Moore, W. F. Whyte, B. B. Gardner, Elton Mayo, C. Barnard, E. W. Bakke, D. C. Miller, B. M. Selekman, to mention but a few, to carry on further research in industry.*

This paper is the presentation of a session conducted at the Sociometric Institute, 101 Park Avenue, New York. The session was originally suggested by Dr. Theodore Jackson. Dr. Jackson made arrangements to bring together a number of persons working in various branches of industry who had special interest in dealing with industrial problems. Present at the session were personnel managers, consultants, public relations men, industrial psychologists, and a small number of students and other guests. The session here reported offers a two-fold type of analysis: (1) it provides one example of the type of work which can be done with sociometric techniques; and (2) as a direct by-product of the study of the group participating in the session, we may demonstrate how the processes of group formation may be studied with the aid of diagrams.

Forms were distributed to the group assembled in the theatre of the Sociometric Institute. These forms asked for name, industrial concern with which the person was connected, position in the firm, and two questions to be used in the construction of interaction diagrams. The first question requested a listing of all persons present at the session with whom the respondent was acquainted. The second question was the sociogram criterion: "In regard to a work situation in which you must make a decision, with which person or persons present would you like to consult?" Each member of the audience was asked to stand and introduce him- or herself. When the forms were completed, they were collected and set aside to be tabulated.

Moreno entered the theatre and the session began.

MORENO: In running a session of this kind, we have to have a situation which is actual. Therefore I am asking you, is there anyone here who has a problem within his own plant? A real problem. Have you?

AUDIENCE MEMBER NO. 1: Yes, I do, but not at my plant. It's a personal one.

MORENO: Well, I tell you, I'll give you an individual session later on. (*Audience laughter*) Is there anyone here who has a problem in his plant? What is yours?

AUDIENCE MEMBER NO. 2: I just got fired Wednesday night. I couldn't get along with the fellow over me.

MORENO: Where do you work?

AUDIENCE MEMBER NO. 2: I was working for P. W. Stores.

MORENO: What kind of a plant is that?

*This list comprises business executives, academics, and editors with a special interest in the human aspects of employer-employee relations. (Ed.).

AUDIENCE MEMBER NO. 2: That's an organization of retail stores.

MORENO: What kind of retail stores?

AUDIENCE MEMBER NO. 2: They sell women's wear.

MORENO: How long were you working there?

AUDIENCE MEMBER NO. 2: Three weeks.

MORENO: All right, problem number one. We'll call it "retail" problem. Is there anyone else who has an actual problem within his plant? All right, what do you have?

AUDIENCE MEMBER NO. 3: I don't know whether my problem really would fit. I am a public relations man.

MORENO: Public relations is business; what's your name?

AUDIENCE MEMBER NO. 3: Bryan. A group of school teachers came in to us some time ago and asked us to take on their problem. Their problem was one of trying to get wider recognition and increased salaries. They said to us that they had no money, but that they expected to raise the money in a matter of a week or ten days. That was a month ago. They have not as yet raised the money. My problem is that I have become so emotionally involved in their problem that I find myself working for them without fee. (*Audience laughter*)

MORENO: That's a very interesting situation. You are working without a fee because you got emotionally involved with a client. That happens also to doctors. That is problem number two: emotional involvement with a client and how to get out of it. Anyone might be in a similar situation. Now is there anyone else who has a real problem at the present time? (*No one answers*) I can see that you people have so many problems that you have amnesia for the time being. (*Audience laughter*) Well, nevertheless, we have two problems. Let's start right here. I would like you now to consider which of the two problems you would like to work out. Problem number one, the man who got fired. (*To AUDIENCE MEMBER NO. 2*) Now I want you to stand up and state your problem to the group, and we will then take a vote. The other gentleman will do the same.

AUDIENCE MEMBER NO. 2: (*Stands up, facing the group*) I have a problem of unsatisfactory relations with people I work with.

MORENO: That you got fired from a job. Have you been fired before?

AUDIENCE MEMBER NO. 2: No, never.

MORENO: Who would like to work out a problem of this type? Please raise your hand. For problem number one?

(*A vote is taken; the count is 19*)

MORENO: Let's take count of problem number two. Who is interested in problem number two?

(*Another vote is taken; the count is 6*)

MORENO: For problem number one we have 19 votes and for problem number two we have 6. That's quite a drastic difference. I'm going to ask you to reconsider both problems and to raise your hand once again. Who is for problem number one?

(*The count is taken again; the count is 17*)

MORENO: Two dropped out. What happened? Who did?

ZERKA MORENO: I did.

MORENO: Who else? You? Why did you drop out, Zerka?

ZERKA MORENO: Well I reconsidered and decided to change my mind. . .

MORENO: Changing your mind again! (*Audience laughter*) The group is the patient with a problem. In counselling of this kind the group is the client, so you have to know the structure of the group to let the group determine the problem, and also to determine which of the problems presented is the most interesting one for them. In other words, we are trying to get a problem which is most vital to the group. The more involvement there is in the problem, the better is the problem for you. Don't forget that I'm not the one who is in charge of this session. It is really you. I'm merely warming you up to yourself. It's sort of a reversal procedure. It looks as if I'm the one who is working so hard but it is really you who do the work. In a way we can say that we are in a similar position here as when we are doing group psychotherapy. In group psychotherapy, the group is the patient and so we have always to see that the group is warmed up to its own problem. Therefore as you have probably noticed, we took certain data in advance, in order to determine the structure of the group. We got your acquaintance diagram and your sociogram; they may give us clues when we analyze the session. Now if you are doctors, social doctors in your own plant, you will have to know the structure of the group with which you work. So all these steps are taken in logical sequence in accord with the requirement of the session. After we have determined the problem, we begin to work. It is obvious that this gentleman has a problem. (*MORENO goes over to the subject*) By the way what is your name?

AUDIENCE MEMBER NO. 2: Norton.

MORENO: Now I begin to work with Norton. He is the protagonist. He is first of all Norton, a private person, but then he also represents a collective man, of whom we have numerous duplications in the community: "the man who gets fired." So now tell me, is there anyone here who already has been fired and who was frustrated because of that experience of having been fired? Is there anyone here who is still frustrated because of that experience? (*To Bryan*) Don't worry, I won't use you. (*To another audience member*) You?

AUDIENCE MEMBER NO. 4: Yes, but I lost my frustration a long time ago.

MORENO: How long ago did that happen?

AUDIENCE MEMBER NO. 4: About five years ago.

MORENO: What kind of situation was it? How long did you work before you were fired?

AUDIENCE MEMBER NO. 4: Seven years.

MORENO: What kind of an organization was that?

AUDIENCE MEMBER NO. 4: Public relations.

MORENO: The same kind of business you are working in now? Are you married?

AUDIENCE MEMBER NO. 4: Yes.

MORENO: To the same woman?

AUDIENCE MEMBER NO. 4: Yes.

MORENO: Is she here?

AUDIENCE MEMBER NO. 4: Sure is. (*She is sitting next to him. Audience laughter*)

MORENO: So here we have two exponents of the same problem on both sides of the fence. And now we are moving once again to our primary protagonist. What was your name again?

AUDIENCE MEMBER NO. 2: Norton.

MORENO: (*Taking NORTON by the hand and leading him towards the stage. They are standing on the first step*) Norton, tell me, would you like to go back to that job, or is it all over?

NORTON: No, it is not all over.

MORENO: Why not?

NORTON: I still remember the situation and it affects me. It was very personal and important.

MORENO: What kind of situation is it in which you operate?

NORTON: (*Appears perplexed*)

MORENO: What kind of store is it?

NORTON: It's a chain of stores.

MORENO: What are you doing there?

NORTON: (*Apprehensive*) Are we going to act this out? (*Audience laughter*)

MORENO: Go ahead, just tell me what you are doing there.

NORTON: My official title is sort of a stock clerk.

MORENO: Who is your immediate supervisor?

NORTON: An individual named Morty (*Morton*).

MORENO: When you were fired, what type of situation was it? Can you reconstruct it? Who was there?

NORTON: He was there.

MORENO: Who else?

NORTON: An individual.

MORENO: Well, to whom are you directly responsible?

NORTON: To Morty and the other individuals who are working with me.

MORENO: Well, as far as the situation of actually losing the job is concerned, who was in that situation?

NORTON: Individuals in the office.

MORENO: But who fired you?

NORTON: I couldn't find out.

MORENO: Just a name. What will we call him? Any name?

NORTON: I don't know who it was.

MORENO: Let's call him Mr. X. Why don't you look around and pick a Mr. X for yourself.

NORTON: (*Appears to be peculiarly undecided*)

MORENO: Who would like to portray Mr. X in this situation? Anyone here? You look like a man who would make an excellent executive. Come on, you will be Mr. X. (*MORENO brings a member of the audience up on the stage*) Here he is! Is there anyone else you need in the situation?

NORTON: I need Morty in it.

MORENO: Morty . . . (*looking at the audience*) Is he a younger man or older man?

NORTON: An older man.

MORENO: Here he is. (*He picks out an older man from the audience*) You look just like a "Morty." (*Audience laughter*)

I will give you a few minutes to prepare the situation.

(*NORTON and his two auxiliary egos go towards the rear in order to reconstruct the scene*)

MORENO: We are moving towards this gentleman here (*the other protagonist who got fired*) If you will sit in front for a moment. (*The gentleman gets up and sits in the front row of the theatre*)

MORENO: And you were fired about 7 years ago. Exactly what happened?

AUDIENCE MEMBER NO. 4: A new man was brought in. Now I realize that he was probably a better man than I was.

MORENO: Who was he?

AUDIENCE MEMBER NO. 4: He was an ex-admiral.

MORENO: How much salary were you getting at the time?

AUDIENCE MEMBER NO. 4: $25,000.

MORENO: How many hours did you put in a day?

AUDIENCE MEMBER NO. 4: About 20 hours a day.

MORENO: Well you certainly weren't overpaid there! (*Audience laughter*) Tell me, what circumstances were there that you lost the job?

AUDIENCE MEMBER NO. 4: There were no circumstances. It was an organization of many people, and a few of them decided that they needed someone with a title of ex-admiral. They were absolutely right and I recognize that now. But at that time I thought they were all wrong.

MORENO: Why did you think they were wrong?

AUDIENCE MEMBER NO. 4: I felt they had no recognition of talent.

MORENO: What do you consider your most outstanding talent?

AUDIENCE MEMBER NO. 4: Intelligence, sincerity, hard work...

MORENO: Had you achieved something outstanding for the organization while you were working there?

AUDIENCE MEMBER NO. 4: I left an excellent record behind me and a good reputation in the field.

MORENO: How did they fire you?

AUDIENCE MEMBER NO. 4: There was an eight months period while I was training this man in the job.

MORENO: It took you by surprise?

AUDIENCE MEMBER NO. 4: Well, not completely.

MORENO: How much salary did you get after they fired you?

AUDIENCE MEMBER NO. 4: Six months.

MORENO: Did your wife know about it?

AUDIENCE MEMBER NO. 4: Yes sir.

MORENO: Why do you remember that incident so clearly?

AUDIENCE MEMBER NO. 4: It was the first time that I was ever fired in my life and a terrible blow to my pride.

MORENO: How old a man were you then?

AUDIENCE MEMBER NO. 4: Thirty-two.

MORENO: What did you actually do?

AUDIENCE MEMBER NO. 4: I had a staff of 40 or 50 people under me.

MORENO: In what executive capacity were you?

AUDIENCE MEMBER NO. 4: I was managing director.

MORENO: Was there any personal problem with any member of the group?

AUDIENCE MEMBER NO. 4: No.

MORENO: Was it entirely symbolic, would you say?

AUDIENCE MEMBER NO. 4: Yes.

MORENO: Are you entirely sure of that?

AUDIENCE MEMBER NO. 4: I am now; I wasn't then.

MORENO: How did you feel then?

AUDIENCE MEMBER NO. 4: Very unhappy.

MORENO: The job afterwards—how much did that pay?

AUDIENCE MEMBER NO. 4: There was quite a cut in my income. But I had that severance pay which helped matters quite a bit.

MORENO: Let's go back to that personal problem. Who was the man that fired you?

AUDIENCE MEMBER NO. 4: That was the admiral.

MORENO: The admiral himself? Is he still alive?

AUDIENCE MEMBER NO. 4: Yes, and as a matter of fact we are fairly good friends now.

MORENO: That's very nice to hear. All right, thank you very much. That was very interesting. (*The man goes back to his original seat*) Is there anyone else here who remembers being fired? You?

AUDIENCE MEMBER NO. 5: I do!

MORENO: Oh yes, of course.

AUDIENCE MEMBER NO. 5: What do you mean "of course"?

MORENO: I say "of course" because this is very natural, a frequent finding in group sessions. At first no one remembers and then after being warmed up, people begin to remember quite suddenly their previous collateral experiences. That is a sort of group contagion angle. We speak of a "network" in sociometry. Now what do you remember?

AUDIENCE MEMBER NO. 5: I was working for a newspaper.

MORENO: What newspaper?

AUDIENCE MEMBER NO. 5: The *World Telegram*.

MORENO: How long did you work there?

AUDIENCE MEMBER NO. 5: Four years.

MORENO: How many years ago was this?

AUDIENCE MEMBER NO: 5: About 11 years ago.

MORENO: What salary did you get?

AUDIENCE MEMBER NO. 5: About 75 dollars a week.

MORENO: Who fired you? A woman or man?

AUDIENCE MEMBER NO. 5: A man, the general manager.

MORENO: Do you have a better job now?

AUDIENCE MEMBER NO. 5: Much better.

MORENO: What are you working at now?

AUDIENCE MEMBER NO. 5: Public relations.

(*MORENO stops the interview here. NORTON and his two auxiliary egos have returned back on the scene*)

MORENO: Thank you. And now Norton... Tell me what is the situation? Where are you?

NORTON: We're in the stock room of P.W. Stores right here in New York City.

MORENO: Who is this gentleman?

NORTON: This is the individual who is my immediate supervisor.

MORENO: Who is the other individual?

NORTON: This is the individual who informs me that I have been fired and who has my pay in his pocket.

MORENO: Go ahead! Get into action just as it is! The scene begins.

MR. X: Who is Norton over here?

NORTON: Right here. Don't you remember me from the other day?

MR. X: No, I don't know you. I just looked up your name. How long have you been here now?

NORTON: Three weeks.

MR. X: I don't like to tell you this, but for a great number of reasons we think we will have to dispense with your services. If you will take this voucher up to the cashier . . .

NORTON: But why?!

MR. X: Well, a great many reasons, Norton. You just don't fit into the scheme of things.

NORTON: But I don't understand. My production has increased, and I have been improving right along.

MR. X: Well, that may be so within your own mind. But for a great number of reasons which are too numerous to state. . .(*rather impatiently*) So if you will take this voucher up to the cashier. . .

NORTON: What does Morty have to say to this? He's been working with me right along.

MORTY: Sorry, I have nothing to say about it. The decision has been made.

NORTON: But what are the reasons?

MORTY: I'm sorry but it seems that your work has not been satisfactory. (*There is an embarrassing silence*)

MR. X: (*Determined*) Let's not drag this out any longer. We have just told you that your services were unsatisfactory and "for a great number of reasons." One is...Well, you seem not to mix in with the group in the way you should. You carry some of your load of work, but most of the time it's wanting in a little more pep and initiative. You seem to have things on your mind that interfere with your work. Many instances when Morty asks you to do something, you don't actually do it wrong but you just convey the idea that you're not quite suited for it. So we better not discuss it any further.

NORTON: Couldn't you possibly give me another week of trial? I have only been here for three weeks.

MR. X: No. I'm sorry. Once the decision has been made we can't alter it.

MORTY: All right, Norton, I think we better call it quits.

NORTON: Suppose I see the head of the office here.

MORTY: We can't arrange that now.

NORTON: (Breaking out of role) Well, that individual does see me.

MORENO: All right, let's cut right here. I'd appreciate if you three men would stay right here on stage. Now tell me, Norton, as you are standing here and you know that they want to fire you, how do you feel?'

NORTON: I feel very disappointed in myself and in the firm and also my relations with the various people because of the fact that they notified me so suddenly.

MORTY: How do you feel about Morty? Look at him?

NORTON: I feel very distrustful of his attitude when he was friendly with me.

MORENO: How friendly was he? Did he ever go out with you?

NORTON: No, I didn't want to get personal with him because I had irritations with him. But he was friendly towards my progressing with my work.

MORENO: Did he believe that you were all right?

NORTON: He didn't seem to know too well whether I am all right, just that . . .

MORENO: Is there anything which he did towards you which stands out in your mind.

NORTON: Yes.

MORENO: Any specific thing?

NORTON: His continual nudging of me to do something.

MORENO: What do you mean by "nudging"?

NORTON: Well, if I was working at something he would come over to me and say "do it even better."

MORENO: What is your pay?

NORTON: $35 per week.

(The AUXILIARY EGO contributes to the interrogation)

MORTY: Didn't you say that you were also engaged in too much conversation with the rest of the people at work?

NORTON: Well, during the time I was supposed to rest I talked the same way you did.

MORENO: (Walking over towards MR. X) Confidentially, what is the matter with Norton? Why don't you keep him?

MR. X: The way I see it he seems to have other problems on his mind which keep him from putting his whole self into his job.

MORENO: What kind of problems?

MR. X: Problems of, oh, maybe "some other occupation after work" that keeps his mind off his work.

MORENO: Has someone informed you of this?

MR. X: Yes, Norton himself.

MORENO: What kind of work is he doing in the evening?

MR. X: School in the evening, which is useful, of course. But it seems to me that it is just too much for him and he can't put his whole self into the job. He is also an individual who doesn't fit in with the rest.

MORENO: Morty, what personal experience have you had with Norton?

MORTY: Well, he just doesn't put his whole heart into the job the way he should.

MORENO: Did he do any specific thing?

MORTY: He doesn't carry out the assignments quite as readily as he should and he'll stop, talk, and listen to the other people and that has caused quite a bit of delay in getting jobs done and thus he throws the others off balance.

MORENO: Norton, how many others depend upon you with their job?

NORTON: There is no one that is subordinate to me. You can't put your finger upon one person because we all depend upon each other in the work.

MORENO: Is there anyone who squealed on you? Who carried information about you?

NORTON: I squealed on myself.

MORENO: Now, you take the boss's situation. You are now the boss, Norton, and I want to talk to you.

(NORTON changes his position and takes the part of the boss)

MORENO: What do you think is the trouble with Norton? You are now your own boss, Norton, remember. You have the part of the boss. Tell me now what happened that compelled you to fire that boy?

NORTON AS MR. X: He didn't get along with other people in the organization as well as...(There is a pause here and NORTON seems to be groping for words) The fact that he brought up an issue.

MORENO: Which issue did he bring up?

NORTON: The fact that I was getting too much pay for my work. (NORTON has fallen out of role and answers as NORTON instead of MR. X)

MORENO: You, yourself, how much do you get paid?

NORTON: $35 a week. Well there is a fellow in my office...

MORENO: (Interrupting) Who are you now? You're not Norton, I'm talking to the boss, not to Norton.

(NORTON often falls out of the role when the subject matter becomes "hot"—i.e., very personal and intimate)

MORENO: How much do you get paid?

NORTON: As the boss?

MORENO: Yes.

NORTON AS BOSS: $10,000.

MORENO: And do you really feel that the $35 Norton gets is too much pay?!

NORTON AS BOSS: Well, this is what Norton said. (NORTON's speech is hesitant and slow at this point) There are fellows who have been hired before he was hired and are getting less money for the same work. There are fellows who were hired after he was hired and are getting less pay also. Now Norton was hired to do a more technical job than he was doing and he wanted to go ahead and learn this more technical job, but business was slow—the job was being taken care of.

MORENO: That's what you think about Norton?

NORTON AS BOSS: That's what he told me.

MORENO: Norton told you?

NORTON AS BOSS: Mmm, yes.

MORENO: Is this part of the policy of the organization to use employees of this kind the way you do?

NORTON: (*Falling out of role again*) I as Norton?

MORENO: No, no, I'm talking about Norton to you. Norton is over there, look at him. (*MORENO points to the auxiliary ego*)

NORTON AS BOSS: It seems to me a very stupid thing to do. It seems ridiculous that he was doing work for which he had less experience than the others and for which he was getting more pay. I suppose he was stupefied at this.

MORENO: Norton was stupefied. But how was the organization? How do you as a representative of this organization feel about this employee?

NORTON AS BOSS: Well he's getting paid far more than he is worth.

MORENO: So you feel justified in firing him?

NORTON AS BOSS: Yes.

MORENO: (*Addressing NORTON as NORTON*) Now let's go over here. You be the man with whom you were closest. I'd like to speak to him. So you will take the part of Morty, your immediate supervisor.

(*NORTON has now taken the part of MORTY and is standing in his place. Everyone has a special place assigned to him in the room: the manager, the immediate supervisor (MORTY), and NORTON, so that when NORTON takes their place he also resumes their roles*)

MORENO: What do you think about Norton's being fired?

NORTON AS MORTY: As far as I am concerned, I can be frank now, even though I am not usually frank to myself.

MORENO: Anything personal?

NORTON AS MORTY: Well, I was willing to keep him on, but he himself has brought up the issue that he is getting more pay than the other individuals doing the same job. I didn't realize that before. And I've had some . . . situations where we didn't get along too well.

MORENO: What kind of situations?

NORTON AS MORTY: Well, he griped that he had to continually nudge me to do certain things. (*NORTON has fallen out of role again*)

MORENO: Who is talking now?

NORTON: Norton.

MORENO: You are acting as Morty.

NORTON AS MORTY: As far as I know I have this job as supervisor, and I have to see that everything gets turned out.

MORENO: Did he do anything that would justify you to report him?

NORTON AS MORTY: He made me aware of the fact that he was getting more pay than the other fellows doing the same work.

MORENO: Does he really get too much pay? How many hours a week does Norton work?

NORTON AS MORTY: Thirty-seven hours.

MORENO: Thirty-seven hours at $35 a week. Is that too much pay, Morty?

NORTON AS MORTY: We can get individuals who will work for less money.

MORENO: What do you pay for the type of service which he renders?

NORTON AS MORTY: $32.50 and $34.50 a week.

MORENO: So it's really a matter of $2.50 more a week or even 50 cents more a week than he should be getting? Now, does it really make that much difference to the company?

NORTON AS MORTY: It was very easy to get Norton through the N. Y. State Employment Service, and we got another fellow through the same service and we're paying less money. So we can easily replace Norton.

MORENO: Tell me something else about Norton that bothers you?

NORTON AS MORTY: (*Looking thoughtful*) Mmm.

MORENO: Why don't you come out with it?

NORTON AS MORTY: I didn't get along with Norton too well.

(*Tempo of interaction becomes fast from this point on*)

MORENO: What happened between you two?

NORTON AS MORTY: For one thing he told me that I was overworking myself and was in a nervous state and should go to a doctor.

MORENO: Who should go to a doctor?

NORTON AS MORTY: I, Morty, should go to a doctor. He told me that a couple of others had noticed it and that's why he told me about it. He told me that if I don't go I would get a crack up . . .

MORENO: What's the matter with you, Norton? Now take the part of Norton again. Why did you tell him that?

NORTON: Well, I felt he would get a breakdown.

MORENO: All right. Let's see the way Morty acts in an office. Norton you take the part of Morty again.

NORTON AS MORTY: (*Walking through the plant*) You go over there! You get that over here! Ah... (*Seems rather lost at this point*)

MORENO: (*To auxiliary ego*) You take the part of Norton.

AUXILIARY NORTON: How soon shall I do it?

NORTON AS MORTY: Do it right away!

AUXILIARY NORTON: I can't do it right away. I've got some other things to do.

NORTON AS MORTY: What else do you have to do?

AUXILIARY NORTON: I have to move some stock to the other building.

NORTON AS MORTY: When you get done with that, then do this. (*Points at some stock which blocks the doorway*)

AUXILIARY NORTON: All right.

MORENO: What happens next?

NORTON AS MORTY: You fellows move this box over here. You over there get this out to the shipping department. Make sure that gets done . . .

MORENO: All right, Morty, now you take the part of Norton again. Be your self and go up to Morty. (*Pointing to the auxiliary ego*) This is Morty over here and tell him about the doctor.

NORTON: Listen, Morty, the way you're carrying on it seems to me that you'll get sick. I'm afraid that you'll get a nervous breakdown. You're working too hard.

MORTY: I don't think that anything is the matter with me. What business is it of yours anyway?

NORTON: I'm just trying to help you out, you know. It's for your own benefit that I'm telling you this. Furthermore I'm not the only one that has noticed how nervous you are. The other fellows see it too.

MORTY: Look, Norton, what are you driving at?

NORTON: I think you ought to go see a doctor. Maybe he can help you. You have to be careful. I've had trouble myself and I know what its like.

MORTY: Listen, Norton, if I were you I'd mind my own business. You better get back to work now. I've just about had enough of you . . .

MORENO: What kind of a doctor have you been going to Norton? A psychiatrist?

NORTON: (*NORTON pauses, looks at MORENO, looks at the audience*) Yeah.

MORENO: How long have you been under treatment?

NORTON: Two years. (*Looks uncomfortable, slouches, shifts his feet*)

MORENO: Have you been to a mental hospital?

NORTON: Yes, in Connecticut.

MORENO: Shock treatment?

NORTON: (*No response*)

MORENO: Did you get electric shock treatments? Insulin?

NORTON: (*After pausing*) Yeah. The works.

MORENO: What was the name of your psychiatrist?

NORTON: Dr. Zand.

MORENO: What did he say when you told him about this incident?

NORTON: He didn't think what I said was wise.

MORENO: How do you feel about it?

NORTON: I agreed with him. I learned one lesson out of this. That is to keep my mouth shut!

MORENO: No doubt you did! (*Audience laughter*) You mentioned before that you wanted to see the head of the store. Did you get to see him?

NORTON: Yes, I did.

MORENO: (*To the AUXILIARY EGO*) You take the part of the head of P.W. Stores and Norton comes in to see you. Did you make an appointment with him, Norton?

NORTON: Yes, I did.

MORENO: For what time did you make the appointment?

NORTON: For two o'clock in the afternoon.

MORENO: What does his office look like? Describe it!

NORTON: It is large. It has a big desk in the center and two chairs on the side.

MORENO: Does it have any windows?

NORTON: Yes.

MORENO: How many?

NORTON: Two.

MORENO: Where do they face?

NORTON: I don't remember exactly. But I think they are facing the street.

MORENO: Are there any pictures on the wall?

NORTON: He has one big painting, an oil, I think.

MORENO: Is the man sitting or standing?

NORTON: He is sitting when I come in. His desk is cluttered with papers.

MORENO: When you come in what does he tell you?

NORTON: To sit down.

MORENO: All right, Norton, you are now coming in to see Mr. . . . What is his name?

NORTON: I don't remember. I think it is Mr. Wells.

MORENO: You are now coming in to see Mr. Wells about the fact that you have been fired. What time is it?

NORTON: It is 10:35.

MORENO: Is that the time that you went to see him?

NORTON: Oh no, it was at two in the afternoon.

MORENO: Be exact if you can; then it is two in the afternoon and you are in Mr. Wells' office.

MR. WELLS: Yes, what can I do for you?

NORTON: I've come to see you about my being fired.

MR. WELLS: I'm not familiar with the facts of the case, but if you were fired there must have been a good reason for it.

NORTON: That's just it. I want to know the reason!

MR. WELLS: How do you feel you have been doing in your work?

NORTON: I feel that I have been progressing all along and that my production has increased and I don't see why I was fired.

MR. WELLS: I really have very little time, young man, but it seems to me that if you were let go there must have been something unsatisfactory about your work.

NORTON: I was fired from one day to the next without any notice and I feel that an injustice has been done to me.

MR. WELLS: The officers of this company are all reliable and efficient individuals and I am sure if they have decided to let you go . . .

NORTON: I have been with the company for three weeks and was wondering if you would give me another chance?

MR. WELLS: Well . . .

MORENO: Change parts!

(*NORTON takes the part of MR. WELLS and MR. WELLS the part of NORTON*)

NORTON AS MR. WELLS: I am afraid that we will not be able to do that. Once a decision has been reached it is not altered. That is against the policy of the company.

MORENO: (*Walking over to NORTON, who has the part of the boss*) Just between you and me, Mr. Wells, what do you think of this employee?

NORTON AS MR. WELLS: I think that he has some nerve to be taking up my time like this. After all I am a very busy man and can't be bothered with such things.

MORENO: Don't you think it's a bit unfair to fire someone without a reason and without notice?

NORTON AS MR. WELLS: I think he is just coming up here to make trouble. I am sure a reason was given to him; if it wasn't he should be able to see it himself. It is not the policy of my company to fire our men without reason. That would be poor business procedure.

MORENO: Nevertheless, why won't you give him another chance?

NORTON AS MR. WELLS: I am not able to do it. It is against the policy of this company.

MORENO: All right, Norton, you are your own self again. How do you feel after the interview with that man?

NORTON: I feel that the whole thing is very unfair. I am angry with myself that I was not able to succeed. I feel like a failure. Anyway, I am glad that I went to see him, even though it didn't turn out well. So I feel I did everything I could.

MORENO: Tell me, Norton, have you ever been fired before?

NORTON: No.

MORENO: What was the job you had before this.

NORTON: I worked for my uncle.

MORENO: What did you do there?

NORTON: I just helped him around the place.

MORENO: Why did you leave?

NORTON: I wanted to be out on my own.

MORENO: And what did you do before that?

NORTON: I worked for my father.

MORENO: What did you do for him.

NORTON: I worked around his place.

MORENO: And why did you leave him?

NORTON: My father and I have many different opinions about various things and we just did not understand each other.

MORENO: I see. Have you ever had a job outside of your family?

NORTON: No, I never had. This one for P. W. Stores was the first one.

MORENO: I see. What do you intend to do now?

NORTON: I'm trying to find another job. By the way, does anyone here need a good stock clerk? (*Audience laughter*)

MORENO: Well, I hope someone does, for your sake. If they do they will see you after the session.

NORTON: Well, I hope so too. I really need a job.

MORENO: Norton, thank you very much for your excellent presentation. You were a fine protagonist. I want to thank the other members of the group who acted as auxiliary egos. They gave a very realistic portrayal.

(*Applause. NORTON and the two other men leave the stage*)

MORENO: Now, as usual, we are again moving back into the group. Is there anyone else here who has had a similar experience? Anyone who has been fired? We had one gentleman before who lost his job. Could you identify yourself with any part of the presentation?

AUDIENCE MEMBER NO. 4: Well, my case was different but I do see some similar points.

MORENO: What do you see that you can relate to yourself?

AUDIENCE MEMBER NO. 4: The way Norton felt about being fired. I felt the same way. That is to say, that someone had been unfair to me and at the same time that feeling of disappointment in myself. You know, your vanity is hurt.

MORENO: Don't talk in the "you," always "I."

AUDIENCE MEMBER NO. 4: I felt that they didn't appreciate my talents and I felt that maybe I didn't sell them strongly enough. But now I understand the whole incident and it doesn't bother me in the least. Thank God, I got over it 100%.

MORENO: Lucky boy! How about the lady over there. You started to tell us something.

AUDIENCE MEMBER NO. 5: Yes, I was fired from my first job.

MORENO: From your first job? What happened? What did you do?

AUDIENCE MEMBER NO. 5: I was a reporter for the New York World Telegram.

MORENO: A reporter for the New York World Telegram! What did you do — dig up stories that were not supposed to be dug up?

AUDIENCE MEMBER NO. 5: Not quite but something like it. I was given an assignment to find out how men felt about beauty parlors. (*Audience laughter*) Something trivial like that. As I remember it was very hot at that time and I didn't take the thing too seriously. There was a lot of other work which had to be attended to and I couldn't be bothered with such a side line. At any rate it got to be two nights before the thing was due and I proceeded to pound out what I thought was a pretty good story, gave a few examples, you know, of the confessional type. At any rate I handed it in to the editor and he called me down to his office a little while later. He began asking me questions about my sources and I guess they didn't jive. To make a long story short I found myself confessing the truth and in return got my notice.

MORENO: That was one time you didn't get away with it!

AUDIENCE MEMBER NO. 5: Don't get me wrong. That was the first and last time it ever happened.

MORENO: What are you doing now?

AUDIENCE MEMBER NO. 5: I'm in the same organization that other gentleman is in, public relations!

MORENO: Like it better?

AUDIENCE MEMBER NO. 5: Much better. It was a big step ahead.

MORENO: How did you feel when you got fired?

AUDIENCE MEMBER NO. 5: I got over it pretty quickly. I was rather amused that they were able to see through my trick.

MORENO: You mean to say that it didn't bother you at all?

AUDIENCE MEMBER NO. 5: Well, I was a little angry with myself that I wasn't able to cover it up a little better. It didn't go too deep.

MORENO: I am sure, nevertheless, that your pride must have been wounded, just a little?

AUDIENCE MEMBER NO. 5: I guess so. It was so long ago I really can't remember. Anyway when I look back now it makes me laugh.

MORENO: Is there anyone else who has ever been fired, or who can identify himself with any part of the production?

AUDIENCE MEMBER NO. 6: I have a question that I would like to ask Norton.

MORENO: Yes, go right ahead.

AUDIENCE MEMBER NO. 6: Do you remember the type of interview you had with that company?

NORTON: Yes.

AUDIENCE MEMBER NO. 6: What was it like?

NORTON: Well, they asked me about my background and my experience, my age.

AUDIENCE MEMBER NO. 6: Did they ask you about your activities in the evening? About the fact that you went to school?

MORENO: Excuse me for interrupting here, for a second, but this is a rather interesting point. How do employers feel about their employees attending school in the evening? What would you say?

AUDIENCE MEMBER NO. 6: I think that some would have a lot of respect for a boy who is ambitious enough to want to attend school in the evening. I know that my company recognizes that fact very highly. However, some organizations might feel that the employee is using the company as a stepping stone to further himself and as soon as he finds something better he will leave. This is especially true in a position of a non-executive capacity.

From this point on the discussion took a turn to general considerations of personnel selection in industry. A member of the audience, an executive of a major airline, indicated the steps in selection of personnel in his firm. He also indicated the manner in which persons are fired from the firm, indicating that first there is a "conversation" which is a hidden warning; second there is the direct warning; if no results are gotten by this procedure, the person may be "laid-off" for a week without pay; if this still doesn't get results in modifying the behavior of the worker, the worker is discharged. He indicated that at all points the worker is informed of reasons for dissatisfaction, and that a situation similar to that of Norton's could not arise. Other members of the audience raised questions and made comments, most, however, being of a general nature, indicating dissatisfaction with the personnel policies of the majority of firms.

The discussion was returned to focus on the subjects of the interviews who also reported being fired. They were questioned concerning any identification they might have with the portrayal on the stage. One subject, the person who had been fired from the paper, did not identify with the portrayal at all. The other subject, on the other hand, stated that he had felt the same bewilderment which was so apparent with Norton. Other members of the audience were queried concerning their feelings about the performance. A few identified with each of the positions. What became more apparent was the general dissatisfaction with the inadequate personnel policy of Norton's employer. From this point the discussion moved back to Norton.

AUDIENCE NO. 7: I got the impression that all along he was acting like a person who was was mentally ill.

MORENO: Did Morty know about that? Did you talk to him about it?

NORTON: Well, I asked Morty whether I could leave a little earlier on Monday to go to the doctor because I was nervous.

MORENO: Did he ask you anything more?

NORTON: No.

MORENO: How long after you started to work did you ask him that?

NORTON: One week.

MORENO: And you worked there three weeks in all. The fact of being nervous and mentally ill came out first in an abreactive way on the stage, but now in the discussion we come back to it. This shows again how valuable it is not to leave the production on the stage hanging in mid-air (*some misinformed people think that a sociodrama ends with the production on the stage*), without returning to the audience participants and interweaving their questions and remarks with further interview of the subject, whose stage production now gets him ready for a more intensive interview. The entire production has prepared him, warmed him up for a more complete communication with us, the audience. Now one thing we noticed about Norton in the job-situation: he did not keep his mouth shut. About what one must keep his mouth shut differs of course with the social environment and its top values; in our society one loses prestige if he reveals that he has served a prison sentence, that he has been mentally ill, or that he has no money, et cetera. We should discuss such things in an open group like this. Mental maladjustments are frequent in industrial plants. Whether a psychiatrist is consulted or not, knowledge of psychiatry has become such a necessity that even in simple employment situations there is a need for it; it is a reality. In industrial settings we should have sociometrists and sociatrists employed. There are not only economical problems to deal with. These people, besides working, have to live, too, and there is a tremendous amount of deceit and tricks going on. Sooner or later the manager has to face it. At the same time this man is probably a capable worker, but was scared to tell his superiors the truth about himself. If instead, you could have told them fearlessly, they could have placed you, giving you the four steps this gentleman mentioned before, and you could have learned about yourself step by step, instead of being fired and having to come here because you are upset about it. I am very glad the protagonist came here tonight; we can all learn from such a production. It makes us realize that our community is full of sick people; maladjusted parents rear our children; teachers, sick themselves, teach our children in the schools; in our industries a person with mental illness may frequently be found in the frontier of leadership. (*To* NORTON) Did you understand that they all knew about your mental condition? They did not tell you?

NORTON: I don't know; I don't think they knew until recently.

MORENO: We have to make our industrial plants so flexible that they can absorb people who are somewhat maladjusted, maybe by assignment to special work groups and by grading their wages and employment hours.

AUDIENCE MEMBER NO. 8: Why was Norton so concerned about the fact that he was earning two and a half dollars more than other people?

NORTON: I was concerned about the security of my job. There were fellows there who had had more experience.

MORENO: Yes, but what did you fear about it?

AUDIENCE MEMBER NO. 8: I had the feeling that he wanted to be a member of the group completely rather than being set aside. The "fifty cents" difference is only symbolic.

MORENO: How did you feel about that?

NORTON: I did not understand her.

AUDIENCE MEMBER NO. 8: Maybe you just wanted to be one of the boys.

NORTON: Well, I did feel differently from the other fellows. I did not feel an equality with them. Especially when I asked if they were there longer, and they did not earn more than I did.

AUDIENCE MEMBER NO. 9: How much education did your immediate superior have?

NORTON: He continuously stressed the fact that he thought I was a college graduate.

MORENO: Are you?

NORTON: No. I have had two years at Brooklyn College, at Brooklyn College of Pharmacy.

MORENO: Why did you stop?

NORTON: Because I did not like pharmacy and because my father rushed me into it.

MORENO: What about Morton? How much education did he have?

NORTON: I don't know what education Morty had. But he always assumed that I was a college graduate; I kept talking about being a high school graduate.

MORENO: What education did the man have who handed you the paper?

NORTON: He looked as if he had had a higher education of some sort by the way he handled himself and his work; he seemed to have had some college education.

MORENO: What about the other co-workers?

NORTON: They were high school graduates; there was one who was a Negro and going to college at night; and a fellow who walked with a cane who had a deformity. He was going to City College Business School.

MORENO: (*To audience*) I would like now to make a statement and finish the group part of the session, and explain to you what kind of a process you were undergoing. You remember that when you came in you were handed a blank and we asked you to fill it in. It dealt first with your acquaintance with people here and then with your work, and also whom you would like to choose to have a confidential talk with about a work problem. On the basis of this we immediately could draw a rough acquaintance diagram and a sociogram and obtain a picture of the structure of this group.

During the session I have been careful to divide my time equally between two groups, sitting right and left of the aisle, in about equal numbers. On the one hand, I have conducted interviews with two members of the audience, and on the other I have worked with Norton.

Our intention was to study the resourcefulness of interview as compared with psychodramatic role techniques, their accuracy, depth, and range of information. In order to accomplish this I tried to give the same amount of time to the interview section of the audience (*the two interviewees, audience members 3 and 5*) as to the psychodramatic section (*audience member 2 and auxiliary egos*). At the beginning of the session we did not know which would be the interview half and which the psychodramatic half, on the right side of the aisle or on the left side of the audience. You decided this when you chose the topic "the man who gets fired" to be represented on the stage; it is often useful for the warm up to let the proponent of a topic also be its protagonist. In this case it was Norton. We know from experience that the proponent of a topic has some personal involvement with the subject matter, particularly that he is ready for a work-out at the time of the proposal, now and here. This is then a short-cut; he starts the ball rolling for the rest of the audience and draws into participation those who are similarly involved in the topic. The proponent of a topic and the role playing protagonist are not always the same individual. He may be helpful as a starter but we frequently use different individuals to be the role players. The first role player is succeeded by as many in the audience as have experienced versions of this same problem. Working with two techniques simultaneously puts an additional strain on the conductor of the session. It may not have been noticed by you but whenever the interview time was just beginning I looked encouragingly at the members of the interview audience to arouse their participation; but when the time came to an end I looked the other way, at the role playing part of the audience, engaging some of the auxiliary egos to work with Norton, or engaging Norton himself. Some of the potential interviewees may have been left out of participation but on the other hand some role players may have been left out; I tried to do both parts an equal injustice.

We have recorded these processes and will analyze the data and compare role playing techniques, configurational aspects, techniques of recall with interview technique, and where there are definite advantages for each one. We will analyze this material and send you each a copy, and it will also be published. Of course, we will not use original names and localities. In this field no control study actually exists; we will analyze this material and see what we will get. After we have analyzed this maybe we will meet again. I don't want to tell you what will happen then but it would be a second step in the training, to understand group processes better and how much such understanding is of value to administrative and personnel people. I did not know the subjects and I did not know you. I am like a doctor who sees a patient for the first time; here I am a social doctor examining and testing you as a group, just as there is a physical doctor who examines an individual. I want also to thank you for your courtesy and cooperation.

I further wonder whether the position in the group had a relationship to the number of words spoken, including myself. I spoke a lot more than other members of the group. (*Audience laughter*) That would be something worthwhile knowing for obtaining clues: how much did I speak, and how much did the protagonist speak, and the people who have any position in the sociograms? We would also like to hear from you and to have your comments on the production. But, before you leave, please make another choice as to whom you would like to have as a counselor and confidant now, after the session; the forms are being passed out. We will consider the stimulus which came from the session and to what extent it reflects in a change of the choices for a guide or counselor in the problem situation.

THEORETICAL AND TECHNICAL ASPECTS

We have been trying to maintain the diagnostic aspect of this sociodrama, although the therapeutic impact cannot be avoided. The thing we have to do therefore is to be aware of it and try to assess and measure the therapeutic effect. Our focus in this session was on research and diagnostic procedure, whereas in other cases our focus is on therapeutic procedure. In reality, however, social diagnosis and therapy merge into one another, they cannot be strictly separated.

We have to differentiate (a) the direct and tangible evidence emerging from a session from (b) the unconscious hypotheses projected into the construction and direction of the session (what the conductor and his staff want to show and prove, what the audience participants want to experience and learn), and (c) the interpretations of the session material. By direct evidence we mean the people present, their social roles, the actions and interactions on the stage or in the audience, the volume of words spoken in each dialogue, the duration of the total session, the duration of acts and pauses in the course of role playing, et cetera. As means of recording we used a tape recorder, a [human] observer recording movements and gestures, questionnaires, acquaintance [diagrams] and sociograms.

Audience laughter is a significant part of the session: its volume, duration, tone characteristics, and spread among the members can be assessed in the play back. Often significant are the events which precipitate laughter, at what moments in the session it occurs, and who among the members of the audience participate in a wave of laughter and who don't. From a sociometric point of view one can observe two types of laughter, one type produced by (a) collective stimuli, standardized jokes, slangy remarks emerging spontaneously in the right moment (*then everybody is inclined to join in the laughter*); and (b) private stimuli, jokes, or remarks which have an amusing connotation only for the people who know the protagonist intimately or who are involved in a similar problem. I have frequently pointed out that there is a cleavage within the psychosocial networks between collective and private networks. Using participation in laughter as a criterion, one can draw a series of sociograms in the course of the session, each showing who joins in an outburst of laughter and who does not, the one who laughs first and the ones who laugh loudest and longest. In the present session laughter is recorded as provoked by the director six times, five times by the protagonist, and once by an audience member. Seventy per cent of the total volume of laughter was recorded in the first twenty minutes of the session. It is frequently observed that people laugh particularly in the beginning of sessions; the unusually spontaneous character which they have, the impromptu remarks and gestures of the director and protagonist, the abreactions and interabreactions on the stage, the exhibitionistic side-plays take the onlookers by surprise. As the production goes on and the involvement of the protagonist and audience grow, laughter gradually vanishes. Actors and audience become increasingly serious and tense.

Another significant aspect is the warm up. In this session the participants were entirely unprepared, while in other cases they may be warmed up in advance as to the problem to be worked out. They may come to the session either with an overheated or a negative attitude which may influence the conduct of the session considerably. Then there is the warm up which takes place within the first few minutes of the session. The approach of the director may vary; it is what I often call the "bedside manner of the sociodramatist or group psychotherapist." The form which the warm up takes may come from the director or from the group itself. In this session we used the voting method, letting the group determine the topic and the protagonist. In other sociodrama sessions the audience may come with a problem which they have already formulated in advance. In other cases one member of the audience after another begins to talk and suddenly a large number of participants cluster around a problem. You may have noticed that Norton was the first one to present a topic. It was apparent that he came to the session with the intention to act and to act out his own problem. There were a few in this audience who came with the intention just to look on, by no means to act. We find in audiences several types of participants: (a) those who want to act (an extreme case is the exhibitionist); (b) those who are anxious to see (the extreme case is the voyeur); (c) those who want to analyze; (d) those who would like to be in the place of the director and if they cannot then they will at least analyze or criticize him; and (e) those who like to act and discuss as long as it is not their own problem.

Another significant aspect in sociodrama as well as in psychodrama sessions is the "bodily contact." Whereas in other forms of diagnosis and therapy body contact is unnecessary, it was so natural to psychodrama and role playing from their very inception that the director, the auxiliary egos, and the protagonist would enter occasionally not only into verbal but also into bodily contact. Knowing how far to go with bodily contact requires a special skill and training. Properly applied it aids the warm up and it brings the process of reality testing to a climax. The director, taking Norton by the hand, brings about a quicker rapport than words could. The feeling of a hand may tell the director whether a protagonist is willing to act or whether he resists.

Norton began to fall out of the role frequently at the time when the situation became tense for him; he had to expose the fact that he had been mentally ill. Falling out of the role is often, as here, a diagnostic clue for insecurity in a given situation.

ANALYSIS OF THE ACQUAINTANCE DIAGRAM AND
THE SOCIOGRAMS

In the Acquaintance Diagram [Figure 15-1] persons 1, 12, and 20 did not report acquaintances, nor were they reported as acquaintances. Person 21 was not reported as an acquaintance by any of the session members, but he listed being acquainted with one person present.

Aside from persons 1, 12, and 20, who may be considered as acquaintance isolates, there existed two discrete groups, according to the reports. The smaller group consisted of persons 13, 14, 19, 25, and 26, and the larger group consisted of the remainder of the session members. Person 17 serves as the focus of acquaintanceship for the larger group. Persons 2, 3, 4, 11, and 22 form a distinct subgroup with connections to the larger group converging exclusively on person 17. Persons 7, 8, 15, 16, and 18 form another subgroup with connects to the larger group through the acquaintance of person 17 to person 18, and through the acquaintance between person 8 and 10. Persons 8, 9, and 10 may be considered as another subgroup, with persons 8 and 10 each having a position in an additional subgroup. Persons 5, 6, 10, 17, 23, and 24 represent the last major subgroup of the larger group.

In Sociogram A [Figure 15-2], persons 1, 4, 12, and 20 are isolates—i.e., do not choose and are not chosen. Persons 2, 3, 7, 9, 10, 13, 14, 19, 22, 23, and 24 are not chosen. Person 17 is the primary focus of choice, being chosen eight times. Person 6 is chosen six times and person 8 is chosen five times, and persons 21 and 18 are chosen three times each. Mutual choices occur between persons 5 and 6, 8 and 15, and 15 and 16.

Of the 31 choices exhibited among the session members, 22 were directed to acquaintances and 9 to non-acquaintances. Since only nine of the 24 persons were chosen, it may be assumed that certain strong influences, such as reputation in the field, served as elective factors. While this is true, it is notable that the acquaintance subgroup consisting of person 7, 8, 15, 16, and 18 maintains its form when tested by the criterion of choice.

Eleven persons chose only among their acquaintances, five persons chose only non-acquaintances, three persons chose both acquaintances and non-acquaintances, and five persons made no choices at all.

Of the 33 choices in Sociogram B [Figure 15-3], 22 were the same as in Sociogram A, 6 choices were dropped, and 11 new choices were made. Of the 6 dropped choices, 5 were among acquaintances and only one was a non-acquaintance. Of the 11 added choices, 10 were among non-acquaintances, and only one was an acquaintance.

Persons 6, 17, and 21 were main participants in the discussion period. Person 6 is most chosen after the session, having eight choices. Person 21, who still chooses no one, is also in a more favorable position, being chosen

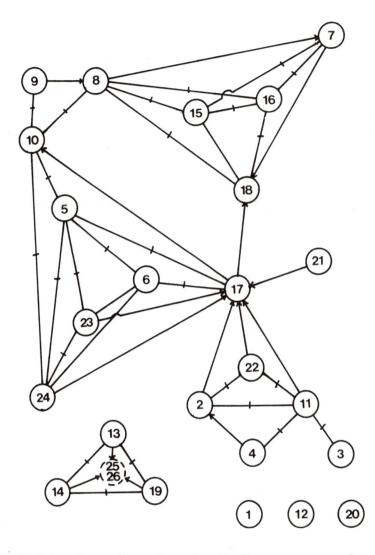

Figure 15-1 Acquaintance diagram. *Instructions:* List all persons present at the session with whom you are acquainted.
Note: Why numbers 25 and 26 have a broken line around them is not clear. Most likely they were staff members administering the test, which would explain why they are not part of the sociograms. (Ed.)

seven times. Person 17 has faded as a star, but still is chosen five times. Persons 7, 8, 15, 16, and 18 maintain the same pattern of choice as in the first sociogram. Person 27, the director, who did not participate in either sociogram, is chosen three times.

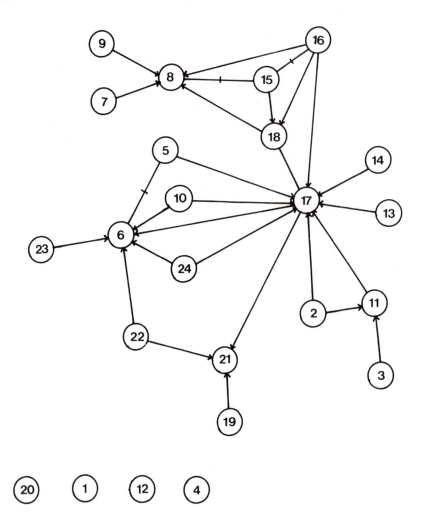

Figure 15–2 Sociogram A. *Criterion:* In regard to a work situation in which you must make a decision, with which person(s) present would you like to consult?

In Sociogram B, eight persons chose only among their acquaintances, eight and non-acquaintances, and four persons made no choices at all.

It is notable that person 12, the protagonist of the session, is unchosen even at the end of the session. Number 12, however, is no longer an isolate. The auxiliaries who worked with the protagonist on the stage maintained their respective positions in terms of the sociograms. The interview respondents, who were unchosen in the first sociogram, continued as unchosen in

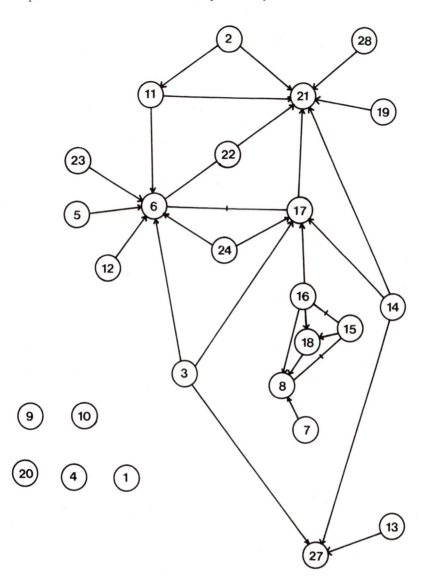

Figure 15-3 Sociogram B. *Criterion:* Now that you have participated in the session: In regard to a work situation in which you must make a decision, with which person(s) present would you like to consult?

Notes: The director, number 27, did not participate in the sociograms. Numbers 9 and 10 did not participate in the second sociogram. Number 28 was a late arrival and participated only in the second sociogram.

the second sociogram. One interview respondent, however, made two additional choices in the second sociogram.

In the analysis of the session it becomes obvious that the session members establish norms for the judgement and advisement of the protagonist, and more generally, for what is to be considered good personnel policy. The sociograms indicate that at the same time, the session members are also establishing norms of judgement for the good social analyst, or more specifically, the good consultant. The analysis of the session tends to corroborate this conclusion. The most chosen persons, 6, 21, and 17, have different approaches from the rest of the session members as seen in the complete transcript of the session. These persons do not merely ask questions or make comments; their part in the discussion is typified by systematic statements set in well defined frameworks, with questions based on their respective statements. At the same time, it is to be noted that these same persons were those most adept in the proper techniques for presentation. When recognized by the director, each stood, faced the larger part of the audience, and controlled the audience while holding the floor.

PARTIAL ANALYSIS

As the title of this section implies, we do not endeavor here to give a complete analysis of the session. It should be noticed that the psychodramatic and sociodramatic sessions have a cumulative content. The director edits the production as it proceeds, and taking the cues and clues from the production itself as it involves the protagonist, he may focus the production to become more and more specific. Information which is elicited serves as the basis for the continuation of the production, and as information is accumulated, the director is able to judiciously select the more important scenes to be portrayed. Each scene progressively provides more information which may be focused in interview.

In the interviews with the two audience members there is merely the reporting of feeling. Only persons who have been in similar situations can really identify with the situations recounted. Very little is known of the attitudes of the other persons involved, or the operation of policy. We have no real knowledge of whether dismissals are personal matters involving the personality of the interviewee, or whether it is a problem of surplus personnel, elimination of positions, et cetera. In the psychodramatic situation, however, it becomes evident that the problem has many ramifications. There is the problem of Norton as the maladjusted person, speaking out of turn and too much. On the stage it could be seen that Norton was not a person who can be characterized as energetic, industrious, or direct. Rather, it became obvious that he is slow and confused. Here we did not have to ask Norton how he worked. We could watch him in operation. We did not have to ask Norton how he felt. We could watch him, identify with his problems, and become aware of his feelings. At the same time, we were introduced to the structure of the organization which fired Norton. We were introduced to the people with whom he worked. We became involved with Norton and his problem. We are able to remain objective. The prejudices of the company are evident, and they are understandable in the context of the definition of community values. We observe the policy of the company, and while as individuals we may not condone it, we may realize the "why" of what has happened.

The efficiency of the psychodramatic procedure is borne out in an interesting way in this particular session. Without building stereotypes, it should be noted that it is possible to make judgements about personality types. Watching Norton on the stage, acting as Norton and being Norton, two trained members of the audience observed that Norton acted "like a mental patient." Speaking with Norton, or interviewing him, might not provide the opportunity for such accurate observation.

Such a session as this is preliminary and suggestive. Here we controlled the factor of time, given equal attention to the interview of two audience members and the psychodramatic session with Norton. Unfortunately the topic chosen by the audience was not of a nature where more persons of the audience could be made to participate as protagonists. This type of study remains to be repeated.

Still, it may be seen in such a procedure that the sociometric approaches can identify the problems of the individual worker, not only in the impersonal terms of a category such as "maladjusted," but also in the terms which are real to the person. We do not only identify the problem of the workers, but we also begin to identify some of the problems of the industrial concern. While most of the session members present felt sympathy for Norton, there was, even with the recognition that the personnel policy of the P. W. Stores is not the most enlightened, an understanding of the circumstances which would lead the firm to dismiss Norton.

Probably the most notable contribution that a session of this sort makes is in making evident the possibilities for the further application of the techniques. The psychodramatic work here centered around Norton, a worker with a specific set of problems. What problems exist for the foreman, the junior supervisor, the supervisor, the junior executive, the executive? Norton is one case, and we learn a great deal from him, but we must study many workers and many executives in their social contexts to begin to really understand the dynamics of group structuring. We must learn to distinguish between aspects of personality which are associated with the statuses a person holds, and those aspects of personality which make the person in the status unique.

A further implication to be investigated is in the process of establishment of the norms of judgement and conformity which is evidenced in the production. These norms did not only refer to the individual, Norton, but also to the situation in which he was found. The group judgement concerned itself with what is proper procedure for selection of personnel. Equally important, in the procedure we not only found the limitation of the person in the job, but we also began to explore the limitation of the job, and the structure in which the job is found. What is especially to be noted in the presentation and in the analysis is that the divergence of interests mentioned in the introduction of this paper, those of "management" and those of the "worker," lose their discreteness. The approach lends itself to the analysis of the system in which these operate, and thus, for the treatment of both simultaneously rather than as unified entities which stand independent of each other.

The experimental design constructed in this sociodrama session has strong and weak points. One strong point is that the experimental group (the role playing portion) and the control group (the interview portion) are processed simultaneously and within the same setting. There is certainty here that the conditions and the stimuli to which they are exposed are for both groups identical. A weak point is that the conductor of the role playing part and the interview part is one and the same person. He may have a bias in favor or disfavor of either of the two techniques he is applying. His bias might have influenced the course and results of the production. Unless it is proven that a conductor is trained in both skills and unless it is certain that his scientific curiosity is greater than his bias, it is of advantage that the role of the psychodramatic director and that of the interviewer be assigned to two different individuals.

CHAPTER 16

Fragments from the Psychodrama of a Dream

1941

Editor's note: The exploration of dreams played a significant part in Moreno's treatment approach. In this dream enactment from the 1940s, the subject is an outpatient coming to Beacon for therapy. Moreno's directing emphasizes the warm-up to the dream, the enactment of it—in which "analysis is submerged into the production"—and the extension of it. He does not give the instruction to role reverse as frequently as would be done today, although the technique is employed at key moments.

. . . . The patient, Martin Stone, came to Beacon for treatment, at times together with his wife, once a week during the summer of 1941. Two days after his second treatment session this dream took place. Its psychodramatic production was recorded by means of a [tape] recorder, and an observer in the audience recorded the actions and interactions between the dream characters. Besides the couple, the psychodramatist and a staff of auxiliary egos, six other patients took part in this session. The wife was absent. After Martin's

From *Group Psychotherapy, Psychodrama & Sociometry* 3 (1950), 344-355. Another version appears in *Progress in Psychotherapy* 4 (1941).

dream was produced the patients were encouraged to relate themselves to the production and to communicate some of their own dreams.
(*At the start of this session, MORENO and MARTIN sit on the center, or interview, level of the psychodrama stage.*)

MARTIN: Well, doctor, where shall we begin?

MORENO: Martin, thank you for the letter and for your notes which I read. I also received the dream, which I didn't want to read since I planned to work the dream out with you here today. We will have some control in comparing the data which you put down yourself with that which we will work out psychodramatically. When did the dream take place? What date?

MARTIN: This was Sunday night, just after I left here.

MORENO: That was . . .

MARTIN: July 6th.

MORENO: (*Getting up, has MARTIN by the hand, takes him from interview position to top level of stage*) Let's see that. Was it during the night?

MARTIN: I'll have to take that back. It would be Saturday night or sometime between midnight Saturday and early Sunday morning.

MORENO: Do you sleep alone? (*Drops MARTIN's hand, takes a step away from him*)

MARTIN: Well, in this case I slept alone.

MORENO: You slept alone. Well, suppose you fix your bed up the way it was. Is your wife sleeping in another room?[. . .]

MARTIN: No, that's the particular circumstance of the dream. I am in my father-in-law's house. My wife is not here.

MORENO: (*Walks to side, off stage*) You are in your father-in-law's house? Where is your wife?

MARTIN: (*Alone on stage*) She is in Worcester and this is in Boston. I went from here [Beacon] to New York on Saturday and then on up to Boston on Saturday night. Here I am, in Boston.

MORENO: And, of course, your in-laws . . .

(*MORENO changes lights to soft midnight blue*)

MARTIN: They are in the back of the house and this room is more to the front.

MORENO: Is it a bedroom?

MARTIN: Yes.

MORENO: Have you ever slept in this house?

MARTIN: I slept in this house but never in this particular room.

MORENO: Try to describe the room as best you can.

MARTIN: The room is ordinarily occupied by the grandmother in the family who happens to have gone away to visit another daughter. There's a table right by the bed and it is about 39 inches long.

MORENO: Why don't you put the bed up the best you can, just the way it is. (*The scene is being set. MARTIN uses chairs to set up the bed, table, and other simple furnishings to represent the room*) Why don't you move the bed further to the front?

MARTIN: (*Indicating*) This is the position the bed has in the room, next to the window.

MORENO: In what position do you sleep?

MARTIN: I sleep in all ways but usually toward my left side.

MORENO: All right then, go to bed and sleep on your left side.

MARTIN: (*Lies down on three or four chairs representing the bed*)

MORENO: Have you a pillow?

MARTIN: Yes.

MORENO: How many pillows do you use? (*Steps upon the stage again, stands behind MARTIN, puts his hands on his shoulder*)

MARTIN: Just one.

MORENO: And when you are in bed is that how your legs are placed?

MARTIN: I think so, about like that. They usually are crossed at the ankles, like this. (*Crosses his legs[. . .]*)

MORENO: What are you doing with your hands?

MARTIN: The right is usually under me and the left is at my side.

MORENO: And you try now to fall asleep slowly. Are you comfortable? Try to make yourself as comfortable as possible under the circumstances. Try to concentrate on the dream. That is to say, try to have in your mind as clear a perception of the dream as you can. Are you concentrating now? (*Closes MARTIN'S eyes with his hands, gently strokes his hair*)

MARTIN: Yes.

MORENO: Do you see the dream?

MARTIN: Yes.

MORENO: The sequence of the dream? (*MARTIN nods his head*)

MORENO: Try to concentrate now and try to visualize it the best you can, but don't tell us anything about it. Just concentrate on the dream. Do you have it now? Let it pass just like a sequence of scenes through your mind. Do you have it? (*MORENO'S voice is suggestive, gentle, and softer than usual*)

MARTIN: (*Beginning to look more at ease*) Yes, I have it.

MORENO: Do you see people in it? Do you see the media, the environment in which it takes place? (*Continues to stroke MARTIN'S head, his hair, forehead, helping him to relax*)

MARTIN: Yes, I see it now.

MORENO: Close your eyes. Try to fall asleep, deep asleep. Concentrate the best you can. As you are falling asleep all kinds of images go through your mind, don't they? What goes through your mind as you are trying to fall asleep, Martin? Relate yourself to that dream which you are going to have . . . You know you are going to have that dream, right?

MARTIN: (*Looking quite relaxed, body at ease, warming himself up to an increased degree of consciousness, as if in a creative mood*) Yes.

MORENO: In a few minutes you are beginning to have that dream, so try now to visualize what kind of images go through your mind as you are going to have that dream? What is going through your mind?

MARTIN: Well, I seem to see an office of some kind.

MORENO: An office?

MARTIN: There is particularly someone at the desk, a doctor whom I know.

MORENO: A doctor whom you know. Do you see the doctor? Who is the doctor? You see him before you start the dream, of course, right? What kind of a doctor is it?

MARTIN: I think this is Dr. Miller, an eye doctor.

MORENO: Mmm. And what else goes through your mind now as you are trying to fall asleep? (*Softly steps away from MARTIN*)

MARTIN: (*After a short silence*) I see my wife.

MORENO: What is she doing? Is she doing anything?

MARTIN: No, she is . . . (*hesitates*) she is sitting in the kitchen.

MORENO: All right now, Martin, close your eyes, breathe deep, breathe deeper, and try to fall asleep. Concentrate on that dream. Very soon you are going to dream the same dream all over again which you had five days ago when you were sleeping in your father-in-law's house. Here you are, the dream is emerging now. Now the dream is emerging, what do you see first in the dream? What happens first?

MARTIN: Well, I see a group of women.

MORENO: A group of women! What are you doing there?

MARTIN: I don't know . . . I'm just watching them.

MORENO: Are you sitting or standing?

MARTIN: I am standing.

MORENO: Well, then get up and stand! Just as you stand in the dream.

MARTIN: (*Gets up[. . .]*)

MORENO: Where do you stand? Where are you? What kind of a scene is it.

MARTIN: We are in a room in my house.

MORENO: Which room is it?

MARTIN: It's the dining room.

MORENO: Which house is it?

MARTIN: It's the house I used to live in, in Boston.

MORENO: Where are you standing there?

MARTIN: I am standing near the kitchen door.

MORENO: Move towards the kitchen door! What else do you see?

MARTIN: There's a group of women. Quite a group of them.

MORENO: Where are they?

MARTIN: They are in front of me, in the dining room.

MORENO: They're in the dining room. Do you recognize any of them?

MARTIN: Yes.

MORENO: Who are they? (*Motions to two female AUXILIARY EGOS to come up on the stage. They get up from the audience and come forward*)

MARTIN: My mother; there's a sister of mine.

MORENO: Your mother (*motions to one AUXILIARY EGO that she is to take the part of MARTIN's mother*), a sister of yours (*motions to the second AUXILIARY EGO to represent his sister*), who else?

MARTIN: There's the wife of a professor friend of mine. Her name is Kay. My sister's sister-in-law is there, her name is Caroline. My mother is there. And my wife is there, too.

MORENO: (*Motions to three more AUXILIARY EGOS to come upon the stage*) What are they doing?

MARTIN: They are discussing something.

MORENO: (*To MARTIN, the AUXILIARY EGOS, and audience*) You see, Martin, the characters in your dream are like wax figures on the stage; the AUXILIARY EGOS representing them move, act, speak or spring to life only as you and when you, the dreamer, direct them. They have no life of their own, therefore, you tell them what to do. What are they discussing?

MARTIN: They're talking about the fact that my wife has to go to the doctor.

(*The AUXILIARY EGOS in their various roles immediately begin to act; they are talking about MARTIN's wife and the fact that she should go and see a doctor. They are standing around in a huddle and make a compact group*)

MORENO: What else do they say?

MARTIN: They're trying to decide to which doctor she should go.

MORENO: All right.

(*The women begin to question which doctor MARTIN's wife should consult*)

MORENO: What else do they discuss?

MARTIN: They wonder what my attitude is going to be. They murmur.

(*The women begin to murmur about how MARTIN will take JEAN's visit to the doctor. The whole audience joins them*)

MORENO: What is your attitude?

MARTIN: (*He is bending over, trying to listen to what they are saying, his eyes are half-closed*) I am perturbed. I'm worried about it. I don't want her to go. I seem to feel she ought to go, but I don't want her to go. They're discussing the fact that I went with her to the doctor once and they don't think that this is the way to proceed.

(*The discussion among the women is getting more intense*)

MARTIN: I listen and move closer to them, like this (*steps closer to the bunch of women*). They seem to think that I have no place being there, that it's not my place to be there.

MORENO: Who is talking? Who says that?

MARTIN: My sister says that. Mary says that.

MORENO: (*Prompting*) Mary! Mary!

MARY: He has no business going to the doctors with her! (*She talks to all the women and points her finger at MARTIN*) That's no place for a husband to be!

MORENO: Is this your older sister?

MARTIN: Yes, all of my sisters are older, but this is one of my sisters.

MORENO: To whom does she say that?

MARTIN: I think she says that to Kay, the professor's wife.

MARY: Kay, it's not right that he goes to the doctor's office! It's not right! He has no purpose there. What's the use of it?

MORENO: What does Kay say to that?

MARTIN: Kay doesn't say much of anything in response. The conversation is largely dominated by Mary.

MORENO: (*Prompting again*) Go on, Mary.

MARY: You know he gets so upset. Every woman has to go and see a doctor once in a while. Why, Jean wouldn't go along if he had to see a doctor. It looks funny. It's silly!

MORENO: What is next?

MARTIN: They decide that the doctor she should consult is a doctor by the name of Stone, of a partnership. I think, at this point I see something, I see . . .

(*Speech of the women in the background*)

MORENO: What do you see?

MARTIN: I see a piece of paper. It's got the name Stone and something like . . . it begins with B. I'm not sure.

MORENO: Take the paper in your hand and read it!

MARTIN: (*Taking out a piece of paper*) Like . . .

MORENO: What's the name? Look at it.

MARTIN: The paper is a doctor's bill. It says Stone & Bridge on it.

MORENO: All right. What do they decide?

MARTIN: They decide that she is to go and ask for Doctor Stone. And then I become angry at their discussing all this and not taking me in. So I rush into the room . . .

MORENO: Then rush into the room!

(*MARTIN runs towards the center of the stage*)

MARTIN: (*Angrily*) I don't like your talking about this . . . without my being here. It's my business not yours, mine and Jean's. What are you talking about anyway?

MORENO: What does your sister say?

MARTIN: She condemns me for doing something which I have no right to do.

MARY: You always get so upset. It's useless. Why do you have to go with her to the doctor?

MARTIN: It's my business if I get upset. I think I have a right to be there! I think I ought to know what's going on!

MARY: What do you think is going on?

MARTIN: Well, I don't know. That's just the trouble. I want to find out. No one ever tells me anything about this sort of business. I want to find out what's going on.

MARY: What do you suppose goes on in a doctor's office but examinations?

MARTIN: Well, that's what I mean. I don't know anything about this doctor. I'm taking him on . . . well, whose recommendation are we taking him on?

MARY: He's a perfectly well-known doctor in this town.

MARTIN: I know there are lots of well-known doctors. I don't like him. I don't know . . . I don't like him!

MARY: There you go, getting upset again.

MORENO: What is next in the dream?

MARTIN: Well, someone else is mentioned, another doctor, Doctor Magnus.

MARY: Well, Jean could go to Dr. Magnus.

MARTIN: I don't think he's a good man.

MARY: How do you know?

MARTIN: I don't know, I just think so.

MARY: Oh, you just think so! You always get full of ideas about what you think.

You never even try to find out whether it's true what you think. You just think so! She shouldn't go to a doctor just because you get upset when she goes to a doctor? Is that the idea?

MARTIN: Then all of a sudden they reject me. They push me out of the room.

MORENO: Push him out of the room!

(*The five women push him out, off the stage. MARTIN resists*)

MARTIN: Then I go outside.

MORENO: Where do you go outside? Where are you now?

MARTIN: I don't know exactly. I can see a drugstore downtown in some kind of large city. I don't know where.

MORENO: What are you doing there?

MARTIN: I'm outside the drugstore. I'm just looking into the window.

MORENO: What do you see there?

MARTIN: (*Moves towards the front of stage and points with his right arm at various objects which he sees*) I notice some razor blades, shaving brushes, various kinds of instruments.

MORENO: Instruments? What kind of instruments?

MARTIN: Oh, knives, scissors, and . . . they look as though they might be doctor's instruments. I'm not sure.

MORENO: Doctor's instruments. What else do you see in the window? Do you see anybody in the drugstore?

MARTIN: No.

MORENO: What else do you do in front of the drugstore?

MARTIN: Well, I'm trying to make up my mind whether to go back to the house or not. I don't know what to do. I want to go back and I don't want to go back. Finally I decide to find out what I'm doing, so I go into the drugstore and I go into a phone booth that's in the drugstore. Here is a telephone booth (*moves towards the left column on the stage*) and I go into it. I call the number. (*Dials a number*)

MORENO: What number?

MARTIN: It's 734128. And then I notice the number on the phone, I can't see it all the way, but it ends in 997.

MORENO: Nine nine seven.

MARTIN: Jean answers the phone.

JEAN: Hello. Who's this?

MARTIN: Hello, this is Martin. (*Prompting auxiliary JEAN*) You're surprised at my calling.

JEAN: (*In a surprised tone*) Hello Martin, where are you? I didn't expect you to phone me! I expected you to come home!

MARTIN: (*Uncertain of himself*) Well, I'm downtown someplace. I didn't know whether to come home or not.

JEAN: What do you mean, you didn't know whether to come home or not?

MARTIN: Oh, I don't know. What have you been doing right now? (*Explains to AUXILIARY EGO*) She tells me she's been taking a bath. She says . . . something about Scotch bathing. I don't understand it. She says she's been taking a bath, Scotch bathing.

JEAN: I've been taking a bath, Scotch bathing.

MARTIN: Well, that sounds funny. I suppose that means you're going to the doctor. You always bathe before you go to the doctor.

JEAN: I hope that's not the only time I bathe?

MARTIN: No. But I know that you always do before going to the doctor. That means, if you bathe at this time of the day it usually means that you're going out somewhere, if it's about one or two o'clock in the afternoon and you're taking a bath. Well, I guess I'd better come home. I don't know what to do!

JEAN: OK, fine, you come home. (*MARTIN hangs up the receiver*)

MORENO: Where are you now? From where do you phone?

MARTIN: I walk out of the telephone booth and somehow I'm not in the drugstore at all. (*Walks across stage and looks searchingly around*) It's a grocery store. I keep seeing a grocery store. It's about two blocks from my house.

MORENO: What are you doing there? What do you see?

MARTIN: I see fruits, a stack of apples and grapefruits right here in this box. (*Indicates fruits*) Frozen fruits over here. Then there are shelves down this way. (*Indicates shelves behind him*)

MORENO: Who else is there besides you?

MARTIN: No one. I'm alone. That's all.

MORENO: Are you standing and looking at them?

MARTIN: Yes, just standing and looking at them.

MORENO: Do you buy anything?

MARTIN: No.

MORENO: Do you think that's a grocery store?

MARTIN: Yes.

MORENO: How do you feel as you are standing alone in this grocery store with so much merchandise around?

MARTIN: I feel as though I'm about to lose something. I mean, something is going on which I know nothing about and that represents a loss of some kind to me and I don't know what to do. It seems to be something which I must accept and I'm debating this question back and forth. I know Jean must go to the doctor and I don't want her to go but if she goes I feel that I ought to go with her. I feel very badly about it. I was still wondering while I was telephoning whether she was really going to go or not. I suppose I was hoping that she wasn't, but when I called up and found out that she is taking a bath, then I knew for sure that she is going to the doctor. I feel very unhappy. I have the urge to do something. I raise my arm as if to hit someone. At this point the dream ends.

MORENO: (*Walks up the stage to interview MARTIN*) Whenever she takes a bath she goes to the doctor?

MARTIN: Well, it seems to me that way whenever she takes a bath in the middle of the day. Otherwise she takes it in the early morning or late evening. But whenever she takes it in the middle of the day she goes to the doctor.

MORENO: While you are standing there you are fearful and displeased and anticipating a catastrophe or something extremely undesirable to happen to you. Now go back to bed in the same position in which you were before awaking, take the same position which you had, Martin. (*MARTIN does this*) You are now closing your eyes. (*MORENO stands behind MARTIN and strokes his head sooth-ingly*) Close your eyes, try to fall asleep, deep asleep. And now concentrate on that last moment in the dream. You are standing there in the grocery store, you have a feeling of anxiety. You feel unhappy, anticipating something to happen. Concentrate on it! Do you see yourself?

MARTIN: Yes.

MORENO: And what happens now?

MARTIN: I . . .

MORENO: Does the dream come to an end and do you continue sleeping?

MARTIN: It comes to and end and I wake up.

MORENO: Then wake up! Wake up! Are you up now? You are sitting up in your bed?

MARTIN: (*Sitting up*) I wake up very slowly, though. It's a very peculiar thing. As I'm more than half asleep I realize that I'm waking up and that I've been dream-ing and that I ought to make some kind of record of it. I had this impulse to make a record of it. So while I'm still really half asleep I concentrate on the whole dream and try to bring it back into sequence and try to remember until I'm quite sure that I have it. And then I suddenly come wide awake and sit up. And I reach out to the table and snap on the light. Immediately I jump out of bed and I go and look at the clock and it's over on my dresser. (*Gets up*)

MORENO: What time is it? (*Takes off-stage position again*)

MARTIN: It's 5:45 a.m. I walk out the door and when I'm in the living room, I go toward the desk and get some note paper that is there and also a pencil. I come back and close the door and come over to the desk and sit down. Then as fast as I can I commence to write down what I remember about the dream. (*Writes*)

MORENO: Did you have another dream since then or is this the only dream that you had that night?

MARTIN: I go back to sleep after I write this since it is so early in the morning. The sleep is quite dreamless and I sleep another six hours.

MORENO: Then go back to bed, go back into the dream. (*Resumes his position near MARTIN*)

MARTIN: (*Protests*) But that is all I dreamt.

MORENO: Just the same, go back into the position you last had when the dream ends.

MARTIN: (*Lies down again in bed, putting his right arm under, his left arm alongside of him*)

MORENO: (*Again using gently relaxing touches*) Concentrate. Now, what do you see?

MARTIN: Now I see the attic in my house.

MORENO: Are you standing there?

MARTIN: Yes, there's a large box of some kind. I look at it and walk towards it.

MORENO: All right then, get up and do that.

MARTIN: (*Gets up, walks across the stage, looks intensely at the floor and indicates the location of the box*) I bend down and try to lift it.

MORENO: Then bend down and try to lift it. (*MORENO keeps fairly close, but off stage*)

MARTIN: (*Trying to lift the box*) It's too heavy. I decide that I have to take something out.

MORENO: Go ahead then. What do you see in the box?

MARTIN: All kinds of things, books, articles of clothing, trousers, shoes . . . Someone is trying to help me.

MORENO: Who is it?

MARTIN: It's a woman, a stout woman, I think.

MORENO: (*Motions to an AUXILIARY EGO to come upon the stage. She stands besides MARTIN, trying to help him lift the box*)

MARTIN: I start to take some things out (*Goes through the motions of taking things out of the box, as AUXILIARY EGO helps lift them*) They are small articles, like rolls of paper. They're of no value and I'm going to force the box wider because we're going on a trip and we have to make it wider. I give the things to her. (*Hands objects to AUXILIARY EGO*) The woman throws them on the floor. (*AUXILIARY EGO throws things on the floor*)

MORENO: Look at her! Who is she?

MARTIN: (*Peers at AUXILIARY EGO*) I guess . . . It's my mother-in-law! Yes, that's who it is. She's not terribly stout but she's not terribly slender, either.

MOTHER-IN-LAW: Let me help you, Martin.

MARTIN: Yes, mother. Finally, when we've taken these articles out, I see this rug. It's quite large. It's in several folds. It's about this thick. (*Demonstrates*)

MORENO: What kind of rug?

MARTIN: It seems almost like canvas. It's a cotton rug of some kind.

MORENO: What are you doing with it?

MARTIN: My mother-in-law grabs it.

(*Auxiliary ego grabs the rug*)

MARTIN: (*Spreads rug over the stage together with AUXILIARY EGO*)

MORENO: What are you doing?

MARTIN: We are spreading the rug.

MOTHER-IN-LAW: It's not in very good condition, is it?

MARTIN: No, it's badly stained.

MOTHER-IN-LAW: (*Trying to rub the stains off*) I wonder if we can do something with it.

MARTIN: It doesn't seem worth while to take it along. Then suddenly my wife appears. (*Another AUXILIARY EGO comes up, taking the part of the wife*)

MORENO: Whose rug is it?

MARTIN: It's our rug. It's very badly stained and it has a hole or two in it.

MORENO: A hole or two . . .

MARTIN: And then my wife comes in. I say to her "Let's throw it away!" (*Prompting AUXILIARY EGO*) You want to keep it, you're very anxious to keep it.

JEAN: (*Horrified*) Oh no, no, no, no!

MARTIN: But it isn't any good. It's all stained. What can we do with it?

JEAN: Oh, no, let's keep it.

MARTIN: (*Becoming irritated with her*) It has to be fixed, it has to be redyed and the holes patched up.

JEAN: I'm going to have it fixed. I'm going to have the holes patched up and I'm going to have it redyed. It's very important to me.

MARTIN: (*Getting more upset*) But that will cost a great deal of money to have that rug repaired. I don't know how much.

JEAN: How much do you think it will cost?

MARTIN: (*More agitated*) I don't know. Well, is this your own idea? (*Suspiciously*) On whose advice do you think we ought to have this rug fixed up? (*Turns to MORENO*) This is where Doctor Lowrey comes in.

MORENO: Where is Doctor Lowrey? Is he in the scene?

MARTIN: No, he's not in the scene. He flashes in and flashes out.

MORENO: You take the part of Dr. Lowrey, Martin.

MARTIN AS DR. LOWREY: I think you ought to take this rug along with you, to have the rug done over.

JEAN: Doctor Lowrey also seems to think it is worth fixing.

MARTIN AS DR. LOWREY: (*Very businesslike*) After all, it's too valuable to be discarded. Of course, it will cost a great deal to have it fixed up but it will at least be worth it. You better have it fixed up and take it along with you, Martin, I can send you to someone who will renovate that rug for you all right.

MARTIN: (*Taking his own role and also his own position in the group, pensively, his irritation gone*) It certainly seems odd to me to go fixing up an old rug like that, but if you say so, it seems all right to me. But I personally think it will take a tremendous amount to have something like that done, something like a couple of thousand dollars. Maybe it would be better to discard it or get a new one, or something like that.

MARTIN AS DR. LOWREY: (*MARTIN moves off stage again and takes DOCTOR LOWREY's position*) I know it will cost a great deal but it certainly will be worth it. Don't discard it.

MARTIN: (*Moving across stage to his own position again, disconsolately holding the rug*) All right, if you say so. If she wants the rug I guess we'll have to take it along. (*Looks deflated*)

MORENO: And now, what happens, Martin? (*Comes closer to MARTIN, takes his hand*)

MARTIN: I remember now. This dream which we just enacted, the one about the rug precedes and is immediately followed by the other dream, the first one we produced.

MORENO: The dream which starts with the women talking about you?

MARTIN: Yes, it jumped immediately to that one.

MORENO: It jumped immediately from one to the other. Now this took place in a different room?

MARTIN: Yes, this was up in the attic and the other was down on the second floor.

MORENO: Now, in the second dream, is your mother-in-law there, or isn't she? I am referring to the one with all the women in it.

MARTIN: (*Thinking hard, tries to recall*) No.

MORENO: She's only in the first, but not the second.

MARTIN: (*More certain now*) No, she isn't in the second.

MORENO: Now tell me, in that dream, did you awake from the first or did it all merge into one dream? (*Drops his hand, continues to stand near MARTIN*)

MARTIN: (*Tries to remember*)

MORENO: When the dream ends, therefore, Martin, you have two feelings. One isn't a pleasant one, you didn't feel happy about it. On the other hand you have the urge to record the dream. You felt it might be useful. To whom?

MARTIN: To me, I mean, just to put it down, or maybe to you. I thought it was a good idea to get it down before it slipped away from me.

MORENO: You tried to put it down the best you could.

MARTIN: (*Affirmatively*) Hmm.

MORENO: I want to ask you a few questions and you just muse about them the best way you can. The first one is: You think in your dream that your wife, Jean, before she has an intercourse with a man, takes a bath. Taking a bath and making yourself clean and neat, you make yourself attractive. In this case Jean makes herself attractive to the man with whom she is going to have intercourse. The second is: in the dream you resent very much that your wife should be examined by a doctor. Gynecological examination is something like a sort of sexual intercourse with the doctor. Going to a doctor to be examined is like having intercourse with a man. Is that what you think?

MARTIN: That is my reaction. I mean, I have the same kind of reaction as though it would be real intercourse. If it were necessary to describe intercourse, I have the feeling that that's what this is.

MORENO: You think that a woman preparing to go to a gynecologist has very many components which relate themselves easily to what a sexual act is: she takes a bath, she makes herself clean, she makes herself attractive. A woman, when she makes herself attractive to go to the doctor feels: "I want him to feel that I'm good looking, I want him to like me. I don't want him to feel that I'm neglecting myself and that I'm not clean and neat when I appear." In other words, it is for you, the husband of Jean, the same as if she would have an affair with a man. It is true that it is an affair that is highly dignified by custom and has a professional meaning. I know that you realize this, but, at the same time, you can't help having this compulsive thought that it has so many factors which are similar to the way in which a woman prepares herself for sexual intercourse. In fact, she takes more care of herself when she goes to the doctor than when she goes to bed with you. The doctor is a novelty, like a new and unknown lover whom she wants to conquer. She does not have to conquer you.

MARTIN: Yes, yes.

MORENO: She takes a longer bath, she cleans herself more when she goes to the doctor. She makes herself as attractive as possible. She thinks of it as being a major adventure.

MARTIN: Come to think of it, she puts lipstick on when she goes out but I don't see her with too much lipstick on around the house. She does this only when she goes out. And when she goes to see doctors she appears to be most attractive.

MORENO: So, in your dream you can't stand the idea that she takes a bath because that means to you that she will have a sexual act, intercourse with the doctor. You resent very much that doctors have a privilege of doing that, just to examine and being paid for it in addition. Under the pretext that they are doctors they become very intimate with your wife. You don't want your wife to be available to every doctor's fancy. But the worst of it is: she seems to like to go. She doesn't put up any particular resistance. She takes every opportunity to go to the doctor to be examined. You feel that she should be stopped. What's the idea? She almost acts as if she and you were strangers. She doesn't want you to go along. That is exactly how a woman acts when she has a date with a stranger. Then she doesn't want another man to be around. She wants to be alone with him. Here she is alone with a man in a room and he does the same thing to her that a lover would do. Now, you didn't marry her for that. There is no excuse for it! So you resent it violently and you are amazed that your own sister agrees to it. All the women seem to agree on this point. But you feel that it is the same thing as being intimate with another man. Who is Doctor Stone? Do you know who he is?

MARTIN: No, I was struck by the name. As I think of it, it's my own!

MORENO: It's your own name. To top off everything else she goes to another Stone. Who is the other one you mentioned, the one on the hill?

MARTIN: Bridge.

MORENO: Yes, Bridge.

MARTIN: I don't know how to make that out. She's never visited a Doctor Stone. There are a number of doctors, one by the name of Farrell, another by the name of Swanson, whom I mentioned to you before, one by the name of Brewster, and another by the name of Hoffman. But no one by the name of Stone.

MORENO: Why does she go to so many doctors? Why doesn't she have only one. Why does she change from one to the other?

MARTIN: She changes because of my reactions. The first doctor I took any notice of was the obstetrician, Farrell. Swanson, before that, I took no notice of him. I transplanted the feeling to him after the experience with Doctor Farrell. I wanted to see him, and because of my reaction I decided that I didn't like him and that she should look for someone else. So we went to Doctor Swanson. I met him and didn't like him. Then we went to a clinic and there we saw Doctors Hoffman and Brewster and I didn't like them. I saw three to five more. I got the same reaction. I just didn't like them at all. I had the same reaction with each one of them.

MORENO: You met them, saw them face to face?

MARTIN: Yes, I met all of them.

MORENO: You went to them to convince yourself that they are regular guys, that they are not in any way upset by it.

MARTIN: I went even further than that. I told one of them that the only trouble with me was that I didn't know what was going on and if I could find out, if I could actually be there I would lose this feeling of anxiety. So on two occasions when I went to this clinic, once with Dr. Hoffman and once with Doctor Brewster, on two occasions at least I went into the examining room. They made special arrangements. They fixed it up with the matron. I just said right out that we had come down together and if it was all right with them we would stay together.

MORENO: In other words, you stayed right in the examining room as she was being examined? You saw her being examined?

MARTIN: Yes.

MORENO: Martin, now let us return to bed and repeat the way your dream ended. (*Moves back toward the bed. MARTIN follows*)

MARTIN: (*Lies down in bed again, with his arms and legs in the position in which they were when he last enacted the end of the dream*) I feel badly. I raise my arm as if to hit someone. But here the dream ends.

MORENO: Are you satisfied with the end? (*Stands near MARTIN*)

MARTIN: No. I have the urge to do something, to hit someone. I feel a grinding pain in my stomach. I can feel it all over again.

MORENO: Are you thinking of anyone in particular?

MARTIN: I'm thinking of myself . . . You know, I would like the dream to continue so that I'm the doctor.

MORENO: (*Nodding*) Let's see you as the doctor. (*Moves off stage*)

MARTIN: I see myself coming to the examining room. I stand over there . . . (*Points to right side of stage*)

MORENO: Then get up and stand over there.

MARTIN: (*Gets up and steps eagerly across the stage*) My wife is over at the other side of the room. When I am the doctor I am between them.

MORENO: Your wife is over at the other side of the room. (*Motions to same auxiliary ego who took JEAN'S role before; she comes up and goes to the side of the stage indicated by MARTIN*)

MARTIN: Then I suddenly turn into the doctor. (*Moves towards the middle of the stage, walks slowly*)

MARTIN AS DOCTOR: I want to make all the examinations myself. I see Jean before me, but she is not the patient, she is apparently the nurse. Suddenly she is gone. I'm talking to someone who is angry. I see his big eyes staring at me. I think it is Martin, I'm not sure, it may be the eyes of any man whose wife goes to a gynecologist. I say to him: "I see that you are suspicious of doctors. You think that I have performed a hymenectomy upon your wife, before she married you."

MARTIN: Yes, that's it. (*Explains*) I'm continuously changing from the doctor's role to myself . . . when I do that I'll change my position on the stage; when I'm over here I'm the doctor, over here I'm myself.

MARTIN AS DOCTOR: (*Shakes his head, acts embarrassed, face red*)

MARTIN: (*Moving closer to DOCTOR, soliloquizing*) He wants to know why I believe this. (*To the DOCTOR*) Why? Because on the first night we were married our sexual intercourse was not as difficult as I imagined it would be.

MARTIN AS DOCTOR: (*Doesn't speak, acts guilty*)

MARTIN: (*Soliloquizing*) I become excited. (*To DOCTOR*) My wife was a virgin and I expected difficulty, a rupturing of the hymen, a barrier to be broken through! I feel sure the hymen was missing.

MARTIN AS DOCTOR: I didn't do it, didn't do it!

MARTIN: But my wife was a virgin, she had no previous sexual relation. There is no alternative. It must be. You did it.

MARTIN AS DOCTOR: (*Comes close to where Martin stands, speaks gently*) Your wife was a virgin on the first night of your marriage. It was you who performed the operation, you, Dr. Martin Stone.

MARTIN: (*Turns to MORENO*) At this point I'd like the dream to end.

(*MORENO comes upon the stage. MORENO and MARTIN stand in the center of the stage, facing each other*)

MORENO: And where do I come in?

MARTIN: You mean, in the dream? Of course you, too, are a doctor. (*Walks a few steps away and returns*) But there is a difference. You are my doctor. I came to you just like Jean went to her doctors.

MORENO: Is that why you did not bring your wife along? (*Affectionately puts his arm on MARTIN's shoulder*)

MARTIN: (*Begins to smile*) Maybe the situation is now reversed. Now it is she who is anxious to come to my doctor. I'm trying to keep her away from you, just as she was trying to keep me away from her gynecologists. It's a sweet revenge. (*MORENO and he both smile, shake hands*)

Moreno ends the session with a discussion of other patient's responses to the dream. These are omitted here.

DISCUSSION OF DREAM PRODUCTION TECHNIQUES

The objective of psychodramatic techniques is to stir up the dreamer to produce the dream instead of analyzing it for him. Even if one could be sure that the analysis is objective and reliable it is preferable if analysis is turned into production by the dreamer.

The first stage of the production was the dream which Martin actually had on the reality level on a specific date; then Martin was unconsciously his own producer. The stage of production was in the mind of the sleeper; the dreamer hallucinates all his auxiliary egos and auxiliary objects. There was no one to share the dream with him; he was the sole agent of his warming up process, and the end which the dream had, pleasant or unpleasant, had only him as a witness and observer.

The second stage of production takes place in a theatre of psychodrama; it is here that therapy beings. As the dreamer begins to reenact his own dream with the aid of a director and auxiliary egos, the manifest as well as the latent configurations of the dream come forth naturally. Whatever a verbal analysis could reveal to the dreamer is brought out in direct, actional terms. The dreamer does not have to "agree" with the analyst. His own actions tell him and the audience what processes take place in his mind. One might say that instead of being analyzed through analysis he is analyzed through production. Analysis becomes submerged into the production. It is of advantage that learning does not have the form of analysis but the form of living out in action, a form of self-realization through the dream. Beyond this the dreamer brings forth experiences which are in analysis as well as in all verbal communication frequently guess work and as such often unreliable or at least limited.

The third stage of the dream production is stirring the patient up to extend the dream beyond the end which nature has set for the sleeper, or at least the end which he remembers. He is encouraged to redream the dream, to continue the dream on the stage, and to end it in a fashion which appears more adequate to him, or which brings him to a better control of the latent dynamics upsetting him. Such a procedure becomes a veritable "dream test" and leads to an intensive form of catharsis which may be called "dream catharsis." This kind of "dream learning" leads up to the next stage.

The fourth stage finds the patient again back in his own bed, sleeping as he was in the first phase *in situ,* in reality. He is again his own director, hallucinating his own dream characters and objects. But what he has learned in the course of active dream production he is apt to apply now—to the same dream if it is a recurrent one, or to a similar dream emerging in him. One could speak here of "post-psychodramatic suggestion" as one talks about post-hypnotic suggestion. In both cases an operation reaches into the patient's unconscious activities long after he has been exposed to it, and it reaches him on a deep action level, for instance here during sleep; he becomes his own dream therapist . . . .

PART IV: Autobiographical Selections

"I had my own theatre. Even if it was against the theatre, it was still a theatre. It's hard to draw the line sometimes."

(From *Autobiography*, unpublished, Chapter 8, 40)

CHAPTER 17

The Man in the Green Cloak

1972–73, 1946, 1972, 1956

Editor's note: These fragments are meant to convey a sense of Moreno as protagonist. Most come from autobiographical writings which Moreno worked on during 1972-3, the last two years of his life. In the selections we can connect the concept of creativity that lies at the heart of psychodramatic theory with Moreno's life-long compulsion to be a God-player. We get a glimpse of where Moreno saw himself in his own social atom. And we read a description of the mystical experience he had as a young man that confirmed his deep belief in human perfectibility. The final selection, written in 1956, is a fantasy in which Moreno likens himself to Johnny Appleseed.

PLAYING GOD*

One Sunday afternoon my parents went out to visit friends. I stayed home and played with some neighbor's children. We were in the basement of my house, a large room, empty except for a huge oak table in the middle of the floor. We were trying to think of a game to play when I came up with "Let's play God and his Angels."

"But who will play God?" "I am God and you are my angels," I replied. The other children agreed to the game.

"We must build the heavens first," one of the children declared. We dragged chairs from all over the house to the basement, put them on the big table, and began to build one heaven after another by tying several chairs together on one level and putting more chairs above them until we reached the ceiling. Then all the children helped me to climb up to the top chair where I sat pretty. The children then circled around the table, using their arms as wings and singing. One or two of the larger children held up the mountain of chairs we had assembled. Suddenly one of the children asked me, "Why don't you fly?" I stretched my arms, trying it. The angels who were holding the chairs flew away, too. A moment later I fell and found myself on the floor, my right arm broken . . . .

I have always felt that I am a special case with God. Although it is as-sumed that we are all God's children, I have often had the powerful feeling that I am a favorite child of God's. When I was very young the idea of death, my own death, never entered my mind. Even the death of my grandmother and the death of our neighbor in the fire were short distractions in my life, although I missed my grandmother very much and was terrified by the fire. Like many young people I thought I would live for ever. I was endowed with good health and was rarely ill. I felt I was protected from falling ill, but if I did get sick, I would recover fully and quickly. I knew that I was always guided, and that nothing could ever happen to me that would hinder me from a significant life. I was in direct communication with God. I spoke to

---

*"Playing God" from *Autobiography* (unpublished), Chapter 1, 11-12, 15; "Young Man in Search of a Calling" from *Autobiography* (unpublished), Chapter 2, 3-4, 16-17, 22-24; "A Life of Service" from *Autobiography* (unpublished), Chapter 3, 4-6; "Among the Prosti-tutes" from *Autobiography* (unpublished), Chapter 4, 7-9; "Superintendent of a Refugee Camp" from *Autobiography* (unpublised), Chapter 5, 18-20; "At the Theatre of Spontane-ity" from *Psychodrama*, Vol. 1, 3-5; "A Religious Experience" from Religion of the God-Father: in Johnson, Paul (1972), *Healer of the Mind: A Psychiatrist's Search for Faith* Nashville, TN: Abingdon Press, 200-203; "The Story of Johnny Psychodramatist" from *International Journal of Sociometry and Sociaty* 1 (1956), 3-4.

Him or He spoke to me. We had a silent contract, one which I expected him to keep.

I was twice picked up by the gypsies and brought to their camps, according to my mother. I had no fear. The gypsies brought me back after a short time . . . .

YOUNG MAN IN SEARCH OF A CALLING

My behavior was very much out of order. I was totally without sensibility. In order to test my God-likeness, I tried to jump from an oak tree. I jumped from a branch ten feet up and I was not injured. I felt good about that. I took it as a sign.

One day I jumped out of a window nude and walked the streets of Vienna. People stopped me and I went back home. I was not offended by their intervention. I maintained my dignity.

I was, under it all, frightened by what might become of me. I was quite isolated from other people at the time, although I was not lonely. Neither was I completely out of touch with other people. My mother was very worried about my future. All of my brilliant promise seemed destined to be burned out by what she thought was my craziness.

I began to wonder if there had been others in a state of mind like mine. My attention was particularly drawn to Dante and to Swedenborg, the Swedish mystic . . . .

I wore a dark green mantle which fell almost to my ankles. Everyone began to identify me with it, "the Prophet's Mantle." I wore it summer and winter, perhaps with the intention of making myself easily identifiable, like an actor who wears the same costume in every performance of a given role. At times it seemed to me that I was creating a type, a role, which once encountered, could never be forgotten.

I had the *idee fixe* that a single individual had no authority, that he must be the voice of the group. It must be a group; the new word must come from a group. Therefore, I went out to find friends, followers, good people. My new religion was a religion of being, of self-perfection. It was a religion of helping and healing, for helping was more important than talking. It was a religion of silence. It was a religion of doing a thing for its own sake, unrewarded, unrecognized. It was a religion of anonymity.

I felt that, even if my modest effort should remain entirely ineffective and be forgotten, it would have been important from the point of view of eternity that such things were tried and existed, that such things were cultivated, and that such purity was maintained regardless whether it paid off. The new religion required a mood of resignation, of just being and having the immediate satisfactions of such a state of being. If love or comradeship should arise, it should be fulfilled and retained in the moment without calculating the possible returns and without expecting any compensation . . . .

The first encounter I tried to have was with the child. I turned to the offspring, the babes, to the child, and I moved into places where the children played, where they were left by their parents when mothers and fathers had to go to work. Instead of talking to the children in plain language I told them fairy tales. I discovered that I could never repeat the same fairy tale. I noticed that I felt an obligation to myself and to the children to maintain their sense of wonderment even when the plot was the same, to maintain myself on a level of spontaneity and creativity in order to live up to the rigorous demands of my creative ego which did not give me the prophetic license for less. I watched with astonishment my transformation from a humdrum student into an adventurous prophet. I was aroused to greater deeds every day by the imaginative pleas of the children.

When I look at a child, I see "yes, yes, yes, yes." They do not have to learn to say, "Yes." *Being born is yes.* You see spontaneity in the living form. It is written all over the child, in his act hunger, as he looks at things, as he listens to things, as he rushes into time, as he moves into space, as he grabs for objects, as he smiles and cries. In the very beginning he sees no barriers in objects, no limits of distance, no resistances or prohibitions. But as objects hinder his locomotions and people respond to him with,"No, no, no," he starts on his reactive phase, still reaching out, but with growing anxiety, fear, tension, and caution.

I found a deep meaning in children's God playing. As a student I used to walk through the Gardens of Vienna, gathering children and forming groups for impromptu play. I knew, of course, about Rousseau, Pestalozzi, and Froebel.* But this was a new slant. It was kindergarten on a cosmic scale, a creative revolution among children. It was not a philanthropic crusade of adults for children, but a crusade of children for themselves, for a society of their own age and their own rights. I wanted to give the children their capacity to fight against social stereotypes, against robots—for spontaneity and creativity.

It was in my work with the children that my theories of spontaneity and creativity crystallized. Inevitably the older the child the less spontaneous he was, and the less creative he was. The two factors, spontaneity and creativity, went together. Also I found that whenever a child repeated himself in the playing out of an idea of a dramatic sketch, his portrayals became more and more rigid. . . .

One day I walked through the Augarten, a park near the Archduke's palace, where I saw a group of children loafing. I stopped and began to tell them a story. To my astonishment other children dropped their games and joined

*Pestalozzi and Froebel were pioneers of the kindergarten movement in Europe. (Ed.)

in. So did the nurses with their baby carriages, the mothers and fathers, the policemen on horseback. From then on one of my favorite pastimes was to sit at the foot of a large tree and let the children come and listen to a fairy tale. The most important part of the story is that I sat at the foot of a tree, like a being out of a fairy tale, and that the children were drawn to me as if by a magic flute. It seemed to me that they were bodily removed from their drab surroundings and brought into a fairy land. It was not so much what I told them, the tales themselves, but it was the act, the atmosphere of mystery, the paradox, the becoming real of the unreal.

A LIFE OF SERVICE

Like me, Chaim [Kellmer, a friend] made his living by tutoring. One day, following my example, he stopped charging for his work. The families he had been with for several years were embarrassed. They invited him for extra meals. They kept a bed for him so he could stay overnight any time he wanted. They gave him clothing and showered him with gifts. He was such a wonderful teacher and friend to those families that they did not want to lose him. In the end he was the best-dressed and best-fed tutor I knew. He laughed when I teased him about it. "If you give love to people, they give it back to you," he replied.

Chaim also visited people and gave them his counsel, trying to help them solve their problems. People would call on him whenever they needed help. Often they insisted on giving him money for his help, but he always refused, saying, "There is only one thing I can accept. We have a fund for renting a home in the city for people who need shelter. Give money to the fund."

Thus the Religion of the Encounter came to life in the years between 1908 and 1914. My group of followers and I numbered five young men. We were all committed to the sharing of anonymity, of loving and giving, living a direct and concrete life in the community with all we met. We left our homes and families and took to the streets. We were nameless but were easily recognized by our beards and our warm, human, and gay approach to all comers. None of us would accept any money for the services we rendered to others, but we received many gifts from anonymous donors. All the gifts received went into the fund for the *House of the Encounter.*

In the years before World War I the turmoil and political instability of the Austro-Hungarian empire expressed itself in the vast numbers of people who were seeking new homes, either in the Americas or in Palestine. They poured into Vienna, as refugees still do, and they often had a long wait before they could get passage, sometimes as long as a year. Frequently during the long wait they exhausted their meager savings . . . .

We found a house in one of the central districts of Vienna. Anyone who came was welcome and could stay without paying any rent. So they came from all over. They did not know our names, but they carried pictures or descriptions, often quite bizarre, of the founder of the house and his helpers. They heard of us through letters from relatives and friends and from newspaper accounts of our work. Some came alone, some with wives and children. They rarely came by prior arrangement but just showed up at the house holding the much-handled letters or clippings.

On the walls of the house were colorfully drawn inscriptions with the following pronouncement: "Come to us from all nations. We will give you shelter." It still amazes me that so many people crowded into that house and shared with one another whatever they had, without fighting or rancor. We tried to keep families together, but there was little privacy. Nonetheless, there were several babies conceived and born during the long wait for passage. We held nightly sessions after supper in which problems were brought forth and grievances were settled . . . .

AMONG THE PROSTITUTES

I began to visit their houses, accompanied by a physician, Dr. Wilhelm Gruen, a specialist in venereal diseases, and Carl Colbert, the publisher of a Vienna newspaper, *Der Morgan.* Our visits were not motivated by any desire to "reform" the girls, nor to analyze them. The girls were suspicious of us at first because the Catholic Charities in Vienna had frequently tried to intervene in their lives. Nor was I looking for the "charismatic prostitute" among them. She is the creature of a social worker's fantasy—a strong, attractive woman who could be induced to change her ways and to lead her sisters out of lives of corruption.

I had in mind what Lassalle and Marx had done for the working class, ideology aside. They made the workers respectable by giving them a sense of dignity; they organized them into labor unions which raised the status of the entire class. Aside from the anticipated economic benefits to the workers, this organizational activity was accompanied by ethical achievements. I had in mind that something similar could be done for the prostitutes. I suspected, to begin with, that the "therapeutic" aspect would be far more important here than the economic, because the prostitutes had been stigmatized for so long as despicable sinners and unworthy people that they had come to accept this an an unalterable fact . . . .

But we were optimistic and started to meet groups of eight to ten girls, two or three times a week in their houses. It was during the afternoon when the Viennese had what is called "Jauze," a counterpart to the British afternoon tea. Coffee and cake were served and we sat round a table. The conference, at first, simply dealt with everyday incidents which the girls experienced: being arrested, being harassed by a policeman for wearing provocative clothing, being jailed because of false accusations from a client, having venereal disease but being unable to get treatment, becoming pregnant and giving birth to a baby, but having to hide the child under an assumed name in a foster home and having to hide one's identity from the child. At first the women were fearful of persecution and opened up very slowly, but when they began to see the purpose of the group and that it was to their benefit, they warmed up and became quite open.

The first results we noticed were quite superficial. For instance, we were able to find a lawyer who would represent them in court. We found a doctor to treat them and a hospital to admit them as patients. Gradually they came to recognize the deeper value of the meetings. It became possible for them to help one another. The girls volunteered to pay a few dimes a week towards the expenses of the meetings and towards a small savings account for emergencies.

By the end of 1913 the prostitutes held a mass meeting in one of the largest halls in Vienna, the Sofiensaal. By this time there was a real organization with elected officers. They led the meeting . . . . In the end it turned into a wild affair. There was a conflict between the pimps and the prostitutes. The police finally forced their way into the hall and broke up the meeting . . . .

SUPERINTENDENT OF A REFUGEE CAMP

A whole population [of Italian-speaking Austrian subjects from the Southern Tyrol] was interned near Vienna for the duration of the war. The people were not free to leave the camp; it was really like a concentration camp. When I arrived there in 1915 there were more than ten thousand people there, most old people, women, and children. I never met one individual in the early days of the war who was not a loyal subject of the Emperor. They were, however, very proud of their Italian heritage. The community consisted of cottage dwellings, each holding several families. . . . I studied the psychological currents that developed around various elements of community life: nationality, politics, sex, staff vs. refugees, and so on. I considered that the disjunction of these elements was the chief source of the most flagrant symptoms of maladjustment I witnessed in the camp. It was through this experience that the idea of a sociometrically planned community came to me . . . .

Using the methods of sociometry, albeit in a very primitive form, I moved families around on the basis of their mutual affinities for one another. Thus the groundwork by which the community was organized was changed for the better. My theory was borne out by the fact that when people were able to live with those to whom they were positively attracted, the families tended to be helpful to one another, and the signs of maladjustment diminished both in number and in intensity. We also rearranged work groups in the factories whenever possible to create greater harmony and productivity among the workers.

The German-speaking police continued to hinder our work. They relished their godlike power to run the camp. I always had a great number of complaints about police abuses. I wrote many letters to the Ministry of the Interior trying to get the government to discipline the police. Fortunately the Ministry removed or transferred some of the worst, which had a chastening effect on the others, at least for a while.

Although my efforts ameliorated some of the gravest problems in the camp, Mittendorf never became a utopia. There was still hunger, illness, corruption, abuse of innocent people. There were so many fine, wonderful people there who had to suffer and who had no alternatives. Maybe that was the worst part of all. Whenever things got too difficult for me I could get into Vienna in the evening and relax at one of the cafes . . . .

AT THE THEATRE OF SPONTANEITY

We had a young actress, Barbara, who worked for the theatre and also took part in a new experiment I had started, the extemporaneous, living newspaper. She was a main attraction because of her excellence in roles of ingenues, heroic and romantic roles. It was soon evident that she was in love with a young poet and playwright who never failed to sit in the first row, applauding and watching every one of her actions. A romance developed between Barbara and George. One day their marriage was announced. Nothing changed, however; she remained our chief actress and he our chief spectator. One day George came to me, his usually gay eyes greatly disturbed. "What happened?" I asked him. "Oh, doctor, I cannot bear it." "Bear what?" I looked at him, investigating. "That sweet, angel-like being whom you all admire acts like a bedeviled creature when she is alone with me. She speaks in the most abusive language and when I get angry at her, as I did last night, she hits me with her fists." "Wait," I said, "you come to the theatre as usual. I will try a remedy."

When Barbara came backstage that night, ready to play in one of her usual roles of pure womanhood, I stopped her. "Look, Barbara, you have done marvelously until now, but I am afraid you are getting stale. People would like to see you in roles in which you portray the nearness to the soil, the rawness of human nature, its vulgarity and stupidity, its cynical reality, people not as they are, but *worse* than they are, people as they are when driven to extremes by unusual circumstances. Do you want to try it?" "Yes," she said enthusiastically. "I am glad you mention it. I felt for quite a while that I have to give our audience a new experience. But do you think I can do it?" "I have confidence in you," I replied, "the news just came in that a girl in Ottakring (a slum district in Vienna), soliciting men on the street, has been attacked and killed by a stranger. He is still at large; the police are searching for him. You are the streetwalker. Here (pointing to Richard, one of our male actors) is the *apache*. Get the scene ready." A street was improvised on the stage, a cafe, two lights.

Barbara went on. George was in his usual seat in the first row, highly excited. Richard, in the role of the *apache*, came out of the cafe with Barbara and followed her. They had an encounter, which rapidly developed into a heated argument. It was about money. Suddenly Barbara changed into a manner of acting totally unexpected from her. She swore like a trooper, punching at the man, kicking him in the leg repeatedly. I saw George half-rising, anxiously raising his arm at me, but the *apache* got wild and began to chase Barbara. Suddenly he grabbed a knife, a prop, from inside his jacket pocket. He chased her in circles, closer and closer. She acted so well that she give the impression of being really scared. The audience got up, roaring, "Stop it, stop it!" But he did not stop until she was supposedly "murdered."

After the scene Barbara was exuberant with joy. She embraced George, and they went home in ecstasy. From then on she continued to act in such roles of the lower depth. George came to see me the following day. He instantly understood that it was therapy. She played as domestics, lonely spinsters, revengeful wives, spiteful sweethearts, barmaids, gun molls. George gave me daily reports. "Well," he told me after a few sessions, "something is happening to her. She still has her fits of temper at home, but they have lost their intensity. They are shorter and in the midst of them she often smiles, and as yesterday, she remembers similar scenes which she did on the stage and she laughs and I laugh with her because I, too, remember. It is as if we see each other in a psychological mirror. We both laugh. At times she begins to laugh before she has the fit, anticipating what will happen. She warms up to it finally, but it lacks the usual heat."

It was like a catharsis coming from humor and laughter. I continued the treatment, assigning roles to her more carefully, according to her needs and his. One day George confessed the effect which these sessions had upon him as he watched them and absorbed the analysis which I gave afterwards. "Looking at her productions on the stage has made me more tolerant of Barbara, less impatient." That evening I told Barbara how much progress she had made as an actress and asked her whether she would not like to act on the stage with George. They did this and the duets on the state which appeared as a part of our official program resembled more and more the scenes which they daily had at home. Gradually her family and his, scenes from her childhood, their dreams and plans for the future were portrayed. After every performance some spectators would come up to me, asking why the Barbara-George scenes touched them so much more deeply than the others. . . .

Some months later, Barbara and George sat alone with me in the theatre. They had found themselves and each other again, or better, they had found themselves and each other for the first time. I analyzed the development of their psychodrama, session after session, and told them the story of their cure.

A RELIGIOUS EXPERIENCE

I suddenly felt reborn. I began then to hear voices, not in the sense of a mental patient, but in the sense of a person beginning to feel that he hears a voice which reaches all beings and which speaks to all beings in the same language, which is understood by all men, and one which gives us hope, which gives our life direction, which gives our cosmos a direction and a meaning, that the universe is not just a jungle and a bundle of wild forces, that it is basically infinite creativity. And that this infinite creativity which is true on all levels of existence, whether it is now physical or social or biological, whether it is in our galaxy or in other galaxies far away from us, whether it is in the past or in the present or in the future, ties us together. We are all bound together by responsibility for all things, there is no limited, partial responsibility. And responsibility makes us automatically also creators of the world. And I began to feel that I am, and I began to feel that I am the father and that I am responsible, I am responsible for everything which happens, I am responsible for everything which will happen in the future, for everything which happened in the past, and even if I am helpless to do anything, to remove the causes of suffering or to do anything, that I have now the operational link to the entire world. Everything belongs to me and I belong to everybody. Responsibility is the tie which we share and which brings us into the cosmos. And responsibility for the future of the world, a responsibility which does not always look back, but which looks forward. And so I saw the cosmos as an enormous enterprise, billions of partners, invisible hands, arms stretched out, one to touch the other, all being able, through responsibility, to be Gods.

And it was in such a mood of utter inspiration that I rushed into the house in which I lived. It was a house in the midst of the Valley of May, in a little town near Vienna. The only thing I heard was a voice, words, words, coming, going through my head. I didn't have the patience to sit down and write them down, so I grabbed one red pencil after another, went into the top room of the house near the tower and began to write all the words upon the walls, all the words which I heard and which were spoken to me aloud . . . .

I heard "I." I did not hear "He" or "Thou." I heard "I." There is deep meaning in this. "He" would have been wrong; it would have pushed responsibility upon the cosmic God. "Thou" would have been wrong. It would have pushed responsibility upon Christ. It's "I." It's my responsibility.

And I wrote and wrote and wrote that morning, until I fell exhausted upon the floor.

THE STORY OF JOHNNY PSYCHODRAMATIST

Among the many pioneers who arrived in this country in the early part of its history was Johnny Psychodramatist. As the story goes, he was born one stormy night on a ship sailing on the Black Sea in the southern parts of Europe. He crossed the Atlantic and settled here on the shores of the Hudson River.

Johnny was a strange fellow who lived all by himself. He had little to offer except for an odd gift of seeing through people's minds and persistently trying to figure out how they felt about each other. Whenever he saw a man, as a pastime he would draw a line from him to his neighbor, from the neighbor to the blacksmith across the street, and from him to the pastor in the churchyard nearby, and so a line after line after line from one to the other, until the entire village was charted like the map of the landscape, or of a starry sky above him. He drew red lines when he saw love and charity; black lines when it was hostility, greed, and anger; green lines when it was jealousy and envy; blue lines for the lonely and forgotten ones. People often stopped to look wonderingly at the magic map which Johnny was drawing. It was the picture of the village how it really was and not what the people pretended it to be when they put on their artificial masks, covering up their real face underneath. When some of the villagers stopped, Johnny let them in on the secret, and they blushed when they saw themselves exposed. And so Johnny's little lawn and yard became the place to which people secretly came at night as the place where they could truly see themselves, as if through a mirror.

One day he had another inspiration. Looking at the map, he saw himself on it. He was surrounded by blue lines, a lonely man, entirely cut off from humanity. He cried bitter tears and he wondered how he could show the world how truly loving he [was],[4] so different from his external picture, and how much he could share with people who ignored him. In this black moment, a seed fell from his mind to the ground. It made circles, one above the other. It was a stage upon which the moon shone its friendly light. He stepped upon it and acted the friendly neighbor, the strong, courageous man, and the bringer of luck. As he did this, he felt transformed, the stage underneath him grew bigger and bigger until it was as powerful and complete as any stage every built. It had lights which simulated day and night. All the stage needed was a world to act upon it. From now on he initiated every man who came to him to be and act what he was in his fantasy. The story of Johnny who can build a stage for everyone out of the seed in their mind spread, and stages began to blossom and to grow all over his lawn.

One day Johnny's quiet life was disturbed by the unusual sight of automobiles, airplanes, helicopters, driving and flying by. They were full of people. They were on their way west to conquer the country and challenged him to come with them. Johnny stopped and retreated. Why, he couldn't, he had nothing to offer, he could not compare with them. They were brimming full of ideas and zest. In this moment of desperation, his guardian angel stopped him and talked to him: "Don't be afraid, Johnny, have courage, go ahead!" "But," said Johnny, "what can I do? I have nothing. These people have schemes for houses and skyscrapers, huge airplanes and space ships, trying to build a new world out of their dream. I have nothing, I could not go." "You are wrong, Johnny, look! See the stages you have built out of nothing, out of tiny seeds of thought. Look at them, here, there, everywhere. Go from place to place and build the stages for people everywhere."

Johnny saw the light and began to move across the country. First he drew the lines from one man to another and to another, from house to house, from town to town, wherever he stopped, and the maps of the world became thousand fold. And wherever people saw them, they wondered and became enthralled by the magic pictures. And out of the lines grew the seed of stages on which the people could be and feel themselves. He carried the torch of light and did not rest until there was a stage in every yard, in every home, in every forest, for animals as well as birds, wherever he put down his feet.

But time flew by and Johnny became an old man; his hair was white and he saw the shadow of death nearing him. And when death had come and taken him from the earth, he wondered what to do next. At this juncture his guardian angel appeared again. Johnny looked at him: What shall I do now? My life is over. It is the end." "No," said the guardian angel, "look, see." And Johnny saw the universe filled with millions, seeds of new beings, of newborns, coming and going, going and coming, living and dying like stars that shine and stars that perish. He began to draw lines from one newborn to the next, and to the next, and the next, through the vast spaces of the universe, infinite as his dreams, and each time, the seed of a new stage blossomed on the spot.

In his wanderings he suddenly found himself higher and higher, high above the clouds in a white land, and his guardian angel whispered into his ear: "This is heaven." He saw there angels of all sizes and sexes, of all ages and ranks, and high above everything the mysterious center of the universe itself, where the Supreme Being was resting. Johnny was shaking like an aspen leaf, full of anxiety. In this moment of stress he followed his old impulse to draw lines, his red and blue and green and black lines which flew like powerful lights in all shades and intensity of color from angel to angel, right up to God.

And here he was, holding in his hand the map of heaven itself. But it was so different from the heaven which people were taught it was like on earth, and it was different from the heaven the angels thought it was, and the angels looked at it with curious eyes, discovering their most inner secrets exposed. The angels, and God, too, have an unconscious, and so they all began to laugh. The laughter grew and filled the entire heaven with the joy of a new day.

Johnny was frightened because he thought that punishment would result from his deeds. But as he looked up, he saw to his astonishment that every figure on his heavenly map had turned into a star, and as he looked, farther and farther, more and more stars took their places, millions and millions of them, on the heavenly firmament. And from star to star sprang the lines, in all the colors he had ever envisioned, until they became what they were from the beginning of time, the starry skies of the universe. Every star was the picture of a man he had known when he was on earth, and their emotions were written in the lines that ran between them. The map he had drawn as a boy was now hinged to the skies above.

Notes

CHAPTER 1

[1] See *Einladung zu einer Begegnung* (1914). Translated and reprinted in *Psychodrama*, Vol. 1, frontispiece.

CHAPTER 3

[1] Moreno refers here to elsewhere in *Sociometry* 1 where he lists "some of the communities in which the work has been progressing." The list includes "a resettlement community near Vienna" (Mittendorf), 1915-1917; Plymouth Church, Brooklyn, NY (1928); Mt. Sinai Hospital, New York City (1928); Hunter College, New York City (1929); Grosvenor Settlement House, New York City (1929); Sing Sing Prison, Ossining, NY (1931); Riverdale Country School, Riverdale, NY (1932-33); and the New York State Training School for Girls, Hudson, NY (1932-1937). (Ed.).

[2] References for this article include: Lukács, Georg (1928), *Gesichichte und Klassenbewusstein*, Berlin: Walik Verlag [*History of Class Consciousness*, (1971), Cambridge, MA: M.I.T. Press]; Mannheim, Karl (1936), *Ideology and Utopia: An Introduction to the Sociology of Knowledge*, New York: Harcourt, Brace & Co.; and Brown, J. F. (1934), *Psychology and the Social Order: an Introduction to the Dynamic Study of Social Fields*, New York: McGraw-Hill. (Ed.).

CHAPTER 4

[1] This research is reported more fully in Moreno, J. L. & Jennings, H. H., Sociometric Measurement of Social Configurations, Based on Deviation from Chance, *Sociometry* 1 (1937), 274-342. See Chapter 12 for a similar study, also conducted at Hudson. (Ed.)

CHAPTER 5

[1] A sterling illustration of the fact that physical concepts such as energy cannot be transferred onto a social or a psychological plane is the process of catharsis, which brings about fundamental changes in a situation without effecting any alteration in the energy-pattern situation.

[2] See Moreno, J. L. (1938), Creativity and the Cultural Conserve, *Sociometry* 2, 31.

[3] Breuer and Freud called their early hypnotic treatment of hysteria a "cathartic" procedure. Later, Freud replaced hypnosis with free association and the idea of a cathartic procedure was abandoned. Their concept referred to the patient's discharge of memories in a state of hypnosis. Obviously, their cathartic procedure had no relationship to the drama.

[4] Trends in psychotic patients and patterns of society towards reduction should not be taken as "regression" to an infantile level in the psychoanalytic sense.

[5] It has been a significant finding in the course of psychodramatic work that schizophrenic patients experience complicated patterns of emotion, thought, and interpersonal relations. This is contrary to the general view of Freud and Bleuler that the experiences of schizophrenics are almost entirely confined to the verbal level and that verbal suggestion of an event is just as satisfactory to them as the actualization of an event would be.

CHAPTER 6

[1] Zilboorg, Gregory and Henry, G. W. (1941), *A History of Medical Psychology,* New York: W. W. Norton.

[2] See Mead, G. (1934), *Mind, Self, and Society,* Chicago: University of Chicago Press; Linton, R. (1936), The *Study of Man,* New York: Appleton-Century-Crofts; and Parsons, T. (1951), *The Social System,* Glencoe, IL: The Free Press.

Other references for this article have been omitted because of their incomplete nature, as well as a table of role classifications, which can be found in *Psychodrama,* Vol. 1, Beacon, NY: Beacon House, 77.

CHAPTER 8

[1] Freud, Sigmund (1924), On Narcissism: An Introduction, *Collected Papers,* Vol. 4, New York: International Psychoanalytic Library, 30-60.

CHAPTER 11

[1] See Danielsson, Bengt (1949), Attraction and Repulsion Patterns Among the Jibaro Indians, *Sociometry,* 12, 83–105.

CHAPTER 15

[1] See, for example, such works as *The Theory of Business Enterprise* (1904), *The Instinct of Workmanship* (1914), and *The Vested Interests and the State of the Industrial Arts* (1919).

CHAPTER 16

[1] Three explanatory interjections have been omitted because they are neither particularly useful nor consistent with the rest of the protocol. They are indicated by ellipses within brackets. (Ed.).

CHAPTER 17

[1] See Moreno, J.L. (1946), *Psychodrama*, Vol. 1, Beacon, NY: Beacon House, 2-3. (Ed.).
[2] See Moreno, J.L. (1947), *Theatre of Spontaneity*, Beacon, NY: Beacon House, 3. (Ed.).
[3] See Moreno, J.L. (1953), *Who Shall Survive?*, Beacon, NY: Beacon House, pp. xxix-xxx. (Ed.).
[4] The original has "is," a verb tense error which is of psychological interest: ". . . he wondered how he could show the world how truly loving he is . . " (Ed.).

Chronology of Jacob Levy Moreno

1889   Born Iacov Moreno Levi, Bucharest, May 18.

1894   Moves to Vienna.

1909–17   Student of philosophy and medicine, University of Vienna.

1914–17   Serves in Tyrolean Medical Corps, Austrian Army.

1917   Receives M.D. degree from University of Vienna; director, children's hospital, and superintendent, Mittendorf resettlement community.

1918–20   Publishes *Daimon* and *Der Neue Daimon*, quarterly journal of existential literature.

1918–25   Resides in Bad Vöslau, near Vienna: public health officer, Bad Vöslau; medical director, *Kammgarn Spinnerei* (Kammgarn textile mill); private practice in medicine.

1921–23   Directs *Das Stegreiftheater* (Theatre of Spontaneity), Vienna.

1925   Emigrates to United States.

1926   Marries Beatrice Beecher.

1927   Awarded New York State medical license.

1928   Conducts spontaneity tests with children at Plymouth Institute and at Mount Sinai Hospital's Department of Pediatrics, both in New York City.

1929   Conducts psychodramatic work at Grosvenor Neighborhood House and Hunter College, New York City.

1929–31 Director, Impromptu Theatre, Carnegie Hall, New York City; founder-editor, *Impromptu*, a journal devoted to improvisational theatre and music.

1931   Conducts sociometric studies at Public School 181, Brooklyn, NY, and Sing Sing Prison, Ossining, NY.

1932   Featured speaker, Conference on Group Methods, American Psychiatric Association Annual Meeting.

1932–38 In collaboration with Helen H. Jennings, directs long-term sociometric research, New York State Training School for Girls, Hudson, NY.

1934   Advisor, Subsistence Homestead Division, U.S. Department of the Interior; becomes U. S. citizen; legally changes name to Jacob Levy Moreno.

1936   Founds Beacon Hill Sanitarium, Beacon, NY; founder-editor, the *Sociometric Review*.

1937   Founder-editor, *Sociometry*.

1938   Marries Florence Bridge.

1939   Birth of daughter, Regina.

1941   Inaugurates psychodrama theatre at St. Elizabeths Hospital, Washington, DC, at invitation of William A. White; incorporates Beacon Publishing House.

1942   Opens Sociometric Institute and New York Theatre of Psychodrama
                in New York City, renamed Moreno Institute in 1951; founds the
                Society of Psychodrama and Group Psychotherapy, incorporated as
                the American Society of Group Psychotherapy and Psychodrama in
                1951.

1945   Founds the American Sociometric Association.

1946   Elected Fellow, American Psychiatric Association.

1947   Founder-editor, *Sociatry*, renamed *Group Psychotherapy, a Journal of
                Sociopathology and Sociatry* in 1950; renamed *Group Psychotherapy
                and Psychodrama* in 1970; renamed *Journal of Group Psychotherapy,
                Psychodrama and Sociometry* in 1976.

1948   Special lecturer, Harvard University.

1949   Dedicates theatre of psychodrama at Psychological Clinic, Harvard
                University, under aegis of H. A. Murray; conducts psychodrama at
                Mansfield Theatre (Broadway), New York City; marries Celine
                Zerka Toeman.

1951   Founds International Committee of Group Psychotherapy.

1951–66   Adjunct professor of sociology, Graduate School of Arts and Sci-
                ences, New York University.

1952   Birth of son, Jonathan.

1954   First International Congress of Group Psychotherapy, Toronto.

1956   Transfers *Sociometry* to American Sociological Society, which re-
                names it *Social Psychology* in 1976; founder-editor, *International
                Journal of Sociometry and Sociatry*, renamed *Handbook of International
                Sociometry* in 1971.

1959   Lectures in Soviet Union.

1964   First International Congress of Psychodrama, Paris.

1968 First International Congress of Sociometry, Baden, Austria; receives honorary doctorate from Medical Faculty, University of Barcelona.

1969 Receives Golden Doctor diploma from University of Vienna; commemorative plaque fixed to former home in Bad Vöslau.

1973 Founds International Association of Group Psychotherapy.

1974 Dies at home in Beacon, NY, May 14, age 85.

Bibliography

SELECTED PUBLICATIONS OF J. L. MORENO

Einladung zu einer Begegnung [Invitation to an Encounter]. (1914). Vienna: Anzengruber Verlag.

Das Testament des Vaters [Words of the Father]. (1920). Berlin: Gustav Kiepenheuer Verlag.

Das Stegreiftheater [Theatre of Spontaneity]. (1924). Berlin: Gustav Kiepenheuer Verlag.

With E. Stagg Whitlin. *Application of the Group Method to Classification*. (1932). New York: National Committee on Prisons and Labor.

Who Shall Survive? A New Approach to the Problem of Human Interrelations. (1934). Washington, DC: Nervous and Mental Diseases Publishing Co.

The Words of the Father. (1941). Beacon, NY: Beacon House.

Psychodrama (Vol. 1). (1946). Beacon, NY: Beacon House.

Editor. *Group Psychotherapy: A Symposium*. (1945). Beacon, NY: Beacon House.

The Theatre of Spontaneity. (1947). Beacon, NY: Beacon House.

Sociometry, Experimental Method and the Science of Society. (1951). New York: Beacon House.

Who Shall Survive? Foundations of Sociometry, Group Psychotherapy and Sociodrama (2nd ed.). (1953). Beacon, NY: Beacon House.

Preludes to My Autobiography. (1955). Beacon, NY: Beacon House.

Editor, *Sociometry and the Science of Man*. (1955). Beacon, NY: Beacon House.

Editor, with Frieda Fromm-Reichmann. *Progress in Psychotherapy* (Vol. 1). (1956). New York: Grune & Stratton.

The First Book on Group Psychotherapy. (1957). Beacon, NY: Beacon House. (A reprint of *Application of the Group Method to Classification*).

Editor, with Jules H. Masserman. *Progress in Psychotherapy* (Vol. 2). (1957). New York: Grune & Stratton.

Editor, with Jules H. Masserman. *Progress in Psychotherapy* (Vol. 3). (1958). New York: Grune & Stratton.

Editor, with Jules H. Masserman. *Progress in Psychotherapy* (Vol. 4). (1959). New York: Grune & Stratton.

With Zerka T. Moreno. *Psychodrama* (Vol. 2). (1959). Beacon, NY: Beacon House.

Editor, with Helen H. Jennings, Joan H. Criswell, Leo Katz, Robert R. Blake, Jane S. Mouton, Merl E. Bonney, Mary L. Northway, Charles P. Loomis, Charles Proctor, Renato Tagiuri, & Jiri Nehnevajsa. *The Sociometry Reader.* (1960). New York: The Free Press.

Editor, with Jules H. Masserman. *Progress in Psychotherapy* (Vol. 5). (1960). New York: Grune & Stratton.

Editor, with A. Friedemann, R. Battegar, & Zerka T. Moreno. *The International Handbook of Group Psychotherapy.* (1966). New York: Philosophical Library.

With Zerka T. Moreno. *Psychodrama* (Vol. 3). (1969). Beacon, NY: Beacon House.

Secondary Bibliography

JOURNALS

Dramatherapy. England.

International Journal of Sociometry and Sociatry. United States. From 1956 to 1971.

Journal of the British Psychodrama Association. England.

Journal of Group Psychotherapy, Psychodrama & Sociometry. United States.

Sociometry. United States. (Published by Beacon House from 1937, transferred to American Sociological Society in 1956, renamed *Social Psychology* in 1976.)

BOOKS

General

Arieti, Silvano (Ed.). (1959-66). *American Handbook of Psychiatry*. New York: Basic Books.

Back, Kurt W. (1972). *Beyond Words: The Story of Sensitivity Training and the Encounter Movement*. New York: Penguin.

Bromberg, Walter. (1959). *The Mind of Man: A History of Psychotherapy and Psychoanalysis*. New York: Harper & Row.

Gendron, Jeanine M. (1980). *Moreno: The Roots and the Branches and Bibliography of Psychodrama, 1972-1980; and Sociometry, 1970-1980*. Beacon, NY: Beacon House.

Graham, Thomas F. (1966). *Parallel Profiles: Pioneers in Mental Health*. Chicago: Franciscan Herald Press.

Greer, Valerie J. & Sacks, James M. (1973). *Bibliography of Psychodrama*. Unpublished manuscript.

Hare, A. Paul. (Ed.). (1976). *Handbook of Small Group Research*. New York: Free Press.

Hare, A. Paul. (1985). *Social Interaction as Drama*. Beverley Hills, CA: Sage.

Homans, G. C. (1950). *The Human Group*. New York: Harcourt, Brace.

Howard, Jane. (1970). *Please Touch: A Guided Tour of the Human Potential Movement*. New York: McGraw Hill.

Johnson, Paul E. (Ed.). (1972). *Healer of the Mind: A Psychiatrist's Search for Faith*. Nashville, TN: Abingdon Press.

Jones, M. (1953). *The Therapeutic Community*. New York: Basic Books.

Kaplan, H., Freedman, A., & Sadock, B. (Eds.). (1980). *Comprehensive Textbook of Psychiatry III* (Vol. 2). Baltimore: Williams & Wilkins.

Kaplan, H. & Sadock, B. (1971). *Comprehensive Group Psychotherapy*. Baltimore: Williams & Wilkins.

Kovel, Joel. (1976). *A Complete Guide to Therapy*. London: Penguin.

Lindzey, G. & Aronson, E. (Eds.). (1968). *Handbook of Social Psychology*. Reading, MA: Addison-Wesley.

Murphy, Gardner. (1947). *Personality: A Biosocial Approach to Origins and Structure*. New York: Harper.

Pines, Malcom. (1982). *The Individual and the Group: Volume 1,* Theory. New York: Plenum Press.

Sahakian, William S. (Ed.). (1965). *Psychology of Personality*. Chicago: Rand McNally.

Sahakian, William S. (Ed.). (1969). *Psychotherapy and Counseling: Studies in Technique*. Chicago, IL: Rand McNally.

Sills, David L. (Ed.) (1979). *International Encyclopedia of the Social Sciences* (Vol. 18). New York: Free Press.

Siroka, R., Siroka, E., & Schloss, G. (1971). *Sensitivity Training and Group Encounter*. New York: Grosset & Dunlop.

Wedding, Dan & Corsini, Raymond J. (Eds.) (1979). *Great Cases in Psychotherapy*. Itasca, IL: F. E. Peacock.

Wolff, Werner. (1956). *Contemporary Psychotherapists Examine Themselves*. Springfield, IL: Charles C. Thomas.

Wolman, Benjamine B. (Ed.). (1983). *The Therapist's Handbook: Treatment Methods of Mental Disorders*. New York: Van Nostrand Reinhold.

Psychodrama and Role Theory

ASGPP Commission on Accreditation of Training Programs. (1986). *Standards for Program Recognition and Accreditation*. New York: American Society for Group Psychotherapy and Psychodrama.

Berne, Eric. (1947). *The Mind in Action*. New York: Simon & Schuster.

Biddle, Bruce J. (1979). *Role Theory—Expectations, Identities, and Behaviors*. New York: Academic Press.

Biddle, Bruce J. & Thomas, Edwin. (1966). *Role Theory: Concepts and Research*. New York: Wiley.

Bischoff, Ledford J. (1964). *Interpreting Personality Theories*. New York: Harper & Row.

Blatner, H. A. (1973). *Acting-In: Practical Applications of Psychodramatic Methods*. New York: Springer.

Blatner, H. A. (Forthcoming) *Foundations of Psychodrama*. New York: Springer.

Boas, Phill, & Armstrong, Dick. (1980). *Experiential Psychotherapies in Australia*. Bundoora, Vic.: Preston Institute of Technology Press.

Corsini, Raymond J. (1967). *Role Playing in Psychotherapy*. Chicago: Aldine Press.

Fagan, Joen & Shepherd, Irma Lee. (1970). *Gestalt Therapy Now*. London: Penguin.

Goldman, Elaine E. & Morrison, Delcy S. (1984). *Psychodrama: Experience and Process*. Dubuque, IA: Kendall/Hunt.

Greenberg, Ira A. (Ed.). (1974). *Psychodrama: Theory and Therapy*. New York: Behavioral Publications.

Hardy, Margaret & Conway, Mary. (1978). *Role Theory: Perspectives for Health Professionals*. New York: Appleton-Century-Crofts.

Hare, June Rabson. (1979). *Psychodrama: Theory and Method*. Capetown, South Africa: Department of Sociology, University of Capetown.

Haskell, Martin. (1975). *Socioanalysis: Self-Direction Through Sociometry and Psychodrama*. Long Beach, CA: Role Training Associates.

Heisey, Marion J. (1982). *Clinical Case Studies in Psychodrama*. Washington, DC: University Press of America.

Kahn, Samuel. (1964). *Psychodrama Explained*. New York: Philosophical Library.

Kipper, David A. (1986). *Psychotherapy Through Clinical Role Playing*. New York: Brunner/Mazel.

Leveton, Eva. (1977). *Psychodrama for the Timid Clinician*. New York: Springer.

Nye, Ivan F. (1976). *Role-Structure and Analysis of the Family*. Beverly Hills, CA: Sage Publications.

Psychodrama Research Information Service. (1984). *Abstracts of Psychodrama Research*. Tucson, AZ: Tucson Center for Psychodrama.

Schutz, William C. (1967). *Joy: Expanding Human Awareness*. New York: Grove Press.

Smilansy, S. (1968). *The Effects of Sociodramatic Play on Disadvantaged Schoolchildren*. New York: Wiley.

Starr, Adeline. (1977). *Psychodrama: Rehearsal for Living*. Chicago: Nelson Hall.

Warner, G. Douglas. (1975). *Psychodrama Training Tips.* Hagerstown, MD: Psychodrama Institute.

Yablonski, Lewis. (1976). *Psychodrama: Resolving Emotional Problems Through Role-Playing.* New York: Basic Books.

Sociometry

Evans, K.M. (1962). *Sociometry and Education.* London: Routledge & Kegan Paul.

Hale, Ann. (1985). *Conducting Clinical Sociometric Explorations* (rev. ed.). Roanoke, VA: Royal.

Homan, George C. (1961). *Social Behavior: Its Elementary Forms.* New York: Harcourt, Brace & World.

Jennings, Helen H. (1943). *Leadership & Isolation: A Study of Personality in Interpersonal Relations.* New York: Longmans Green.

Klineberg, Otto. (1940). *Social Psychology.* New York: Henry Holt.

Kretch, David & Crutchfield, Richard. (1948). *Theory and Problems of Social Psychology.* New York: McGraw Hill.

Lewin, Kurt. (1948). *Resolving Social Conflicts.* New York: Harper.

Lundberg, George. (1942). *Social Research: A Study in Methods of Gathering Data.* New York: Longmans Green.

Northway, Mary L. (1952). *A Primer of Sociometry.* Toronto: University of Toronto Press.

Group Psychotherapy

Berne, Eric. (1963). *The Structure and Dynamics of Organizations and Groups.* New York: Grove Press.

Christensen, Oscar & Schramski Thomas. (Eds.). (1983). *Adlerian Family Counseling.* Minneapolis, MN: Educational Media Corp.

Corsini, Raymond. (1957). *Methods of Group Psychotherapy.* New York: McGraw Hill.

Foulkes, S. (1957). *Group Psychotherapy: The Psycho-analytic Approach.* London: Penguin.

Foulkes, S. (1964). *Therapeutic Group Analysis.* London: Allen & Unwin.

Gazda, George M. (Ed.). (1984). *Basic Approaches to Group Psychotherapy and Group Counseling* (3rd ed.). Springfield, IL: Charles C. Thomas.

Greenberg, Ira A. (Ed.). (1977). *Group Hypnotherapy & Hypnodrama.* Chicago: Nelson Hall.

Mullan, Hugh & Rosenbaum, Max. (1962). *Group Psychotherapy: Theory and Practice.* New York: Free Press.

Naar, Ray. (1982). *A Primer of Group Psychotherapy.* New York: Human Sciences Press.

Nichols, Mary. (1984). *Change in the Context of Group Therapy.* New York: Brunner/Mazel.

Ohlsen, Merle M. (1969). *Group Counseling.* New York: Holt, Rinehart & Winston.

Rosenbaum, Max & Berger, Milton. (Eds.) (1963). *Group Psychotherapy and Group Function.* New York: Basic Books.

Rosenbaum, Max & Snadowsky, Alvin. (Eds.) (1976). *The Intensive Group Experience.* New York: The Free Press.

Shaffer, John & Galinsky, M. (1974). *Models of Group Therapy and Sensitivity Training.* Englewood Cliffs, NJ: Prentice Hall.

Sigrell, Bo. *Group Psychotherapy: Studies of Processes in Therapeutic Groups.* (1968). Stockholm: Almqvist & Wiksell.

Slavson, S. (Ed.). (1956). *The Fields of Group Psychotherapy.* New York: International Universities Press.

Smith, Peter B. (Ed.). (1980). *Small Groups and Personal Change.* London: Methuen.

Yalom, Irvin D. (1975). *The Theory and Practice of Group Psychotherapy.* New York: Basic Books.

Education, Industry, & the Arts

Anderson, Walt. (Ed.). (1977). *Therapy and the Arts.* New York: Harper & Row.

Bentley, Eric. (1967). *The Life of the Drama.* New York: Atheneum.

Bentley, Eric. (1972). *Theater of War.* New York: Viking.

Bonney, M., Grosz, R. & Roark, A. (1986). *Social Psychological Foundations for School Services.* New York: Human Sciences Press.

Corsini, R. J., Shaw, M. E., & Blake, R. R. (1961). *Role Playing in Business and Industry.* New York: Free Press.

Courtney, Richard. (1968). *Play, Drama & Thought.* London: Cassell.

Fleshman, Bob & Fryrear, Jerry L. (1981). *The Arts in Therapy.* Chicago: Nelson Hall.

Hass, Robert Bartlett. (1949). *Psychodrama and Sociodrama in American Education.* Beacon, NY: Beacon House.

Kase-Polisini, Judith. (Ed.). (1985). *Creative Drama in a Developmental Context.* Lanham, MD: University Press of America.

Landy, Robert J. (1982). *Handbook of Educational Drama and Theatre.* Westport, CT: Greenwood Press.

Landy, Robert J. (1986). *Drama Therapy: Concepts and Practices.* Springfield, IL: Charles C. Thomas.

McNiff, Shawn. *Arts and Psychotherapy.* (1981). Springfield, IL: Charles C. Thomas.

Northway, Mary. (1957). *Sociometric Testing: A Guide for Teachers.* Toronto: University of Toronto Press.

Shaftel, Fannie & Shaftel, George. (1967). *Role-Playing for Social Values: Decision-Making in the Social Studies.* Englewood Cliffs, NJ: Prentice Hall.

Shaftel, Fannie & Shaftel, George. (1982). *Role-Playing in the Curriculum* (2nd ed.). Englewood Cliffs, NJ: Prentice Hall.

Schattner, Gertrud & Courtney, Richard. (Eds.). (1981). *Drama in Therapy* (2 vols.). New York: Drama Book Specialists.

Schloss, Gilbert A. (1976). *Psychopoetry: A New Approach to Self-Awareness through Poetry Therapy.* New York: Grosset & Dunlop.

Shaw, Malcom E., Corsini, R., Blake, R., & Mouton, J. (1980). *Role Playing: A Practical Manual for Group Facilitators.* San Diego, CA: University Associates.

Stanford, G. & Roark, A.E. (1974). *Human Interaction in Education.* Boston: Allyn & Bacon

Torrence, E. Paul. (1970). *Encouraging Creativity in the Classroom.* Dubuque, IA: Wm. C. Brown.

Torrence, E. Paul & Myers, R. (1970). *Creative Learning and Teaching.* New York: Dodd, Mead.

FOREIGN LANGUAGE PUBLICATIONS

Danish

Møller, Marchen. (1981). *Psykodrama og Undervisning* [Psychodrama and Education]. Copenhagen: Borgen.

Dutch

Maandblad Geestelijke volksgezondheid. Netherlands.

Souget, Frits. *De achterzijde van de menselijke geest* [The Dark Side of the Human Mind]. Lisse: Swets & Zeitlinger.

French

Folia Psychodramatica. Belgium.

Le Journal des Psychologues. France.

Revue du S.E.P.T. France.

Ancelin Schützenberger, Anne. (1970). *Précis de psychodrame: Introduction aux apects techniques* [Handbook of Psychodrama: A Technical Introduction] (2nd ed.). Paris: Ed. Universitaires.

Ancelin Schützenberger, A. (1986). *Le Jeu de Rôle* [Role Playing] (2nd ed.). Paris: Editions E.S.F.

Anzieu, Didier. (1956). *Le Psychodrama analytique chez l'enfant et l'adolescent* [Analytic Psychodrama with Children and Adolescents]. Paris: Presses Universitaires de France.

Fanchette, Jean. (1971). *Psychodrame et théâtre moderne* [Psychodrama and Modern Theater]. Paris: Buchet Chastel.

Lemoine, Gennie & Lemoine, Paul. (1972). *Le Psychodrame* [Psychodrama]. Paris: Robert Laffont.

Leutz, Grete. (1985). *Mettre sa vie en scène: le psychodrame* [Psychodrama: Putting Your Life on Stage]. Paris: EPI-DDB.

Marineau, R. (Forthcoming) *Un homme et son double: La vie et l'oeuvre de J. L. Moreno* [A man and His Double: the Life and Work of J. L. Moreno].

Salome, Jacques. (1984). *Les Mémoires de l'oubli* [Memoirs of Forgetfulness]. Plombières-les-Dijon: Ed. Le Regard Fertile.

German

Gruppen Psychotherapie und Gruppendynamik. West Germany.

Integrative Therapie. West Germany.

Leutz, Grete. (1974). *Psychodrama Theorie und Praxis: Das klassische Psychodrama nach J. L. Moreno* [Psychodrama Theory and Practice: Classical Psychodrama According to J. L. Moreno]. Heidelberg: Springer Verlag.

Petzold, Hilarion G. (1979). *Psychodrama-Therapie: Theorie, Methoden, Anwendung in der Arbeit mit alten Menschen* [Psychodrama Therapy: Theory, Methods, and Applications in the Treatment of the Elderly]. Paderborn: Junfermann Verlag.

Petzold, Hilarion G. (1982). *Dramatische Therapie: Neue Wege der Behandlung durch Psychodrama, Rollenspiel, Therapeutisches Theater* [Drama Therapy: New Methods of Treatment with Psychodrama, Role Playing, & Therapeutic Theater]. Stuttgart: Hippokrates-Verlag.

Plöger, Andreas. (1983). *Tiefenpsychologisch fundierte Psychodramatherapie* [Psychodrama Therapy Based on Depth Psychology]. Stuttgart: Verlag Kohlhammer.

Straub, H. H. (1969). *Erfahrung mit psychodramatischer Behandlung von Zwangsneurosen* [Experience with the Psychodramatic Treatment of Compulsion Neurosis]. Heft 5: Zeitsschrift fur Psychotherapie.

Hebrew

Naharin, Eliav. (1985). *Bamah bimcom sappa.* [The Stage Instead of the Couch]. Tel Aviv: Tzerkover.

Italian

Atti dello Psicodramma. Italy.

Boria, Giovanni. (1983). *Tele: Manuale di Psicodramma Classico* [Tele: Manual of Classical Psychodrama]. Milan: Angeli.

Montesarchio, Gianni & Sardi, Paola. (1986). *Dal Teatro della Spontaneita allo Psicodramma Classico: contributo per una revisione del pensiero di J. L. Moreno* [Spontaneity Theater in Classical Psychodrama: A Contribution to a Reevaluation of the Thought of J. L. Moreno]. Milano: Angeli.

Rosati, Ottavio. (Ed.). (1983). *Questa sera si recita a soggetto: Pirendello, Moreno e lo Psicodramma* [Tonight we improvise: Pirandello, Moreno, and Psychodrama]. Rome: Astrolabio Ubaldini.

Rosati, Ottavio. (1985). *Il teatro di Esculapio: Psicodramma e Sociodramma per tossicodipendenti* [The Theater of Esculapius: Psychodrama and Sociodrama with Toxic Dependents]. Rome: CeIS.

Japanese

Shuudan seishin ryohou [Group Psychotherapy]. Japan.

Shinrigeki, Shuudan Shinri Ryouhou, Rorupureiingu [Journal of Psychodrama, Psychotherapy, and Role Playing]. Japan.

Mashino, Hajime. (1977). *Shinrigeki to sono Sekai* [Psychodrama and Its World]. Tokoyo: Kongo-Shuppan.

Matsumura, Kohei. (1961). *Shinrigeki—Taijin Kankei no Henaku* [Psychodrama: Revolutionary Improvement in Interpersonal Relations]. Toyoko: Seishin-shobo.

Tanaka, Kumajiro. 1959. *Soshiometori no Riron to Houhou* [The Theory and Method of Sociometry]. Tokyo: Meiji-Tosho.

Utena, Toshio. (1984). *Shinrigeki to Bunretubyo Kanja* [Psychodrama with Schizophrenics]. Tokyo: Seiwa-shoten.

Utena, Toshio & Mashino, Hajime. (Eds.). (1986). *Shinrigeki no jissai* [The Practice of Psychodrama]. Tokyo: Kongo-Shuppan.

Norwegian

Røine, Eva. (1978). *Psykodrama: Psykoterapi som eksperimentelt teater* [Psychodrama: Psychotherapy as Experimental Theatre]. Oslo: Aschehoug.

Portuguese

Revista de Psicodrama. Brazil.

Ancelin Schützenberger, Anne & Weill, Pierre. (1975). *O Psicodrama Triadico* [Triadic Psychodrama]. Belo Horizonte: Interlivros.

Bustos, Dalmiro. (1982). *O Teste Sociometrico* [The Sociometric Test]. Sao Paulo: Brasiliense.

Fonseca Filho, Jose. (1984). *O Psicodrama de Locura* [The Psychodrama of Madness]. Sao Paulo: Agora.

Naffah Neto, A.. (1983). *Psicodrama* [Psychodrama]. Sao Paulo: Brasiliense.

Weil, Pierre. (1969). *O Psicodrama* [Psychodrama]. Rio de Janiero: Cepa.

Spanish

Momento. Argentina.

Revista de la Sociedad Argentina de Psicodrama. Argentina.

Bustos, D., Bustos, E., Calvente, C., Alegre, C., Galina, C., Freire, D., Bustos, G., & Bini, M.. (1974). *El Psicodrama* [Psychodrama]. Buenos Aires: Ed. Plus Ultra.

Bustos, Dalmiro. (1985). *Nuevos Rumbos en Psicoterapia Psicodramatica* [New Directions in Psychodrama Therapy]. La Plata: Momento.

Garrido Martin, Eugenio. (1978). *Jacob L. Moreno: Psicologia del Encuentro* [J. L. Moreno and the Psychology of Encounter]. Madrid: Atenas.

Manegazzo, Carlos M., Sauri, J., Zuretti, M., Noseda de Bustos, E., & Severino, J. (1982). *El Psicodrama: Aportes para una Teoria de Roles* [Psychodrama: Its Contributions to Role Theory]. Buenos Aires: Docencia.

Rojas Bermudas, Jaime. (1964). *Que es Psicodrama?* [What is Psychodrama?] Buenos Aires: Ed. Genitor.

Swedish

Gralvik, Elisabeth. (1975). *Psykodrama* [Psychodrama]. Stockholm.

Schulze, R. (1957). *Psykodrama* [Psychodrama]. Stockholm: Medens.

Index